# Perspectives on Business Modelling

Understanding and
Changing Organisations

Springer
*Berlin*
*Heidelberg*
*New York*
*Barcelona*
*Hong Kong*
*London*
*Milan*
*Paris*
*Singapore*
*Tokyo*

Anders G. Nilsson · Christofer Tolis
Christer Nellborn (Eds.)

# Perspectives on Business Modelling

## Understanding and Changing Organisations

With 78 Figures
and 8 Tables

Springer

Prof. Anders G. Nilsson
Karlstad University
Department of Information Technology
SE-651 88 Karlstad
Sweden

Christofer Tolis
Stockholm School of Economics
Department of Information Management
Box 6501
SE-113 83 Stockholm
Sweden

Christer Nellborn
KTH and Stockholm University
Department of Computer and Systems Sciences
Electrum 230
SE-164 40 Kista
Sweden

ISBN 3-540-65249-3 Springer-Verlag Berlin Heidelberg New York

Library of Congress Cataloging-in-Publication Data
Die Deutsche Bibliothek – CIP-Einheitsaufnahme
Perspectives on business modelling: understanding and changing organisation /
Anders G. Nilsson ... (ed.). – Berlin; Heidelberg; New York; Barcelona; Hong
Kong; London; Milan; Paris; Singapore; Tokyo: Springer, 1999
    ISBN 3-540-65249-3

© Springer-Verlag Berlin · Heidelberg 1999
Printed in Germany

Hardcover-Design: Erich Kirchner, Heidelberg

SPIN 10700571    42/2202-5 4 3 2 1 0 – Printed on acid-free paper

# Preface

We have for many years perceived a great need for innovative and systematic ways of working with change processes in organisations. Business modelling is a field that provides valuable knowledge for performing development work more professionally in companies and public services. An important prerequisite for success is to understand the underlying values and principles of the models and methods being used in practice.

The leading idea behind this book is to present different perspectives on working with business modelling based on established theories and practical experiences. Instead of "pushing" a specific method or view, you will be able to appreciate a whole smorgasbord of different experiences and ideas. Recognising different alternatives gives you a stronger position when involved in development work in organisations. Especially, we have written this book for you who are interested to learn more about:

- bridging the communication gap between business people and systems experts in development work

- understanding and changing organisations by combining established models and methods on the market

- exploring different aspects and points of view when developing corporate strategies, business processes and information support

Organisational change is an integrated part of most people's work. Many types of models and methods are being used to facilitate the development work. Unfortunately, in many organisations there is still a lack of deeper understanding of the possibilities and limitations involved. This book provides much needed insights for you who want to do something about that.

The overall goal is to give advanced knowledge and relevant information on the key issues in business modelling for today's organisations. The book contains contributions from active researchers and senior consultants from the field. The contributions are based on a common frame of reference that have been tried out in change projects in both private industry and public service sector.

The authors of this book are involved in the Business Modelling research consortium. The consortium is an active network of researchers from academia and participants from industry. It has been funded by NUTEK, the Swedish National Board for Industrial and Technical Development, during the period of 1995-1997.

This book is the result of extensive cooperation within the consortium. We want to acknowledge Christofer Tolis' work with designing and implementing the joint layout for the book. We also wish to express our gratitude to all other people who in different ways have contributed to making this book possible.

Stockholm, January 1999

*Anders G. Nilsson*            *Christofer Tolis*            *Christer Nellborn*

# Contents

# Part III: Description of Different Aspects

# Perspectives on Business Modelling: Understanding and Changing Organisations

*Anders G. Nilsson*
*Christofer Tolis*
*Christer Nellborn*

*Business Modelling is the use of models and methods to understand and change organisations. The main objective is to bridge the communication gap between business people and systems people. In this chapter, three important themes in business modelling are presented: development on different levels, explorations of different points of view, and descriptions of different aspects. Overviews of the following chapters are given in order to highlight each perspective on business modelling.*

## Introducing Business Modelling

Business Modelling is the use of models and methods to understand and change business operations together with information systems in organisations. In this book, twelve authors from the Business Modelling research consortium present their perspectives on the field. This introductory chapter aims to provide an overview of Business Modelling and a foundation for the following fourteen chapters.

Our mission with this book is to give a broad range of perspectives on what we perceive as key issues for business modelling in organisations and industry today. We believe this book to be of interest and importance for you working as:

- a practitioner, involved in business development or information systems development in an organisation;

- a management consultant, giving professional advice on corporate or information technology matters to your customer organisations; or

- a student or researcher, focusing on business administration or information systems.

In order to fully appreciate the content of the book, a basic knowledge of business analysis and systems development is helpful. By providing different perspectives on business modelling, the book has a character of "follow-up" studies for people who are interested in both theoretical and practical aspects of change work in organisations.

# Understanding and changing organisations

In today's business world, information systems and information support have become a more integrated part of business operations and, in many cases, a vital part of the business mission itself. The information systems can also create new business opportunities for the companies to reinforce their competitive edge in the market place. Product quality and delivery times have gained importance in the business world, in order to achieve enhanced customer value. This puts pressure on the functionality and flexibility of information systems in responding to business changes. The information support is also becoming more critical in order to achieve sustainable business results in organisations.

Understanding and changing an organisation is two crucial skills needed to succeed in a competitive environment. People working within an organisation, as well as those coming in from the outside, e.g. consultants and researchers, need to be able to explore new situations and opportunities. Structuring and sense-making are important in order to understand and assess a situation. Working towards goals and influencing others are important in order to change and improve it.

Within an organisation, there are different people and groups trying to understand and change it. In many cases, the development of business activities and its information support are carried out as separate change processes and in independent projects. There is very limited, or no, organisational co-ordination between business development and information systems development. This situation leads to long turn-around times and unnecessary duplication of work. Sometimes business and systems development are based on contradictory prerequisites and assumptions (e.g. decentralised business functions versus centralised information support).

Business managers and systems experts often experience frustration when information support for business activities is being discussed. A major part of the problem is due to lack of essential communication. Accusations from both sides are often the result: "The business people do not know what they want!" or "The systems people do not understand what we need!" However, communication is more than talking. It requires a firm base for shared understanding, in terms of common languages and tools.

# Using models and methods to bridge the communication gap

The main objective of business modelling as a field is to bridge the communication gap between business people and systems people by using shared models and methods as a means for understanding and change. Business models have proved to be effective tools for supporting and specifying communication between different actors involved in development work. Models can be instrumental in creating shared images of the business and systems for current as well as future situations. Both model and method are important concepts in the chapters of the book:

- A "model" (description) in this context can be characterised as a representation of an organisation and its information support. The basic goals of understanding and change have a parallel in two variations of business models: "is" models describing the current situation and chiefly aiding understanding, and "should" models describing future situations and chiefly aiding change.

- A "method" (methodology, approach) in this context can be characterised as concrete guidelines for a systematic way of working with development tasks in organisations. A method prescribes how different actors should behave during a change process. It gives recommendations for efficient work and is normative in this sense.

There are a large number of model types and methods in use today. Apart from developing new ones, there is a strong need to explore the relationships among the ones that are already established. Being able to evaluate and combine different model types and methods are a key skill for success in today's development work.

The following chapters have been divided into three parts corresponding to three basic themes within the field of Business Modelling. Part I deals with development on different levels, part II with exploration of different points of view, and part III with description of different aspects. In the following, each part will be described in more detail together with overviews of the different chapters. As will become evident, there are no definite boundaries between the themes. Most chapters relate to all three in varying degree – although each has a main focus on one of the themes.

# Part I: Development on different levels

Today, we have many methods and approaches for development work. Many of them share a focus on the vital and critical business processes that flow through the organisation. This is the case of, for example, Total Quality Management (TQM), Business Process Reengineering (BPR) and Process Management. These three approaches are mainly focused on organisational development, something that can be seen as the middle of three general levels of development work:

- *Corporate development.* The development of corporate strategies in a company, concretised in business plans with information technology policies. Corporate strategies explore the company's relations with different actors in the environment and the market.

- *Organisational development.* The development of business processes in the organisation, such as order-handling and material flows. Business processes are linked with both strategic questions and the use of information systems in the company and can be seen as a mediating link between the other two levels.

- *Information systems development.* The development of information support in the form of in-house applications, business systems packages and component based solutions. Information systems (IS) and information technology (IT) are regarded as resources or enablers in running the business professionally.

A widespread problem in companies today is that the interplay between the three levels of development work doesn't function satisfactorily. There are communication gaps between people performing the different development activities. There is also a communication gap between people focusing on development work and those more involved with normal day-to-day activities.

# Content of part I

The first part of the book (chapters 2-6) focuses on development on different levels. It illustrates the different emphasis put on the three levels of development work and some problems in linking them to each other. The cases give concrete illustrations from larger organisations in Sweden, both private industries and public services. The case companies demonstrate critical issues in performing business modelling with a high degree of international relevance. To get an overview of the situation also for small and medium-sized companies, this first part is concluded with some interesting results from a recent survey. The content of the five chapters in part I is as follows:

Chapter 2: *Process Ownership in a Rapid Growth Situation: The Ericsson Radio Case.* "Process owner" is a new role in many companies as a result of the increased interest in business processes. In this case study Christofer Tolis and Christer Nellborn report on the things that occupies the minds of ten process owners in Ericsson Radio and what they regard as important in their work with developing new products and services. "Process" is found to be a complicated concept in practice, several problematic relationships have to be dealt with, and issues of IS/IT are not in focus.

Chapter 3: *A Monopoly Facing Competition: Sweden Post's Exploration of Processes and Descriptions.* Changing a functionally organised, 360 year old, state monopoly into a flexible commercial communications provider on a competitive market has been the challenge for Sweden Post. To meet this, a number of exploration and development activities have been deployed. In this case study, Christer Nellborn and Christofer Tolis present how Sweden Post investigated the issues of process orientation and business descriptions in order to fulfil the ambitions.

Chapter 4: *Process Management in Public Administration: The Social Insurance Office Case.* Establishing a process-oriented view on a business has up until now been carried out mostly in private companies. Jörgen Andersson shows in this case study how a public authority has proceeded to change its operations towards process orientation. The Social Insurance Office has used TQM and process management to increase quality in its operations and at the same time make considerable reductions in the economic resources, following demands from the government.

Chapter 5: *Business Modelling in a Historical Perspective: Experiences from Statistics Sweden.* Production and dissemination of statistics is the "business" of Statistics Sweden. In this case study, Bo Sundgren describes a long tradition at Statistics Sweden aiming at the integration of systems development and statistical work. How did it start? Which were the obstacles? Was it successful? Which are the plans for the future? Taking a historical perspective he tries to answer these and other questions.

Chapter 6: *Business Process Development and Information Technology in Small and Medium-sized Companies.* Computer maturity is at a high level in smaller and medium-sized Swedish companies (SMEs) today! Based on the results from a European Commission project, Jörgen Andersson illustrates a shift in SMEs from having concentrated computerisation to opening up the company's communication with the external world, using new technology. However, SMEs still have a certain lack of competence in the IT area, particularly regarding the planning of information systems.

# Part II: Exploration of different points of view

Organisations are complex phenomena. In order to be successful in understanding and changing, one has to reflect on the points of view used. People use different points of view depending on their personal background and the values they hold. By exploration of the current view one can discover new ones. Two main sources of inspiration are:

- *Different practices:* Work that takes place in different organisational contexts. Looking at what's being done in other departments, other companies, and other countries can be highly relevant. Comparisons, benchmarking, and best practices all represent ways to gain new insights.

- *Different academic fields:* Existing knowledge from various disciplines, such as Business Administration and Information Systems. Relevant areas include corporate strategies, business control, material/production control, marketing management, IS/IT support, and IS development methodologies. But also other areas and disciplines are important, for example philosophy, psychology and pedagogy.

It is the comparison and combination of current ideas that give rise to new ones. By exploration of underlying assumptions and future consequences of various points of view, opportunities and limitations can be discovered. Recognising the current point of view might help in exploring alternative ones, but also the other way around.

Exploring ideas from different contexts, both practical and academic, is important in Business Modelling. In development work and research, people with different background contribute their own views of the situation. When bridging communication gaps among the people involved, it is an important skill to be able to recognise and employ different points of view.

## *Content of part II*

The second part of the book (chapters 7-11) focuses on exploration of different points of view. Each chapter takes on one or several points of view and explore their background and consequences. Issues discussed include modelling activities, process models, business relationships, and methods. The content of the five chapters in part II is as follows:

Chapter 7: *Facilitating Understanding and Change: The Role of Business Models in Development Work.* A common element of much development work is the use of various types of business models. In model work, there are a number of differences that affect the process and outcome of the development work. Drawing on theories of signs, learning, and knowledge, Christofer Tolis presents a conceptual framework of model work. The framework examines alternatives in three areas: model artefacts, model activities, and model assumptions.

Chapter 8: *Lessons Learned from Applying Business Modelling: Exploring Opportunities and Avoiding Pitfalls.* In applying Business Modelling, what issues have proved to be most relevant? Where have we succeeded, what pitfalls could be noted, and why did they probably occur? Claes-Göran Lindström gives a practitioner's viewpoint and advocates a "multiple simple model" strategy. Confluence from business style, participativeness and group dynamics is brought into the picture. The effects of recent trends like BPR and Object Orientation are discussed.

Chapter 9: *Business Process Models Revised: Challenging the Physical Metaphor.* The present modelling techniques have shown severe shortcomings in handling many types of computerised business processes. Gösta Steneskog claims that behind today's process models are implicit concepts inherited from the physical world view. That heritage prevents us from creating models which makes it possible to fully utilise the potential of the virtual world. The present ways of modelling business processes have to be radically changed in order to realise the IT potential!

Chapter 10: *Principal-Agent and Transaction Cost Theories in Business Modelling.* New models are introduced, they are used, and they disappear. Many of them are launched as the final model that will overcome all obstacles with existing models. However, we can see that the models are not as good as promised and that they do not solve the problems they were aimed to solve! Birger Rapp shows how two theories, principal-agent theory and transaction cost theory, can broaden the perspective on business model building.

Chapter 11: *Business and Systems Development: Opportunities for an Integrated Way-of-Working.* Important problems with information systems requirements engineering include traceability and validation. Christer Nellborn argues that requirements validation is a cross-disciplinary topic. It involves both business and systems developers and has much to do with communicational problems. A framework for classifying methodologies according to their ability to cover the span from strategic planning to information systems design is discussed and presented with examples.

# Part III: Description of different aspects

An important tool in successful development work is rich and precise business models. Being able to effectively describe business activities as well as supporting information systems is crucial in a situation where different people work together. Business modelling is therefore a key activity in such development work. Using models for description not only explores the organisation or information system in focus, but also the minds of the people that are involved in the modelling.

Instead of searching for one superior way of description, there is room for different types of models. Each model type focuses on a certain aspect of what is being described, e.g. the processes going on in an organisation or the structure of its departments. Together, models focusing on different aspects give a broader picture of the organisation than a single model ever might do. Different model types emphasise different aspects, for example:

- *Behaviour models* (e.g. routine sketches) describing processes from an internal perspective, focusing on the persons who carries out the process

- *Transformation models* (e.g. process maps) describing processes from an external perspective, focusing on transitions of core objects giving value to outside customers

- *Category models* (e.g. conceptual data models) describing important phenomena in the business and their relationships

- *Factor models* (e.g. goal models) describing important conditions in the business and their influences on each other

The first two examples can be called process models. They share a focus on processes, i.e. dynamic flows and courses of events in the business. The last two examples can be called content models. They share a focus of content, i.e. static conditions and structures in the business.

## Content of part III

The third and final part of the book (chapters 12-15) focuses on descriptions of different aspects. Each chapter presents and uses combinations of model types covering a set of aspects. The models are used for describing methods, organisations, and information systems. The content of the five chapters in part III is as follows:

Chapter 12: *The Business Developer's Toolbox: Chains and Alliances between Established Methods.* Many companies are trying to create useful toolboxes for their method application in business development work. The main problem here is to build fruitful links between different methods in use. Anders G. Nilsson shows a framework for method integration using chains and alliances of established methods in the market. The perspective taken is how a business manager can communicate with a systems expert by applying common methods.

Chapter 13: *Improving the Quality of Requirements Specifications by Enterprise Modelling.* An enterprise model is a system of knowledge about the enterprise and is regarded as an essential part of a requirements specification. The framework of the enterprise model can reflect different views of the enterprise. Janis A. Bubenko jr. and Marite Kirikova argue that enterprise modelling supports and amplifies human thinking, reasoning and co-operation. The quality of an enterprise model is supported by continuous participation by relevant stakeholders and by different control procedures.

Chapter 14: *On Why to Model What and How: Concepts and Architecture for Change.* Having spent more than a quarter of a century in practical modelling work, Björn E. Nilsson feels that we tend to model the wrong things, during the wrong work phases, for the wrong reasons, using the wrong instruments. Searching remedies for these problems, he will look into the basic reasons for introducing modelling concepts as well as an architecture within which to apply selected concepts in a profitable manner.

Chapter 15: *Business Modeller's Checklist: "Dos" and "Don'ts" in Hands-on Practice.* There is a multitude of approaches, models and methods in the marketplace giving opportunities for combination in business modelling. However, good performance in business modelling practice demands more! Hans Willars sums up some hints and requirements for success in a "Business Modeller's Checklist" collected from different practical experiences throughout the years. Issues from the other chapters are brought together and related in this concluding chapter.

# Perspectives on Business Modelling

In this introductory chapter, three main themes of business modelling have been introduced. The chapters in each part of the book have also been briefly described. As seen, each chapter deals with the issue of perspectives in some way: In the first part, the chapters deal with perspectives as levels, in the second as points-of-view, and in the third as aspects. As mentioned earlier, there are no clear-cut boundaries; although each chapter has a main focus on a certain theme, most touch on issues of all three.

Not only does each chapter *deals* with perspectives, each one also *represents* a certain perspective on business modelling. Together the contributions provide a varied mixture of theoretical and practical views on business modelling. They all have different focus, background and arguments. We believe that this diversity is a great strength when it comes to understand and change organisations.

*Figure 1. Business Modelling for understanding and change: Bridging communication gaps by using shared models and methods.*

We hope that you will find the perspectives presented in the following chapters challenging and inspiring for your own work of bridging communication gaps!

# Part I:

# Development on Different Levels

# 2

# Process Ownership in a Rapid Growth Situation: The Ericsson Radio Case

*Christofer Tolis*
*Christer Nellborn*

*"Process owner" is a new role in many organisations as a result of the increased interest in business processes. This chapter reports on the things that ten process owners at Ericsson Radio expressed as important in their work. Their processes all belonged to the early stages of developing new systems for mobile telecommunications. Nine main issues are identified among the things occupying the process owners' minds. In summary, "process" is found to be a complicated concept in practice, several problematic relationships have to be dealt with, and issues of IS/IT are not in focus.*

## Introduction

The concept of business process has been highly influential during the last couple of years. Much of the management literature has focused on the issue, e.g. in terms of Process Management (Steneskog, 1991; Rummler & Brache, 1995), Business Process Reengineering (Davenport, 1993; Hammer & Champy, 1993), Total Quality Management (Bergman & Klevsjö, 1994), etc. Many companies have shown a growing interest in process orientation and its implications for the organisation.

Focusing on business processes introduces a new organisational role: the process owner. A process owner is supposed to "oversee the entire process" (Rummler & Brache, 1995, p. 57), being "responsible for the process' functioning and development" (Steneskog, 1991, p. 14; the authors' translation). He or she "is responsible for development and improvement of the process" (Bergman & Klevsjö, 1994, p. 347), has "responsibility for a specific process and the reengineering effort focused on it" (Hammer & Champy, 1993, p. 102) or, put simply, "has ultimate responsibility for a process" (Davenport, 1993, p. 182).

But what occupies the mind of a process owner in a company that has dealt with business processes for a number of years? Building on Tolis & Nellborn (1997), this chapter tries to answer that question by providing the results of a study involving ten process owners at Ericsson Radio in the summer of 1995.

## The study

In the early summer of 1995, contact was established with Ericsson Radio. They were interested in collaboration regarding business processes and IT-support. The initial idea was to provide support for co-ordination among the different processes within the business unit responsible for European standards for mobile telecommunications. This was to be done by investigating how different process owners perceived their role and the work they were involved in.

The initial contacts led to a focus on the early stages of product development, called Requirement Definition. All ten process owners in Requirement Definition were chosen for interviewing. Before each interview, the process owner received a short list of three broad areas for discussion during the interview: (1) product development, (2) improvement work, and (3) IT-support. The first two areas correspond to the main responsibilities of a process owner's role as expressed in the literature (see above): for the process itself and for its development. The third area, IT-support, is interesting in conjunction with both of the first two as it represents an enabler for large-scale change (cf. the literature on BPR).

Each process owner was interviewed for about two hours by the authors. Notes were taken in parallel and later integrated to an interview document. In order to increase the validity of the result, the document was sent back to the process owner for comments. All the ten interview documents were then used as a base for a "bottom-up" analysis inspired by grounded theory (Glaser & Strauss, 1967). The documents were divided into small chunks of meaning, often on a sentence-level, that were iteratively searched for recurring patterns, and grouped together to form clusters of interest. Labels and descriptions of each cluster were added, refined, and extended as the analysis progressed. The result was presented to people at Ericsson Radio as a feedback of the work and a final check of validity.

## *The business*

Ericsson is one of the leading actors in the international telecommunication market. The business area Radio focuses on radio-mediated communication, such as mobile telephony. Within Ericsson Radio, the focus of the study has been on the business unit working with European standards such as GSM, NMT, and TACS. The responsibilities of this unit include development and worldwide selling of all products and services needed to operate a mobile telecommunication network (the mobile telephones themselves are handled by another business unit). Two examples of systems sold are CME20 (for GSM 900/1800 MHz) and CMS40 (for GSM 1900 MHz USA). The main customers are network operators, who in turn provide their services to end-users.

Within the business unit, the organisation is divided into functional units (such as Product Management), development units, and market operations units. The latter are divided according to geographical markets. Legally, the organisation is spread over a number of different companies. Of the roughly 9000 people working in the business unit in 1995, about 1800 were located in Sweden, and the rest in different local companies around the world. The local companies do not only handle European standards; most of them also form parts of other business units within Ericsson.

In addition to the functional organisation there has been an interest within Ericsson for business processes since the mid 80's. Process management have been actively pursued in different forms since the beginning of the 90's. In process terms, the business unit comprises two main flows transforming customer needs to customer satisfaction. One flow is the Customer Supply Flow that deals with *existing* products and services. The other is the Market Supply Flow that develops *new* products and services.

As shown in Figure 1, Ericsson employs a number of techniques and tools in its development activities (cf. Tolis & Nilsson, 1996). For corporate strategies, Ericsson has developed its own method for strategic planning, called ESP (Ericsson Strategic Planning). Process Management, influenced by Rummler & Brache (1995), is used for developing business processes in many parts of the organisation. In the area of information systems development, MQR (Method for Quality and Results) is used as a toolbox of methods that can be adapted to different situations.

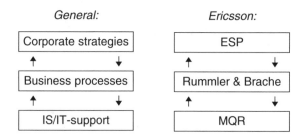

*Figure 1. Three levels of development in general and in Ericsson (adapted from Tolis & Nilsson, 1996).*

# Ten processes and their owners

In the following, the ten process owners describe their work. They are all involved in the early stages of the Market Supply Flow within the business unit for European standards at Ericsson Radio. As Figure 2 shows, this includes the main process Requirement Definition, its four sub-processes (Business Opportunity Tracing, Business Analysis, Product Definition, and Customer Services Definition), and its five control/support processes (Product Control and Support, Product Decisions, Market and Requirement Analysis, Suppliers Management, and Product Market Information). The main process has customer needs as input. As output, it has assignments for the provisioning of new products and services.

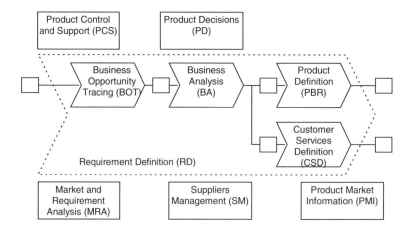

*Figure 2. The Requirement Definition process including its control and support processes.*

## *Requirement Definition (RD)*

The process owner of RD is also head of the organisational function Product Management. The work can be considered a "gap-filler", integrating the market side and the development side of the business. During the development process, wishes from actual and potential customers have to be critically examined and turned into requirements for future products. There are often communication problems between different steps in the chain to the end customer. An enhanced communication is important, especially between product management and the market people, and between them and the network operators. Along the process there are "leaks" where ideas and requirements appear and disappear. These can be minimised by employing a continuous dialogue with the customers.

The GSM-standard has led to a more market-driven development process. Much work is concerned with balancing needs and costs. The expression "return on asses" illustrates the limited personnel resources caused by the rapid growth of Ericsson Radio. The rapid growth also makes it difficult to set priorities and divide responsibilities. The responsibilities within the development side are both technical and commercial and are therefore more complicated than those within the market side.

It is important to ensure that the right decisions are being made, especially in the early parts of the process. One way to do this is to build on a well-structured procedure. Two problems with the approach used for project management is that it risks sequential thinking and requires much documentation work. It is a challenge to get people to work more in parallel, while retaining the ability to keep track of their progress.

The process owner has to define the process and identify sub-processes. The responsibility for the process requires work over organisational borders and might give a new perspective of one's role as line manager. Despite this, seeing the greater picture and facilitating transfers between processes have proved to be two difficult areas.

## *Business Opportunity Tracing (BOT)*

The process owner of BOT is also the Swedish manager for the German market. In BOT, the goal is to develop a specification of customer needs. This specification is later transformed in to a business case in the BA-process. Instead of taking requirements for granted, the aim for BOT is to find the underlying needs. Market competition has led to a need for a more systematic way to analyse customer needs. The overall goal is to cut the lead times within the requirement definition process. An important step towards this is to work with the early parts of the flow, i.e. the BOT process. In BOT, information from various sources is analysed to provide new knowledge. One important source is the Customer Supply Flow, in cases when customer needs could not be satisfied through existing products. Conversely, BOT will deliver information on product ideas to the marketing organisation.

The early parts of the Market Supply Flow are different from the later parts. Especially in BOT, but also in BA, the process is not tied to any specific development project and could be described as "temporally disconnected". Later on, when a project has started, the flow is more "train-like" and easier to describe in process terms. Among the support and control processes, BOT has the strongest connection to Ericsson Strategic Planning (a part of Product Decisions) providing directions, e.g., in terms of prioritised areas.

As BOT is just about to be established, the role of the process owner is currently more like a project manager. Once the BOT process has been defined, a small pilot will be run in order to test the new ideas. It is important to quickly apply the ideas in order to validate them. Process measuring methods will also be defined. When the process is established in the line organisation, the need for continuous follow-up and improvement will become important.

Ericsson has a conservative IT-policy based on IBM mainframes. The MEMO-system for electronic communication has been important for the company's development. One idea for future IT-support is some kind of "structured bill-board" where people working with market analysis and marketing can share input and ideas.

## *Business Analysis (BA)*

The process owner of BA is also product manager for GSM within the organisational unit Product Management. In order to emphasise the importance of the earliest part of the Market Supply Flow, it has been divided into the two processes BOT and BA. Although still a temporary solution, the division is driven by the competition and market needs. As a consequence of the large expansion, it is important to make priorities. Although everything is profitable, the challenge is to find the things *most* profitable. Further on in the Market Supply Flow the process structure become clearer. After BA, a project management approach (PROPS) is employed; although minimising the time required for each part, it does not promote concurrent work.

In the early parts of the product development process, customer needs are being refined into business cases and further on into assignments (if found both technically and economically viable). It is important to get higher quality of the business cases as early as possible in the process. As the lead time for developing a new product is around 18 months, Ericsson would soon be left far behind if they only *followed* their competitors. One idea is to use different development cycles for different products, e.g. using a "fast lane" for smaller projects.

As a process owner, most important is to continually assess the process and to lead the improvement work. In the case of the BOT and BA processes, the first step was to make descriptions of the current situation and suggest improvements. A critical success factor has been to gather people with appropriate competence. Describing the current situation has been an important way to create commitment among people. It is about communicating a "world-view," showing how every part fits into the overall picture. The organisational functions are still strong within Ericsson and can cause problems in the process development work. In addition to the process owner, there is the role of the "process driver" responsible for the day-to-day work in the process. In Ericsson, the latter is the responsibility of the line manager.

Today the flow of information in the BA-process is mainly paper-based, although often complemented by electronic communication. There is a strong need for computer based support in order to minimise the risk of forgetting things. By storing decisions and the information on which they are based, an increased traceability could be achieved. Due to large geographical distances, global systems and global networks are important. Ericsson Strategic Plans, the annual five-year plans, can be viewed as a delimitation for the development work that is being pursued.

## *Product Definition (PBR)*

The process owner of Product Definition (PBR, Product Business Realisation), is also product manager for PCS 1900 (GSM-based products for the American market). As process owner he sees two important tasks: to drive the improvement work and to collect, co-ordinate, and test new improvement ideas. The actual improvement work is handled by a "process developer". Co-operation between Product Definition and Ericsson Strategic

Planning is mainly informal. The product managers provide input to the planning work. Although not directly controlling the Product Definition process, the resulting strategic plan becomes a confirmation of the direction that the company is taking.

One general concern is the consequences of an organisation in three dimensions (line, project, and process). The process is often viewed as the architecture within which projects are performed. One way to increase the commitment to processes within the line organisation would be to employ inter-functional groups for improving and running the processes. Such a solution is currently being used within the Customer Supply Flow. It could facilitate the transfer between different steps in the process and promote concurrent work.

Another issue concerns incentives for improvement work. The managers should be "standing on the barricades", actively showing their interest in process improvement. It is important to facilitate the learning from the process, for example by means of feedback from the project owner to the process owner.

A third issue concerns "Time To Decision", i.e. lead times for decisions. There is a gap between the time when a decision is needed, e.g. when requirements are changed, to when the decision is actually made. Both how the decisions are made and how they are communicated need to be considered. This is the only area where a need for IT support is currently perceived. A related question concerns the flexibility for handling new or changed requirements late in the process. Dealing with so called "disruptive technology" (radically new alternatives) is harder than dealing with "sustaining technology" (existing alternatives). While operating procedures are enough for the latter, the former may require more unconventional solutions, such as creating new companies or new alliances with suppliers and/or competitors.

## *Customer Services Definition (CSD)*

The process owner of CSD is also head of the organisational function Customer Services. They develop and supply services that the customer needs after the hand-over of the equipment, e.g. problem-reporting and modification-handling. Many services have a product number and are listed in the product database. An aim is to develop generic services, especially concerning "core services", i.e. the basic services that are required for customer acceptance. The amount of services in a customer order varies, but many times it is significant (e.g. 20% in a recent order).

The process owner did not quite recognise his process in the process map made by the organisational function Product Management. Instead he preferred the business unit's official process map, where customer needs is a direct input also to CSD, without first going through BOT and BA (cf. Figure 2). Experiences from another part of Ericsson have shown that it might be difficult to get commitment within the organisation for processes. However, process orientation is a critical success factor for long-term economic survival. Customer-oriented processes are more complicated than product-oriented ones. The role of process management is about continuous improvements rather than organisational changes. It can be a way to identify similarities and synergies within the business.

As it is people that in the end influence and are influenced by changes, issues of "people management" and change management are more important than information systems, IT, and methods. "Healthy dissatisfaction" is often good for change. From this perspective, Ericsson's largest problem is its success.

Within the 70-80 countries involved in the CSD process, the process may look quite different depending on the local situation. To manage processes by providing goals might therefore be better than to prescribe a certain way of working. An important prerequisite for improvement is comparison, which in turn requires measurements, e.g. of delivery precision. However, measuring processes is not always easy. Work has been made to document current processes in terms of inputs and outputs. Regarding businesses abroad, it is important to create possibilities for cost and revenue control. The next step is to consider how it ought to be, e.g. in terms of interfaces and transfers between processes. Working with processes leads to stronger commitment. A decision is not taken until it is implemented; it is important with consensus, as it really is the subsidiaries' money and customers that are at stake. Sweden's role is to control and improve, and also to disseminate best practices among the subsidiaries.

## *Product Control and Support (PCS)*

PCS is one of the five processes outside of the main flow of Requirement Definition. The process owner of PCS is also head of Strategic Product Management within the organisational unit for analogue systems (such as the NMT and TACS standards). The unit is responsible for product planning and for providing economic information used for decisions in the development projects.

Although digital systems are requested due to their newness, analogue ones such as NMT are still attractive. Often, issues such as price and coverage are more influential on the decision than the technology itself. It easily happens that employees, network operators, etc., concentrate on the latest products, e.g. GSM. One problem for the analogue side of the organisation is that people working in sales are measured on number of orders rather than profitability. The interest for "cash-cow management" is not prioritised – it is easier to get resources for new (i.e. digital) technology. This is something that may lead to conflict between process and line organisation. It is doubtful whether the best solution is to have strong line managers as process owners.

It is not self-evident how PCS can be viewed as a process. It includes "Economic reporting and feed back" and "Product substitution/termination" – the latter one being the most emphasised part. Questions of lifecycle cost, product substitution, and product termination need higher priority. In cases of product substitution, it can be unclear who is responsible for compatibility issues. Currently, descriptions of the future process of product substitution and termination are being developed. Earlier work focused on defining central concepts: what is meant by e.g. "product", "substitution", and "termination".

It is important to be able to compare profitability measures for different products at different points in time. While service and support earlier were financed through product sales, they might be required to cover their own costs in some product areas, e.g. base stations for NMT. That sales are decreasing in these areas does not mean that the networks' use is decreasing in the same rate. The issue of maintenance represents a cost that needs to be covered and even made profit on. Furthermore, it is important to seriously consider customer queries, the "customer answer process". The queries should be dealt with consistently, questions should be given in the time specified, etc. There is a potential for improvement. Overall, Ericsson Radio is on its way away from a focus on technology development and towards need satisfaction.

There is a risk with a too strong and too narrow focus on processes. If everything is viewed as processes, they loose their meaning. It is through contrasting with something else that the processes gain their appropriate value. For example, experiences from a network operator point to problems with an unmanageable large number of processes, and processes becoming goals in themselves, at the expense of the products.

## *Product Decisions (PD)*

The process Product Decisions (PD) also includes ESP, Ericsson Strategic Planning, where the annual business plans are developed. The process owner of PD is also responsible for two specific releases of Ericsson's GSM-system.

There are problems with measurement and comparison of processes that are not repetitive and have unclear delimitations. This applies to several of the business unit's processes, mainly to the earlier steps of the Market Supply Flow. Much of the work with developing new products is more project oriented in the sense that each project is unique and has its own prerequisites and rules. The projects are always subject to "disturbances" such as competition with other projects for resources, changed requirements from customers, etc. With development cycles of about two years and increased competition on the market, the number of disturbances will hardly decrease.

There is a risk that too detailed control by means of process descriptions hinders creativity, flexibility, and ability to take initiatives. This can be a problem especially in knowledge-intensive companies such as Ericsson. As the concept of process can be applied in various levels of detail in the business, it is an important task to find a suitable level for a given area. There is a greater need for checklists and guidelines than for normative and controlling process descriptions. The approach used for project management has the disadvantage that it builds too much on serial thinking. This might make it harder to achieve parallelism between different parts of the project. In order to reduce project risks and make projects more manageable, large projects with more than 200 participants are avoided. Concerning organisational changes, it is important to be aware of the vacuum that easily appears before a new organisation has come into effect.

The co-operation is more close with the processes BOT, BA, and PD. It is less developed with CSD as this process belongs to another organisational unit and is not yet fully functional. In the product development process, an increased communication between marketing and product management would enable better utilisation of their respective competencies. As a result of increased degree of market control and competition, lead times and the use of resources has to be reduced. Clearer and smother transitions between different stages are also needed, as are earlier contacts with market and suppliers. The role of strategic planning needs to be strengthened; follow-up of business cases and feedback from later stages need clearer routines.

Concerning IT-support, the possibilities for communication are central. Email, networks, and CD-ROM are some examples. For the economic reporting, one has to be able to get information from other systems. It is important to get a good relationship between the IT-systems and their "customers" (the users); it might be difficult to decide what one wants. Two ongoing projects deal with catalogues of products and features (functions). The primary users are marketing, but the projects include participants from different organisational units.

## *Market and Requirements Analysis (MRA)*

The process owner of MRA is also product manager for digital systems. The MRA is not really a homogeneous process but rather a collection of six different activities, e.g. "End user analysis" and "Operator analysis", without closer connections. The work as a process owner accounts to approximately 10% of the work time, i.e. 4-5 hours per week.

Important goals considering work with process-maps are to sort out *what* to do and *why*. The latter becomes a consequence of an increased consciousness of the wholeness that one is part of. Process-maps provide a common world-view. They are especially important when it comes to newly hired employees and training for new positions. Process work can also be a foundation for growth, being a tool for increased effectiveness and efficiency in what is being done. People's knowledge of the more theoretical base for process-maps is minimal.

There is a perceived need for change of the decision process within product development. Not only do the decisions take too long time, it is unsure whether it is the right decisions that are being made. These factors have influenced the coming re-organisation. As a result of all changes in the environment, it is almost a necessity with a re-organisation about every third year. The coming re-organisation will not affect the process descriptions.

In general, it is managers in the line organisation that have got the role of process owner. It is important that there exists diversity in perspectives among the different process owners; several pictures are needed. As a process owner of MRA, much work concerns co-ordinating and managing the process work within the different sub-processes. It is up to each sub-process owner to develop the necessary material, such as process descriptions. Most important is to be able to describe what is being done in process terms – so that people in the main process "recognises themselves". It is the main process that decides if the developed descriptions are sufficient – in a narrow sense the descriptions in themselves, in a wider sense the actual work being done in the sub-process.

As a result of the expansion of the business, and the experience of participating at an exciting time, employees within Ericsson Radio often work hard. It is important that employees combine daily work with more long-term improvement work. These two activities should not be handled independently by different people. New hirings is an area with perceived needs for improvement. There is a large turnover in personnel – annually 25-30% – as a result of the company's growth, required competencies, and internal mobility. The major part of the turnover results from employees moving from one part of the company to another for longer or shorter periods of time.

There is a potential for IT-support in all support processes, although it is currently not being used to any larger extent. Gaps in communication might not only exist between business people and IT-support people but also between business people and production people.

## Suppliers Management (SM)

The process owner of SM is also head of Intelligent Network services within the organisational unit Product Management, dealing with solutions that are customer specific rather than generic and mainstream. The SM process has the purpose of creating added value for Ericsson products by combining them with products from other suppliers. Currently, the work is focused on ways to certify external products for use together with Ericsson products. The integrated operation of the products is checked and a division of responsibilities is negotiated. In order to clarify the relationships with suppliers, an approach to process management was chosen as a tool for discussion of problems and solutions. So far, checklists, test-cases, and pilot-cases has been used to gather and disseminate experiences. The knowledge level about the large degree of complexity that characterises acquisition of complete subsystems is low.

In the middle of 1994, the organised improvement work stopped as a result of too high workload; the operative work took all the time. The ambition now is to scale down central process descriptions and to avoid too detailed control of the processes. The approaches used for process and project management are chiefly focusing on the main development process. Using these approaches also for support processes is not always a simple thing to do. The responsibility of a process owner concerns the commitment for the process in the organisation. Currently, the most important issue is to document the processes. A difficult issue is to know *how* this should be done. How is e.g. feedback represented in process maps; does it exist or are the processes strictly sequential in time? Another difficult issue is that the process descriptions show a mixed "is" and "should" state.

Within the business as a whole, there are a large number of IT-systems in operation; however, they do not seem to be co-ordinated with each other. There seems to be a potential for improvement in this area. It is a challenge to get this heritage of support systems to follow the changes in both organisation and processes. There is no point denying that the support systems are controlling the business to a degree. As the SM-process is so new, not much thinking has been done concerning information support. However, there is a need to better be able to follow the development process, e.g. in terms of product decisions, economic information, and requirements specifications.

## Product Market Information (PMI)

The process owner of PMI is also head of Product Market Support within the organisational unit Product Management. The PMI process is a support process for enhancing communication between the Market Supply Flow and the Customer Supply Flow. PMI provides the market with information about products. Its deals mainly with information and sales support, such as maps, CD-ROMs, information leaflets, and courses for people in sales and marketing.

Two parts of the process owner role are to create continuity in the process work, and to drive the improvement work. The tasks require good descriptions and measurements of the process. In PMI, a consultant from another part of Ericsson is developing process maps of the current process. Too detailed descriptions of processes are to be avoided. There is a risk that they become conserving and leave less room for necessary improvisation and flexibility. Concerning measurements, they are being made mainly by means of surveys that are sent out two times per year to sales and marketing.

While PMI mainly interacts with the early parts of the Market Supply Flow, and sales and marketing in the Customer Supply Flow, it has very little to do with the other support processes. One large difficulty for PMI is to find information about the rationale behind a product or a component. While the descriptions available often contain technical information about *what* the product does, they seldom contain information about *why* it does it, i.e. what need it satisfies.

An important tool for PMI is the "feature database". Currently, a complement to this in the form of a product database is being developed. It is going to contain descriptions of products (collections of features) useful for sales and marketing. As this system might be useful also outside of the business unit, there is a reference group for its development with participants from other parts of Ericsson as well. A special kind of information concerns products that are being developed; this information is much asked for by the customers.

# On the mind of a process owner

Having gone through the descriptions from all ten process owners, it is now time to look for some common patterns. As a result of a bottom-up analysis, nine main issues have been identified. These main issues can be considered as areas of interest and their ordering does not reflect any special order of priority. Each main issue comprises several sub-issues that have been highlighted in the presentation. Key questions, induced from the material, are used as quick introductions.

## *General changes*

Key question: How can we deal with the possibilities and problems of rapid expansion in an environment of increased competition and faster changes?

Concerning the *environment*, the use of standards leads to an increased competition and faster changes. Changes are more and more driven by the market, the network operators and the end-users. Satisfying the needs of the customers is becoming ever more important. A challenge is to offer what the customers actually need – which is not always the same as what they first think or say that they need.

Within the *company*, the large expansion can be both facilitating and hindering for further improvement. Success and good profitability can lead to increased room for action, but also to a decreased motivation for change. As a result of limited resources, especially concerning employees, the expansion forces continuous decisions. To keep reaction times and decision paths short, smaller, autonomous units with clear responsibilities are needed. Well-defined processes are less sensitive to external changes – something to keep in mind as internal change often is a cause of distress. It is felt to be more interesting to work on new products even when the older ones are at least as profitable.

## Process goals

Key question: How can we shorten lead times, accommodate changes in a flexible way, and make the right decisions in the process?

The issue of *decision quality* is important; the consequences of the earlier decisions are large, especially when considering the fast changes in the market. A main concern is to ensure the quality of the information used for decisions, e.g. business cases, during the whole process. It is important to attend to the real problems of the customers – something that put large demands on the ability to look ahead and to articulate the core problems.

Many things can happen along the process. Disruptions, in the form of changes in requirements, tools, standards, etc., have to be managed in some way. Rather than isolating the process from its environment, it is an advantage for it to have enough *flexibility* not to be affected negatively. At the same time, there is an aim to keep the process and its products as generic as possible.

To be able to succeed also in the future, a faster process is needed – both in terms of the work being done, the decisions being made, and the information being spread. Every lead-time has to shorten in order to increase the *speed*; doing more things in parallel is another possible way.

## Process orientation

Key question: How can processes be of help and what are the difficulties, for example in relation to other dimensions of the business?

An important consequence of *process thinking* is to aid the identification of synergies within the organisation. It encourages discovery of wholeness and reflection of your work in a larger context. It can also form the foundation for change work. Although important in the long run, process thinking can be difficult to implement.

A higher *degree of structure* is felt to be of need in the process. However, there are also reasons to avoid too detailed control, because of large local variations and the employees' personal creativity. When it comes to control and support processes, it is uncertain to what extent they can be considered processes at all.

The business is discussed in *multiple dimensions:* processes, the line organisation, projects and products. Relationships between the dimensions are not clear, in particular not concerning responsibility and authority. These uncertainties can lead to confusion, unbalances and inconsistent priorities. The relationship between processes and the line organisation is central, especially since the processes are run within the line organisation.

## Process improvement

Key question: How do we get time and resources for improving and measuring when we hardly have time for the daily work?

Concerning the *way-of-working* to improve processes, it is important to be attentive on how new ideas are created. Questions regarding incentives, initiative and reuse of knowledge are important. The improvement work itself is done differently depending on whether it concerns businesses within or outside Sweden.

*Measuring* the processes is central for improvement. However, this is not always easily done, mainly because of significant variations between different processes and also because of partly undefined boundaries for the processes.

Limited *resources* means that there is a need to constantly balance between the daily work and the improvement work.

## Process descriptions

Key question: How do we create and use descriptions to get overall views and facilitate change, while avoiding to make the descriptions too controlling?

Process descriptions can be a practical way to obtain an *overall view* of the business. A common picture where different groups all recognise themselves and their part of the whole is an important goal. However, due to different perspectives, this goal is not always easy to reach.

*Tools for change* is another function of process descriptions. They can give rise to ideas for change – both within your own process and others'.

Finished process descriptions can be felt to be *controlling* and delimiting, especially for someone who has not been involved in the creation. Steps to rectify this are to involve all people that are affected, and to make the descriptions on an appropriate level of detail.

The *actual creation* of process descriptions is not always easy. Central questions are both what should be described and how the description should be done. Describing a current situation can be as problematic as it is important. Apart from process descriptions, there might also be need of complementary descriptions, such as maps of concepts used and goals pursued.


## The role of the process owner

Key question: How do we get an overview of the whole process, improve it, and integrate it with the line organisation?

The process owner works with a *broader perspective* of the whole. By documenting what the different sub-processes' bring into the picture, as well as their interactions, an overall view is created.

As a process owner, one is responsible of *improvement* and follow-up of one's process. To keep track off the process, and to pick up ideas for change, become important parts of the work.

The process owner aims for *integration* between processes and the functional line organisation. By having process owners that also are functional managers, a larger degree of integration is possible – for better or for worse. Only a small portion of these persons' total workload relates to their role as process owners.


## Personal competence

Key question: How can the knowledge and commitment of existing employees best come to use while supporting newly employed when they get into their new jobs?

*Existing employees* have a key role within the business although that role is not always easy. The rapid expansion of the business has both positive and negative consequences for the employees. An important success factor for process management is the knowledge and commitment that the employees have for process management.

The competence of *newly employed* is especially relevant because of the rapid expansion of the business. There is a high throughput of employees as they often change positions and responsibilities within the company. This makes it important to find ways to support people getting into their new jobs.

## Communication

Key question: How can communication be improved within the organisation, between processes, and with customers and suppliers?

*In terms of processes*, the communication within the main flow is generally regarded as clear and straightforward. However, some of the connections are still unclear. The communication between the main flow and the control- and support processes is significantly more complex and not always defined in terms of input and output.

*In terms of the organisation*, communication and co-operation between different business units concerns mainly products, e.g. telephone switches, and not so much processes or process improvement. Within the business unit, much of the communication in terms of the organisation concerns planning and management, but also the diffusion of ideas and experiences. The communication is not without problems and more extensive contacts are sought after.

*Outside the company*, communication and co-operation with customers is important. This is the case both in connection with the initial identification of customer needs and in connection with final delivery. The communication and co-operation with suppliers is increasing.

## Information support

Key question: What can IS/IT do for our business to facilitate information diffusion, communication and co-operation?

Information support of *today* consists of a variety of systems – some inter-linked, others not. Some systems are global while others are local. Communication and information diffusion through networks and CD-ROM is important.

Coming up with ideas and requirements for *new systems* can be problematic. On a general level there is a need for support systems that are flexible and easy to modify. A main part of the needs concern various ways to communicate and to support co-operation within the business unit.

# Conclusions

As has been shown in this study, there are a number of things occupying the mind of a process owner (cf. Figure 3). In the case of Ericsson Radio, many of the issues are influenced by the context of product development, a successful expansion, and a rapidly changing environment.

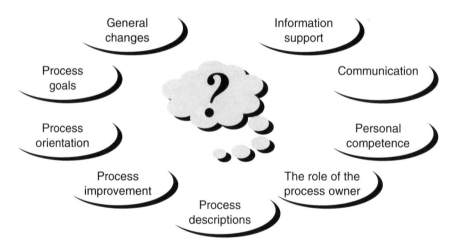

*Figure 3. Nine main issues on the mind of a process owner.*

Going back to the initial broad areas that were identified for the interviews – the process itself (product development), its development (improvement work), and an enabler for change (IT-support) – the results can be summarised in three main points:

(1) The process owners show a strong interest for process orientation and its effects. However, "process" is a complicated concept in practice – even for a company that has been involved with process work for a decade.

(2) The process owners show a strong interest for broad perspectives and co-operation. However, there are a number of complicated relationships where different interests cause problems – not only between processes and organisational functions.

(3) The process owners show a strong interest for communication and information diffusion. However, questions of IS and IT support are not in focus.

# Acknowledgements

The authors would like to thank the people at Ericsson Radio who contributed their experiences as process owners.

The research was funded by NUTEK, the Swedish National Board for Industrial and Technical Development.

# References

Bergman, B. & Klevsjö, B. (1994) *Quality From Customer Needs to Customer Satisfaction*, Studentlitteratur, Lund, Sweden.

Davenport, T. (1993) *Process Innovation: Reengineering Work through Information Technology*, Harvard Business School Press, Boston, Massachusetts.

Glaser, B.G. & Strauss, A.L. (1967) *The Discovery of Grounded Theory: Strategies for Qualitative Research*, Aldine de Gruyter, New York.

Hammer, M. & Champy, J. (1993) *Reengineering the Corporation: A Manifesto for Business Revolution*, HarperCollins Publishers, New York.

Rummler, G.A. & Brache, A.P. (1995) *Improving Performance: How to Manage the White Space on the Organization Chart*, 2nd ed., Jossey-Bass Publishers, San Francisco.

Steneskog, G. (1991) *Process Management: Konsten att styra och utveckla ett företags administrativa processer*, Liber, Malmö, Sweden [*Process Management: The Art of Managing and Developing a Company's Administrative Processes*].

Tolis, C. & Nellborn, C. (1997) "Process Owner, What's on Your Mind? A Case Study within Product Development at Ericsson Radio", in Galliers, R., Murphy, C., Hansen, H.R, O'Callaghan, R., Carlsson, S. & Loebbecke, C.

(eds.) *Proceedings of the 5th European Conference on Information Systems*, Cork Publishing Limited, Cork, Ireland, pp. 1357-1371.

Tolis, C. & Nilsson, A.G. (1996) "Using Business Models in Process Orientation", in Lundeberg, M. & Sundgren, B. (eds.) *Advancing Your Business – People and Information Systems in Concert*, The Economic Research Institute (EFI), Stockholm School of Economics, Stockholm.

# 3

# A Monopoly Facing Competition: Sweden Post's Exploration of Processes and Descriptions

*Christer Nellborn*
*Christofer Tolis*

*Changing a functionally organised, 360 year old, public monopoly into a flexible commercial communications provider on a competitive market – this is Sweden Post's challenge. One way to meet the challenge has been for Sweden Post to explore the topics of process orientation and business descriptions. The work was started in the spring of 1996, in a project called VEPRO. This chapter focuses on the different issues that were discussed in three of the sub-projects within VEPRO. As a conclusion, five important dilemmas that surfaced during the project are presented: degree of process orientation, process "flow", multiple descriptions, amount of analysis, and order of development.*

## Introduction

In 1993, the market for mail delivery within Sweden was opened up for competition. It was the last step in a process of transforming a monopoly into a competitive market. The change was a formidable challenge for Sweden Post. A 360 year old tradition of public monopoly was broken as the government changed the fundamental business rule. For Sweden Post, which had been anticipating this change for a number of years, the loss of the monopoly meant a definite step towards a market situation with increasing competition.

Besides the transformation from public monopoly to competitive market, the situation for Sweden Post is going through another equally dramatic change. The rapidly increasing use of fax, e-mail and World Wide Web has a significant effect on communication habits for both companies and the general public. As a result, the traditional means to communicate in writing – by sending letters – now faces a number of serious alternatives.

A number of ideas and tools for successfully adopting to the changing environment have been explored by Sweden Post over the years. Process orientation and business descriptions are two recent examples. Based on Tolis & Nellborn (1998), this chapter reports on the way Sweden Post, during the spring of 1996, specifically addresses these issues as a way to support the company's transition into a customer-oriented competitive-market situation.

## Sweden Post's business concept and organisation

To match the new requirements, Sweden Post has formulated its business concept in the following way:

> "Through Sweden Post, everyone shall be able to reach everyone with messages, goods and payments. Sweden Post also creates added value for its customers by creatively joining together their own resources with other's in communication processes and financial services. Sweden Post utilises all available media to ensure that messages, goods and payments reach their recipients wherever they are, and whatever means of reception are available. Every person, company, and organisation in Sweden is a customer to Sweden Post. This includes companies located abroad but with connections to Sweden" (Sweden Post, 1995 b, p. 8; the authors' translation).

Sweden Post has a very good starting point for its change process. For example, in an evaluation made by International Post Corporation and Price Waterhouse (IPC, 1997), Sweden Post came out among the top six of 18 European postal services when measuring inter-country mail delivery times. In spite of the good performance relative to other postal services in Europe, the challenge of becoming an actor on a competitive and rapidly changing market has triggered several changes within Sweden Post. Although the concept of being customer-oriented is nothing new to the organisation, it now also has to become competitive.

Sweden Post is organised in different business areas as shown in Figure 1. Supporting the organisation are a number of group executive staffs. One of them is known as Informatics and deals with a multitude of questions concerning information, information systems and the use of information technology within Sweden Post. This area is fast moving forward. Informatics has to stay abreast of the development of concepts, methodologies, and techniques within research and practice and therefore has to be very active. Within Informatics, they have to evaluate, communicate, and adopt new concepts and techniques to the situation in Sweden Post.

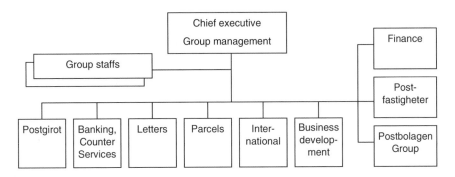

*Figure 1. Sweden Post's organisation (adapted from Sweden Post, 1995 a, p. 3).*

One example is Informatics' heavy involvement in the development of a business development framework, MIPS (Models for Informatics-handling in Sweden Post). MIPS comprises models for systems development, project management, systems maintenance, and data administration. The aim is to cover the complete business systems cycle from strategic business planning to information systems maintenance. For example, in the handbook in data administration one can find recommendations, hints and guidelines for how to go about defining important terms and concepts.

## The VEPRO project

In the beginning of 1996, group staff Informatics launched an investigation project concerning effective information support for the Sweden Post business in the future. The starting point was the assumption that Sweden Post might introduce process orientation some time in the future as a means of managing the organisation. In order to secure the information support for the actors in the processes, there was an important need for useful descriptions of the business. The project was launched to investigate what process orientation and business descriptions (business models) could mean for the organisation. The project was called by its Swedish acronym, VEPRO.

The project might be viewed as a way for Sweden Post to bridge a gap between two dominant models used for development (cf. Tolis & Nilsson, 1996). As shown in Figure 2, one is Sweden Post Business Plan, the model for strategic planning that the company uses. The other one is MIPS, a set of models used for controlling the development and management of information systems. Before VEPRO, there was a gap between these two levels, a gap that process orientation and business descriptions could help to bridge by connecting strategic goals to information needs in the business processes.

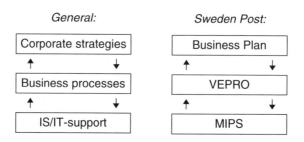

*Figure 2. Three levels of development with associated development models used in Sweden Post (adapted from Tolis & Nilsson, 1996).*

The assignment went to Sweden Post System Service, a company within the Postbolagen Group of Sweden Post (cf. Figure 1 above). The project was divided into sub-projects, each addressing different aspects of the issue. They were executed in parallel and went on for their most intensive parts during the two months of February and March, 1996.

The project manager from Sweden Post System Service ensured that people from all over the organisation participated in the project. In total, around 20 people were directly involved in the project, including several external resources. The authors participated in the project as external resources, providing an external view of the work. Their role was to take an active part in the work done, as well as to observe, reflect, and provide feedback. The sub-projects dealt with:

- *Ongoing process-oriented projects.* Investigating what was being done in other change projects within Sweden Post.

- *Organisational prerequisites.* Addressing what was needed of the organisation for successful implementation of process orientation.

- *Concepts and definitions*. Establishing a conceptual foundation for the new ideas of process orientation and business descriptions.

In the following, each of these sub-projects will be described in more detail. A fourth sub-project, *IS/IT prerequisites*, dealt with the potential use of an object oriented systems architecture as a mean to support process orientation. Although a very important issue in many aspects, it is not within the main focus of this chapter and is therefore not discussed further in the following.

# Ongoing process-oriented projects

As a sub-project within VEPRO, a number of ongoing projects within Sweden Post were examined. They all shared a focus on process orientation in one way or another. Seven projects were chosen among the ones known by the project leaders. Representatives for each project were interviewed in order to gain knowledge of various aspects of the work going on. The aspects, thirteen of them in total, ranged from the concrete purpose of the project to difficulties experienced. As most of the projects were newly started, the focus of the interviews was on their earlier phases. As the projects were quite different in their character, e.g. in terms of purpose and scope, they contributed to give a widespread picture of the process-oriented work that was going on in Sweden Post. Below follow summaries of the seven ongoing projects that were examined.

## *New sales organisation*

The first project was about designing a new sales organisation, where sales people from different business areas co-operate in so called "customer-teams". The purpose was to create one single interface between the customer and Sweden Post in order to keep – and increase revenues from – customers that are common to several business areas. There were many participants in the project from all of the business areas – sales managers, business area managers, sales people, etc. External consultants also played a major role. At the time of the interviews, some pilot cases had been carried out. No special analysis had been done considering information support for the process. In the future, however, the customer system would be of importance.

The choice to adopt process orientation was influenced by consultants; it was believed to facilitate an overall view of the business and its context. A process definition existed but was not considered too important. To help making descriptions, the tool ProcessWise (from ICL) was used in connection with Excel. Team-leaders were owners of the main process, while people from the different business areas were owners of the sub processes. At the time of the interviews, no evaluation criteria for the process had been considered.

The project had created insight into, and understanding of, the business among the participants. It had been noticed that process orientation not always is obvious; it can take some time and work to get used to.

## New process-oriented business

Implementing a new service, including its underlying organisation, was the topic of the second project. Flexibility, customer orientation, world-class performance, and management of complexity and geographical diversity, were all desired goals that required a suitable structure to guarantee quality of project and the service. At the time of the interviews, a relatively small group of people had been involved. Knowledge of process descriptions and quality had mostly been taken from consultants. No implementation had yet been done. Information support was chosen early on, which had resulted in some problems in the match with the needs.

Process orientation was chosen as it was considered a good way to reach the desired goals of the project. A process definition existed, although it needed to be developed further. Qualicycle (from QualiWare and Metcon) with Business Viewer was used as a tool for making process descriptions. Process owners had been appointed, both for development and operations. Although not developed in detail at the time of the interviews, economical and quality measures would be used in future benchmarking procedures.

An important lesson at the time of the interviews was to focus more on process orientation than on the tool being used. Process orientation was believed to be a good way to create shared images of the business. A risk was that the "receiving" organisation did not understand process orientation and management. This work had been found to take time.

## General description of the sales process

The third project had a purpose of developing a general description of the sales process. The work was part of evaluating the benefits of a company-wide customer system. A relatively small group of people – all coming from within Sweden Post – had been involved in the project so far. However, the time had came for communication with the business area. As the first description was almost finished, their comments might lead to it being revised. Information support was considered in the form of the existing customer system: how can it best be used in the sales process?

Process orientation was believed to give a good possibility of co-operation across borders, between both different business areas and different technical platforms. It provided a good foundation for further development and re-use – and perhaps also for a future common methodology. A process definition was not used in the project. Qualicycle with the QA model was used as a tool for making process descriptions. A "sales council" was responsible towards the business area for the resulting general description. No criteria for evaluating the process had yet been discussed.

At the time of the interviews, it was too early to speak of real experiences. However, the way of describing seemed to be effective; at least the possibility of re-use was better than with a more traditional methodology.

## *Existing process-oriented way-of-working*

Evaluating and developing an existing process-oriented way-of-working within a business area was the goal of the fourth project. Concrete purposes were to focus customer benefits, reduce costs, and increase employee's knowledge and sense of participation. The vision of a future way-of-working, having a strong customer orientation, was a reaction to the perception of being stuck in organisational functions and sub-optimisation of the business. A small group of people worked in the project, having commitment from management. The competence was a result from earlier internal projects and from different external consultants. The project further developed earlier work regarding processes; describing the processes was an activity that was going on. Although the existing production systems had not been considered in the project, there had been loose discussions of possible needs for new types of IT support as a result of new ways-of-working.

It was considered that process orientation would be a good means to achieve the project's purposes. The process definition used had been established on a management level. Tools used for process descriptions were the simplest possible; content was more important than form. No process owners had been appointed, but instead people responsible for the descriptions. Despite being considered, no evaluation criteria for the processes had been decided upon.

Lessons from the project were that it had been difficult, fun, and that it had led to a large degree of participation. Descriptions of the business and analysis of the information needs might have been more important than the process concept itself. Also important was to anchor ideas among the management. Difficulties had been that the project was long and had met with a bit of resistance.

## EDI system and consultant service

Electronic data interchange (EDI) was the area of the fifth project. The purpose was to develop a technical solution, an operations model, and a consultant service within the area. This was a way to reach the underlying goal of creating new businesses according to the mission of Sweden Post. Eight to nine people with different background participated in the project. Among them were technicians and people with specialist competence of EDI, data administration, computer operations and accounting. People from Ericsson had a function as sparring-partners. The internal competence of processes was quite varied. A general training programme, the Sweden Post IT School, had provided some knowledge; there was a desire to learn more. The plan was to have the operations model ready in six months time. A process mapping of their own business, in order to learn more, was planned. In terms of information support, the EDI technology was, of course, the base of the new service.

A major reason for process orientation was that EDI and processes naturally support each other. There were many possibilities internally and externally; the environment was turbulent and the reach of new communication media affected the competition. No particular process definition was being used in the project. Neither tools for descriptions, nor process owners or evaluation criteria, had yet come up in the project.

Experiences at the time of the interviews showed that the businesses of different companies had strong similarities. Standardisation was often performed both top-down and bottom-up in the organisation. A potential problem was that it took time to create consensus, time that perhaps did not exist.

## Handling of complaints

Developing new forms for the handling of complaints was the issue of the sixth project. At the time of the interviews, the handling did not sufficiently take into account the content of the complaints in order to improve the business. The purpose of the project was to rectify the problems and create solutions that were independent of changes in services and organisation. A smaller group within Sweden Post had been the driving force in the project. The task had to a large extent been to try to anchor the ideas in the business area. Creating a consensus about the implementation was tried in meetings with the business area. For information support, a top-level analysis and a model of the systems solution had been made. There was co-operation with the customer system project.

It was felt natural to view handling of complaints as an information process. Process orientation ought to result in greater customer orientation and lower costs for quality deficiencies. Apart from viewing the business as an information process, no definition had been made of the process concept. Simple drawing tools had been used in the process. No formal decision of process owners had been made; individual business areas would be responsible for their process. Evaluation criteria had been partly determined but discussions were still in progress.

Lessons from the project were to start with the customer through co-operation, encourage through business plans, follow-up through budgets, make relationships clear through descriptions, and stimulate creativity through networks. Stubbornness was required from a few and engagement from everybody. It was important to anchor the project ideas on a high level in the organisation. It could be difficult to break the borders of the functional organisation.

## *Tool for process descriptions*

The seventh project dealt with evaluating a tool for process descriptions. The concrete purpose of the project was to produce an evaluation report, and a specific business within Sweden Post had been chosen as a test case. This was all done in response to the need for a process description tool. A smaller group was working in the project; the competence had got its base from the Sweden Post IT School. At the time of the interviews, the process report was completed. An information support model existed, with examples of functions and screen layouts. The integration between different systems was important.

The idea to keep track of flows in the business had made process orientation a natural perspective. No process definition existed. The tool being used was Qualicycle with the QA model. No formal decision had been made regarding process owners, but natural choices existed. No evaluation criteria for processes had been formulated.

A lesson from the project was that although there were wishes for standards regarding business descriptions, accurate descriptions easily lead to complex and hard-to-read maps. Another potential difficulty was that new organisational forms lead to new roles that could take time to be accepted. Interest for the project had had both its ups and downs.

### *Summarising the issues regarding ongoing projects*

- There are differences in the *degree of process orientation* that the projects aim for. Some projects regard it as a matter of viewing workflows and activities as processes. Others couple it to a changed way or working. Still others equal it to a whole new organisation.

- There is an aim to increase the *process "flow"*, supporting a strong customer focus. This effort can be more internally oriented, focusing on processes internal to Sweden Post, and more externally oriented, focusing on Sweden Post's role as a part of their customers' processes. However, the integration work takes time and is in many cases quite difficult – for example when crossing organisational borders.

- The projects engage into different *amount of analysis*. The interest of going into details varies, e.g. regarding the interpretation of "process". Their interest is more pragmatic; the content of the descriptions is more important than the form, paper and pen more important than computerised tools. Still, a common standard and tool are believed to be helpful, e.g. by providing a higher degree of unity between descriptions produced in different parts of the organisation.

- The projects exhibits different *order of development*. They begin and end with focus on different types of development activities. Some begin with the process, leaving issues of information support to a later stage; others do the reverse.

# Organisational prerequisites

Within the sub-project dealing with organisational prerequisites for process orientation, four people from different parts of Sweden Post participated together with a researcher. The participants came both from different group staffs and from the more operational side of the organisation.

They all shared an interest in issues of organisational development. Within the sub-project, the work was mostly done in a distributed manner, matched with a couple of physical meetings. Communication within the group was facilitated by the use of an electronic conference system (First Class).

A number of issues and questions were raised in the sub-project. In the following, we have concentrated on those issues that the group focused on and that resulted in the most intensive discussions.

## Goals and changes influencing development

There are several things that influence the work of developing the business of Sweden Post. The group discussed basic goals for the organisation, as well as potential changes in its environment. Both goals and changes were perceived to be relevant as prerequisites for process orientation, although some were seen as having a more direct link to process orientation than others. When it came to basic goals influencing any development activity, the group identified a number of them, based on directives from Sweden Post's management:

- *Everyone shall be able to reach everyone*. Sweden Post shall be a company offering a variety of message-mediating services to all Swedish citizens and organisations. This goal provides a way to focus the market activities.

- *Creating meetings*. Sweden Post shall be an effective link between people, between organisations, and between people and organisations. This goal opens up for new ways of interaction with customers in the form of new products and services.

- *Customer orientation*. This means having a perspective on services and solutions based on customers and customer segments. The business shall be designed from a customer perspective rather than from a product or service perspective.

- *"One Sweden Post"*. Details of the organisational structure shall be transparent to the customer. Although there are different organisational units, customers shall still perceive that they are dealing with one company. This can for example mean that a customer has only one contact point with Sweden Post, irrespectively of the issues at hand.

- *Integrating Sweden Post's resources with other resources in communication processes and financial services*. This means integrating the value chain of Sweden Post with suppliers, customers and other companies (partners) in a creative way.

- *Having the most satisfied customers in the markets of operation.* This means selecting markets and performing in such a way that Sweden Post is able to provide its customers with high-quality goods and services.

- *Having a good local foundation.* This enables the use of small-scale advantages such as direct customer contact and knowledge of local prerequisites.

- *Establishing the workplace of the 21st century.* This means a focus on competence development, participation, responsibility, and objectives.

- *Recognising the "soul" of Sweden Post.* Shared values and management by values are important principles to base actions and decisions on. This gives a more homogeneous behaviour among co-workers, and towards customers and other external parties.

When it came to potential changes in the world around Sweden Post, the group discussed what ought to influence a development activity. To begin with, the customer base may change faster in the future than it previously has. With that will follow demands on fast and flexible acting from Sweden Post. Furthermore, a more competitive situation is expected in the future. There will certainly be more actors willing to compete for the customers. Another change is represented by the technological development for communicative services. This will change the markets significantly. The question is what effect this will have on customer needs, and Sweden Post's ability to satisfy those needs. Also, changes in the society as a whole are important to consider, e.g. in terms of changing value systems and the development of global societies. Finally, changes in the economical situation – for customers, for the country, and of course for Sweden Post itself – need to be considered when developing the company.

## *Process interaction in the value chain*

An important realisation, related to the discussion about potential changes in the environment, was the inter-relatedness of different activities – in and around Sweden Post. In order to create value for the customer, different activities need to interact. From a viewpoint of process orientation, this means that different parts of the value-adding process must work together, whether they are parts of one or several companies. In the context of Sweden Post's value chain, the possible conflict between process orientation and decentralisation was discussed. For Sweden Post, decentralisation of decision making was seen as essential for the ability to adapt quickly to changes. Decentralisation was also seen as a way to fight bureaucracy. At the same time, there was a belief in the integrated workings of "One Sweden Post". The question raised was the relationship between the ideas of decentralisation and process orientation. Are they compatible? Will process orientation lead to more bureaucracy, or less?

Important in the context of value-chain interaction, was the development of virtual organisations and networks of co-operating organisations. What effects will that development have for Sweden Post's role on the market and the way the company works together with its customers? The traditional boundaries of the organisation, and the way other organisations interact with Sweden Post, might very well have to change. The interface towards customers could change, and also vary more between different customers. Some customers might appreciate if Sweden Post took more responsibility for payments and mailing logistics within their organisation. Other customers might want solutions where Sweden Post co-operates with other companies – perhaps even with competitors of Sweden Post.

The increasingly competitive situation, and the ongoing technological development, were other reasons for considering the issue of managing the value chain. The range of products and services that Sweden Post is providing might have to change due to new alternatives becoming available to the customers. Being able to quickly respond to changes in customer habits and needs, e.g. concerning their use of fax, e-mail, and electronic payment, was considered a reason to explore new possibilities of interacting with the environment. Forming alliances and networks with other companies are only some of the alternatives available.

Decentralising an organisation and co-ordinating a network of co-operating organisations (whether within Sweden Post or outside of it), could be assumed to make it difficult for any process to work effectively. Organisational boundaries tend to be boundaries also for the sense of responsibility. However, the discussion was that there are more than one way to structure an organisation. It is not necessarily so that the organisational boundaries have to go between the traditional business functions. They can for instance go along processes instead of along functional borders. Through clever definition of responsibilities, authorities, roles and their organisational relationships, it can be possible to make the processes work over organisational boundaries.

## *Degree of radicality in process orientation*

Given an interest in process orientation, one question was how much to aim for, and how fast. Increasing Sweden Post's focus on business processes, and improving the effectiveness of those business processes, would involve a number of changes to the current way of thinking and working. Different "schools" of process orientation emphasise different degree of radicality in the changes proposed. Business Process Reengineering (BPR), especially as conceived by Hammer & Champy (1993), has traditionally been advocates of radical changes. Total Quality Management (TQM), on the other hand, is often used as a collective name for a focus on smaller changes that take place over a long time with stepwise improvements.

While much of the critique against TQM has been that there very seldom are any major improvements achieved this way, the group also discussed the risks associated with more radical changes. Radical changes might have serious effects on the organisation's behaviour. Its performance might drop dramatically over a period. A radical change comprising vast areas of the organisation under a short period of time may lead to a situation where the organisation is unable to go through all the way with the change, and ends up with a bit of the new and a bit of the old. Another risk lies in loosing the strengths of the current way of working. Organisational knowledge is a lot easier to destroy than to build up.

In the case of Sweden Post, the group identified some specific characteristics that ought to affect the intended degree of radicality. With the size of the organisation comes muscles and a well-recognised name. However, the government does not want Sweden Post to "kill the market" by competing too harsh. Furthermore, Sweden Post continues to have certain obligations to society in terms of not being allowed to abandon certain geographic areas, such as sparsely-populated rural areas. Should a radical change result in a dramatic performance drop, this will not only be a problem for Sweden Post, e.g. by providing competitors with new opportunities. Due to the company's market dominance, it could also be a problem on a larger scale, having serious effects on society as a whole.

On the other hand, Sweden Post has to stay ahead of competition. Current problems, and the expected market position if changes are not made, have to be considered. Although the long-term perspective was hard to predict, the group regarded it as realistic to assume that the market situation would be hard to defend if changes were not made to the organisation's operation. Being big is not always an advantage in a competitive situation.

After a deregulation, the former monopoly often has a difficult position with an inherited reputation of being slow and inefficient, whilst new competitors are viewed as efficient and alert. For Sweden Post this meant that it had to come across to the general public as modern and effective, in order to avoid the monopolistic legacy. If no real changes were made, it was the understanding of the group that the company would have problems due to this legacy.

Instead of hoping to find any conclusive argument for a specific degree of radicality in the case of Sweden Post, the group ended up re-examining the alternatives. It was interesting to note the re-thinking exhibited by Hammer and Champy in the paperback edition of their book (ibid.). In an additional chapter they comment on why many BPR projects have failed. Instead of the earlier focus on quick radical changes as the key to success, they focus on the significance of clear and established processes. The key role that radicality used to play is no longer stressed to the same extent. Another approach to the degree of radicality is to aim for a combination of both small steps and more radical leaps. This makes use of the benefits of the small steps in-between the more radical ones, and does not require investing the whole company future into one major change.

## Success factors within Sweden Post for process orientation

In the group's ongoing discussion of Sweden Post and process orientation, questions such as what will happen in the future, and what ought to happen, led to a number of opinions being expressed. For example, the meaning of the term "process orientation" was considered a bit unclear. There was a need to improve the knowledge within the area – process thinking was believed to be quite shallow in the organisation. Although not everyone would believe that process orientation was the right way to succeed, it was important to get everybody in Sweden Post to understand what it meant. Also the meaning of "customer" had to be sorted out. For example, in one of the large common information systems used, "customer" was the same as "company". However, it is worth remembering that "customer" is not only the one paying; the sender and the receiver are often not the same.

After all, perhaps "customer orientation" would be a better term to use in order to focus on the right problem? In the future, Sweden Post has to focus more on customer needs and offer customer-oriented solutions, working together with other organisations if necessary. Overall, a better understanding of how the organisation works and how it interacts with the environment was seen as needed. Everyone must understand the business foundation of a shared vision, the expected organisational benefits and the personal implications. This is a problem of culture, of management, and – in large organisations – also of volume. There was a demand within the organisation for information about "the whole picture". In order to better create solutions for customers in the future, lots of descriptions will be needed, e.g. of products and service components available. A decision has to be made if processes of the whole business should be described, or if it's enough to describe those that interact with customers. After all, it is easy to get stuck in documentation instead of creating new businesses.

Extensive support in terms of information systems was also required for the future, particularly considering the vision for Sweden Post in the 21st century. There was a need for a "logical undercarriage" that provides proper information, independently of people's position in the organisation. For example, a strong sale support will be necessary as demands on sales representatives will be higher in the future. They will be required to have knowledge in many fields. Still, an increased amount of documentation would facilitate the situation, e.g. in the event of loosing an experienced salesperson. Information is an important strategic resource. However, with increasing amounts of information, e.g. about the customers, ethical issues regarding its handling become more important.

In an attempt to explore process orientation in Sweden Post, it is important to stick to, and support, the valuable aspects of the current organisation. In order to fully succeed with process orientation, the commitment of every-body, including the management, is needed. However, getting commit-ment is hard when the traditional way of working is a "cash cow" – the majority of the business is working fine. There is a challenge to create a sense of urgency, even though there isn't a feeling of impending crisis. It can be hard to avoid the impression of just another one crying wolf. In order to depart from the past to reach the future, Sweden Post has to con-sider the issue of organisational acceptance: how prone to change are the people in the organisation, and how rigid are the current organisational structures? It might be easier said than done to create an environment that recognises and champions the ongoing need for change. To start with, there has to be a recognition of "political" sponsoring, an awareness of the organisation's formal and informal leaders.

Steps towards a successful change also include supporting and institution-alising the change journey. This might involve using a simple implemen-tation plan with goals and responsibilities, pilot studies, workshops (away from the normal workplace), educational programmes, reward systems, and redesigns of the physical workspace. Many insights can be gained from studying earlier changes, both within Sweden Post and in other organisations. There were several pilot projects going on in Sweden Post that could be success projects for process orientation. Moreover, there were a number of experiences from similar development projects in other organisations.

## Conclusions from external business development projects

Reports on process development projects that have failed can be found in journals and conferences every now and then. Discussions with some larger companies in Sweden has confirmed the picture given. The failures have, in many cases, been attempts at extensive, dramatic changes of whole organisations or very large parts of organisations – mainly "classical" BPR projects. However, also more cautious attempts have failed. There are a set of factors that keep being mentioned as critical for successful process orientation. Although a number of them are fairly general, the group felt that they provided valuable background also in the context of Sweden Post:

- *Commitment from management.* The transition from a functional organisation to an organisation that think and work in terms of processes, means a change in the company culture all the way from top management and down. The decision paths in a process-oriented organisation can be very different from those in a traditional functional organisation. So also roles and career paths. To make this happen it is important that the management gets actively involved in the change work, making the necessary decisions and setting a good example.

- *Persistence and patience.* The reason that this kind of change takes time is that it takes place simultaneously on a practical and on a cultural level. Creating an atmosphere of trust and support is crucial to achieving the desired result. Experience from the Japanese car industry shows that it might take ten years to establish process-oriented thinking in a large organisation. This cautions against trying too radical changes too quick – especially if they are not felt to be absolutely needed by the people in the organisation.

- *Small pilot projects to gain experience and set good examples.* Small, well defined, successful examples serve as an inspiration and template for other parts of the organisation. In this way, confidence and commitment will be able to build progressively. It is easy to become too ambitious and try to change the whole organisation in one go.

- *Training in process orientation.* Changing focus from organisational functions to horizontal processes includes a major pedagogical task. While some people see process thinking as quite natural, others see it as difficult to understand and/or as threatening. Knowledge of what process orientation means to the business and to the individual is of vital importance.

- *Clear and supported process maps.* Easily understood process descriptions are a good help when communicating the process thinking. The descriptions need to be at an appropriate level, neither too abstract and generalised, nor too detailed. They also have to be supported by the management as well as the co-workers concerned.

- *Appointed process owners and process teams.* The new organisation should be manifested at an early stage by the appointment of process owners and process teams. Process owners and process teams are essential to get the change work going. Distribution of responsibilities and authorities between the line organisation and the processes has to be dealt with.

- *Co-ordinated process development.* Having a grip on all process development work is very useful in order to avoid co-ordination problems later on. Different projects need to be co-ordinated and aware of what's going on elsewhere in the organisation.

Examining what is considered "common wisdom" in the area, such as the points above, was an important part of the group's discussion. Learning from others includes looking at experiences from similar change projects elsewhere. Although the group felt a need to expand and clarify some of the factors listed, they still considered them as a good source of inspiration. Together with the issues raised from the specific context of Sweden Post, they provided a good coverage of organisational prerequisites for process orientation.

## *Summarising the issues regarding organisational prerequisites*

- There are several possible *degrees of process orientation* with different implications for the organisation. From merely presentational purpose to a thorough process organisation.

- There is a need for maintaining the *process "flow"* and obtaining a high degree of coupling throughout processes. To overcome different boundaries, e.g. in a highly decentralised organisation, is an important goal for well-functioning processes.

- A long-term strategy for introducing process orientation into the organisation is needed, building on a fair *amount of analysis*. However, although the change process requires endurance, quick results are wished for.

# Concepts and definitions

Within the second sub-project, dealing with concepts and definitions, five people from different parts of the organisation participated together with an external consultant and a researcher. All of the participants had previous experience of working with business descriptions. The work was done mostly in a number of common meetings during the project time – although complemented with individual "homework" between the meetings, mostly by the external consultant who documented the work. The focus of the work lied in creating a basis for the future development work in terms of a common terminology.

In the following, a number of important issues in the work are presented. They are critical examples of situations when the participants – at least initially – had quite different opinions. The differences resulted in discussions, at times rather heated, that affected the work and the results. The issues are largely kept in the sequence they appeared in the project, although headings have been added in order to emphasise common themes.

## *Why business processes and business descriptions?*

In order to anchor the work, the group initially analysed top management's vision on what Sweden Post should be. Was there anything that pointed to processes? In the business plan, the business concept was described as "joining together their own resources with other's in communication processes and financial services" (cf. the full quote in the beginning of this chapter).

There was a lot of confusion and discussion concerning the illustration that was used together with the business concept (see Figure 3). One interpretation, which eventually gained acceptance, saw it as an visualisation of the joining together of the business of Sweden Post and its customers. The horizontal arrows were thought to describe Sweden Post's core business, the services it provides to its customers. The vertical arrows were thought to describe areas of the customer's business. The junctions show where Sweden Post can, or should, help the customer. For example, a customer's handling of its financial administration can be helped of Sweden Post's handling of payments and messages.

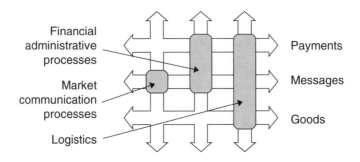

*Figure 3. Sweden post's business (adapted from Sweden Post, 1995 a, p. 8).*

Although the word "process" appeared in the illustration as well as in the business concept, it was not clear to the project group exactly how the term should be interpreted or defined. A further exploration of this issue was considered important, partly as a consequence of the general interest in business processes. Sweden Post had a long tradition of using different types of models to describe the business, e.g. data models and routine sketches. A goal of the project was to examine how the different business models fitted together in an overall framework. In order to examine the need for different model types, an inventory of important questions was made among the participants. Rather than looking for patterns in the questions themselves (bottom-up search for clusters), a match was made with an established framework. The framework used was that of Zachman (1987), differing between six foci of a description, based on the English question-words what, how, where, who, when, and why.

While the framework to be developed was to provide an overall guide of how various business models fitted together, the bulk of the work within the project was done with a so-called meta-model. This was a conceptual data model describing the terminology used to describe the business. Together with textual definitions of the concepts, a model comprising the important concepts in the business and their relationships (cf. Figure 4) was created step-by-step. This type of model itself had a clear data-focus, focusing on the what-question. Sweden Post has had earlier experience with developing data-oriented tools, such as a comprehensive term catalogue. However, those were only partly used within this project. Process models were only used very briefly, as illustrations. Other model types, such as goal models supporting exploration of why-issues, were not used at all.

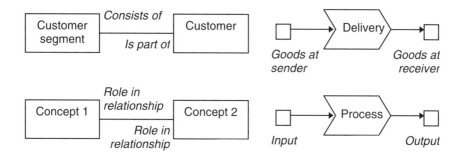

*Figure 4. Example (top) and structure (bottom) of the meta-model (left) and sample process model (right).*

## All processes are equal, but some are more equal than others

The term "(business) process" is often used today, and there are many definitions for it in the literature. The group had looked at work by for instance Steneskog (1991), Davenport (1993), Hammer & Champy (1993) and Goldkuhl (1995). Discussing what should be Sweden Post's use of the term, the group decided that it was important to have a broad definition. It was desirable to keep "process" a relative concept and not restrict it to a certain scope or organisational level. Processes could thus be both large and complex, e.g. distributing mail, or small and simple, e.g. selling stamps. As a result, the definition that was agreed upon allowed processes to consist of, and be parts of, other processes. Other organisations, using "process" as an absolute rather than relative concept, instead need to introduce specific terms like "mega-process" and "sub-process" for large and small processes. In Sweden Post's definition, "sub-process" became a relationship between two processes instead of a concept of its own (see Figure 5).

Given this relative notion of "process," there are sometimes occasions for identifying central processes within the business that are especially important. In the project, these were referred to as "business processes" or "core processes". All other processes, that were not in themselves business processes, were called support processes. Their task is to support the business processes in some way. The criteria for a business process that was agreed upon was that it interfaces to an external "customer" in both ends, e.g. the case of delivering a letter from a sender to a receiver.

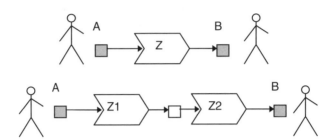

*Figure 5. Processes on different levels; Z1 and Z2 are sub-processes of Z.*

There was an interesting consequence of this criteria that was not realised or consented by all in the group. It was that a sub-process of a business process, e.g. emptying mail boxes as part of the overall business process of distributing mail, is *not* in itself a business process, but a support process. Going back to the example in Figure 5 above, Z is a business process, while its two sub-processes (Z1 and Z2), when discussed in isolation, are support processes. The result of such a criteria is that a focus on business processes becomes an effective means for minimising sub-optimisation, at least from the viewpoint of the customers. Improving only a part of a business process is of no benefit for the customer if there is a bottleneck somewhere else in that process.

## Our processes and theirs

There was a large interest in the issue of process integration and co-ordination, especially towards customers and partners. It was felt important to reach beyond internal processes, e.g. to see how they form part of a customer's business. Consistent with Sweden Post's business concept, the interest was a natural consequence of the company's role as an intermediary, e.g. delivering parcels between two companies. A practical result of the aim for process integration, was the need for describing and keeping track of processes within other companies. Rather than individual companies, the descriptions would more probably concern types of companies, e.g. certain market segments. However, a potential problem in many of the early process descriptions within Sweden Post was that they were quite unclear regarding the transitions between different processes: explicit interface objects were often lacking. Interface objects are important when aiming for another benefit of process descriptions, namely to facilitate re-use of excellent processes.

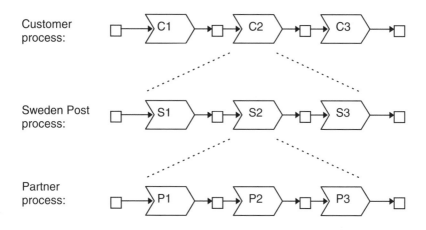

*Figure 6. Example of responsibility for different processes (adapted from VEPRO, 1996, p. 43).*

As important as co-ordinating and integrating processes, as important it was to be able to effectively separate them. For a professional working relation, all parties have to be aware of the boundaries. The division between Sweden Post's processes and external processes, that the group agreed on, was based on responsibility – and not, for example, on the actors' organisational membership. In this sense, it is customers and part-ners that are responsible for the external processes. An example consid-ered was the case illustrated in Figure 6. There, a partner process is part of a Sweden Post process, which in turn is part of a customer process. While the partner is responsible for its process towards Sweden Post, Sweden Post is in turn responsible for its process (including the partner process) towards the customer. The question of responsibility was illustrated – tongue-in-cheek – in a advertisement from another delivery company: "We keep your promises."

## What else is going on in the organisation?

Are there things going on in the business that is outside of any process? Are processes a special kind of activities that are separate from 'ordinary' work?

These are examples of questions that arose in the discussions around business processes. There was a confusion whether "process" described certain phenomena (in this case the answer to the questions above was "yes"), or if it described a certain aspect, resulting from a specific point-of-view (the answer was then "no"). The issue became apparent in the work with the meta-model, also with other concepts than "process". Concepts in the model that were found to refer to "everything" – and thus more of an aspect than a phenomena – were for example "location," "goal," and "concept". As a result of this, the relation between the meta-model and the framework became a bit blurred. Other concepts, such as "person," were not as salient in the meta-model – it appeared rather late in the modelling process as a type of resource being responsible for an actor role.

A concrete difficulty with the process concept was its relation to functions. The concept of function led from the beginning to serious discussions, as it was used in several meanings. One meaning, largely used in the context of BPR and process orientation (cf. e.g. Rummler & Brache, 1995), sees functions as organisational units specialised in certain tasks. Another meaning sees function as a "pure" task or behaviour – independent of organisational structures or type of actor. In the meta-model, the issue was resolved by introducing the term "business function," with relationships to both business process and areas of responsibility. Although intended to facilitate re-use, the difference compared to "process" was somewhat unclear.

## Descriptions for whom?

Descriptions of the business not only focus on certain aspects of the business. Another difference discussed by the project group concerned the intended audience for the model. Zachman (1987) uses the term level of abstraction or perspective when discussing audiences for different models. When working on the framework, this issue came into discussion.

Some of the participants felt that Zachman's framework was too detailed and placed too much focus on the lower, more technical levels. As a complement, a more basic division was introduced: between models intended for audiences external to the business or internal to it (cf. Figure 7). While external descriptions focused on business issues from a consumer point-of-view, internal descriptions focused on technical issues from a producer point-of-view. The question arose whether the central term of "business descriptions", used throughout the project, should be used for all descriptions relevant for the business, or only for external descriptions.

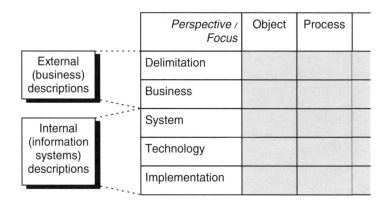

*Figure 7. Example of part of the framework; different types of models belong to each shaded cell (adapted from VEPRO, 1996, p. 25).*

The issue of audience also surfaced when working with definitions accompanying the meta-model. The concept that initiated the discussion was "service," something central both for the company and its customers. It is services, e.g. delivering mail, that customers pay for and that Sweden Post provides. In order to obtain maximum flexibility, it was important to be able to form new services by combining and re-using existing ones. In the meta-modelling, this was shown by distinguishing between elementary and composite services (cf. Figure 8).

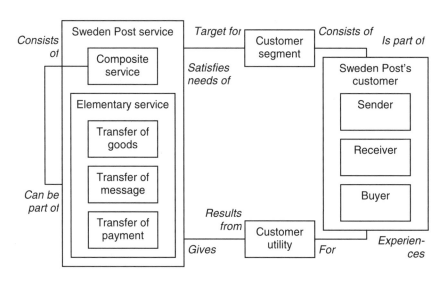

*Figure 8. Example of a small part of the meta-model concerning services (adapted from VEPRO, 1996, p. 83).*

While a composite service was a combination of other services (elementary or composite), the question was what defined an elementary service. From an internal producer point-of-view, it was a service that cannot be *provided* in parts; From an external customer point-of-view, it was something that cannot be *bought* in parts.

Another example of the issue of audience for a description, arose in the work with the actual meta-model. Without any conscious reflection on the way of working, the meta-model had been developed on a detailed level from the beginning. Individual concepts, their definitions and relationships, had been added and modified step by step. When the meta-model became excessively complex (over 40 different concepts and their relationships), the issue of presentation surfaced. It was quite a complicated task to fully understand the meta-model – even for the people who had taken part in its development. To overcome this problem, various ways to aggregate the concepts, and simplify the meta-model, were discussed. The answer came in the form of a overview model comprising nine areas with relationships (cf. Figure 9). Although the overview model proved to be valuable also for the participants themselves, it was widely viewed as "merely" a pedagogical tool. The possibility of actively working also with this more customer-oriented description from the beginning, was never seriously considered.

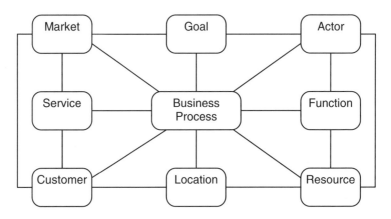

*Figure 9. The areas of the overview model (adapted from VEPRO, 1996, p. 38).*

## Where are we heading?

Throughout the project, the participants returned to the issue of objectives, results, and consequences of the work. On several occasions, there were different opinions about the project's intended results. Should the project only point to possibilities or should it actually suggest changes? How far into the future should it look? How much of the current organisation should be taken for granted? Who benefited from the project? These and other questions partly resulted from a perception of unclear customers to the project as well as unclear users of its results. In spite of this, goal modelling was not used – partly due to lack of time, partly because it was felt more needed for the project as a whole. The objectives were felt to be clear enough not to take valuable time from the "real" modelling work.

Some participants had quite clear pictures of the future use of the results, e.g. as a basis for a database of business descriptions ("Should we really describe the customers' processes as the meta-model indicates?"). There was interest in having people responsible for central concepts in the business – and hence the meta-model – although it was not quite clear what this responsibility would amount to and who would be suitable to have it. Like ordinary business descriptions, the meta-model was believed to be important for continuous improvement of the business. However, there was a perceived risk that the results were not going to come to use, but to stay in some bookshelf. Whatever effects intended for the business, they required that the results were used and continuously updated. As a consequence, it was felt important to appoint people as responsible for maintaining the descriptions, including the meta-model itself.

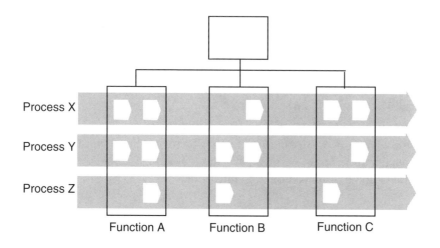

*Figure 10. Relationship between organisational functions and business processes (adapted from Rummler & Brache, 1995, p. 16).*

The longer the project progressed, the more often the participants returned to the central question of process orientation. Much of the concern related to the relationship between the new business processes and the traditional organisational functions (cf. Figure 10 above). Another way of expressing this concern was to ask if processes or organisational functions should be strongest. What should be controlling? What should be controlled? Should processes adjust to the functions or vice versa? As the project progressed, a growing uncertainty could be felt regarding the actual label "process orientation". Was it perhaps a bit too "strong" – compared to alternatives such as "process thinking" and "process view"? However, whatever the label used, there was a strong agreement that processes in one way or the other was going to become a key issue for Sweden Post in the future.

## *Summarising the issues regarding concepts and definitions*

- Interaction with other organisational unit's processes is important to facilitate the *process "flow"*. There is interest in going outside Sweden Post's own organisation. Within the organisation, there is a benefit of being able to re-use processes. This requires a focus on responsibilities and transfers (interface objects) when describing the processes.

- There is a need for *multiple descriptions* using different types of models. Depending on the intended audience, some descriptions might be more appropriate than others. Still, much of the work in the project had a focus on concepts. More than talking "in" processes, the project talks "about" them.

- There is a large *amount of analysis* being done. Much work is done in order to get a clear picture of what, e.g., a process is. Still, it is not always easy to see all consequences. Many concepts are fundamentally complex.

- The *degree of process orientation* that is aimed for is subject to discussion. There is an insecurity of how far to go: how "hard" should the concept of process be pushed? How should processes relate to other things in the organisation, e.g. functions?

# Conclusions

The loss of the monopoly and the increasing use of new communication technologies, have meant quite dramatic changes for Sweden Post. A formidable challenge for any company, Sweden Post has been mobilising resources in its exploration of alternative means to retain a leading position on the Swedish market and a very good position relative to other European postal services. In the VEPRO project, process orientation and business descriptions proved to be two very promising means, giving rise to many new ideas. However, the concepts hwas also shown to be quite complex, much more so than suggested by a lot of the management literature around.

For Sweden Post, the VEPRO project provided valuable insights, three of which have been specifically mentioned by its initiators. First, concerning the use of up-to-date descriptions of the business. This gives a better overview and a shorter start-up time for change work. Second, concerning the use of a common and precise way of description based on a meta-model. This helps identifying important phenomena in the business and their relationships. Third, concerning the use of a method base, comprising models, methods, and tools for change work. This supports the development of the business and its IT support.

As has been shown in this chapter, a great many things were discussed in the sub-projects reported on. In a brief initial analysis, reflecting on the things discussed and searching for common themes, five important dilemmas have been found. The term "dilemma" is used here to emphasise that an issue was found not to have any clear-cut answer or solution. A dilemma can be seen as providing a span of different alternatives, ranging from one extreme to its opposite. The dilemmas are considered important as they all led to extensive discussion. They were repeatedly returned to, at different times but also within different sub-projects. The last three of the dilemmas were also evident in the project work itself. Below is a brief description of all five:

- *Degree of process orientation – keeping the old or trying the new?* A thorough reorganisation according to processes provides an opportunity to increase the focus on customer satisfaction and avoiding the legacy from the former monopoly. However, a large organisation is hard to change, especially when the situation is not felt to be urgent. Acknowledging the value of stability and tradition, a  lower degree of process orientation will mean less "disturbance" of the current work in the organisation.

- *Process "flow" – separating or integrating?* Facilitating process "flow" and integration, e.g. by means of appropriate business descriptions, is considered to be helpful in the future. Developing "One Sweden Post" means avoiding the risk of different parts pulling in different directions, at least as viewed by the customers. However, functional and organisational boundaries make integration more difficult. As an alternative, decentralisation and a higher degree of separation promote competitive structures and agendas, facilitating for smaller and more autonomous units to faster take action, compete, and constructively negotiate responsibilities and goals.

- *Multiple descriptions – being a specialist or a generalist?* Extensive use of multiple descriptions gives a richer view of the business. One type of model is not considered enough, especially when aiming for different audiences. However, multiple descriptions are more demanding to work with and fit together. They require more time and effort, and risk being too complex to understand. Instead, a specialisation in a specific type of description facilitates the development of deep experience and skill in that area. This dilemma was also evident within the project itself, e.g. when arguing for multiple descriptions, although using only one.

- *Amount of analysis – acting or reflecting?* A large amount of analysis, spending time on reflection and planning, gives opportunities to penetrate complex concepts and ideas. It avoids having to rush things and enables the scrutiny of new concepts. However, against this stands a wish for fast results, without too many rules and prescriptions perceived as straitjackets. In a fast-changing market, the ability to act quickly and bring about direct changes in the work performed is considered especially important. This dilemma was also evident within the project itself, e.g. in the concern for how much the analysis done in the project would actually mean to the workings of Sweden Post.

- *Order of development – starting with ends or means?* Exploration of business processes can be facilitated or hindered by other development activities. Developing corporate strategies and IT support have important relationships to process orientation. This dilemma was also evident within the project itself, e.g. how it became influenced, and influenced, other development activities in Sweden Post.

Of course, exploring a dilemma not only means investigating different alternatives within its reach, but also trying to synthesise and transcend the dilemma itself. Viewed in this way, the challenge lies in finding effective ways to *both* keep the old and try the new, *both* separate and integrate, *both* be a specialist and be a generalist, *both* act and reflect, and *both* start with ends and means!

# Acknowledgements

The authors want to thank the people from Sweden Post who participated in the VEPRO project. We also want to thank Jörgen Andersson, Linköping University, for contributing his experiences from the project.

The research was funded by NUTEK, the Swedish National Board of Industrial and Technical Development.

# References

Davenport, T.H. (1993) *Process Innovation: Reengineering Work through Information Technology*, Harvard Business School Press, Boston, Massachusetts.

Goldkuhl, G. (1995) *Processtänkande vid verksamhetsutveckling*, VITS, Research Report LiTH-IDA-R-95-41, Linköping University, Linköping, Sweden [*Process Thinking during Business Development*].

Hammer, M. & Champy, J. (1994) *Reengineering the Corporation: A Manifesto for Business Revolution*, Paperback edition, HarperCollins Publishers, New York.

IPC (1997) *Improving the Quality of International Mail – First Half Year Results 1997*, International Post Corporation (IPC), Brussels.

Rummler, G.A. & Brache, A.P. (1995) *Improving Performance: How to Manage the White Space on the Organization Chart*, 2nd ed., Jossey-Bass Publishers, San Francisco.

Steneskog, G. (1991) *Process Management: Konsten att styra och utveckla ett företags administrativa processer*, Liber, Malmö, Sweden [*Process Management: The Art of Managing and Developing a Company's Administrative Processes*].

Sweden Post (1995 a) *Sweden Post 1994 Annual Report*, Sweden Post, Stockholm.

Sweden Post (1995 b) *Posten Affärsplan 1996-98*, Sweden Post, Stockholm [*Sweden Post Business Plan 1996-98*].

Tolis, C. & Nilsson, A.G. (1996) "Using Business Models in Process Orientation", in Lundeberg, M. & Sundgren, B. (eds.) *Advancing Your Business – People and Information Systems in Concert*, The Economic Research Institute (EFI), Stockholm School of Economics, Stockholm.

Tolis, C. & Nellborn, C. (1998) "Process Orientation and Business Descriptions: The Case of Sweden Post", in Beats, W.R.J. (ed.) *Proceedings of the 6th European Conference on Information Systems – Aix-en-Provence, France*, Vol. III, Euro-Arab Management School, Granada, Spain, pp.1320-1335.

VEPRO (1996) *Förslag till ramverk och innehåll för processorienterade verksamhetsbeskrivningar*, v.1.3., internal report, Sweden Post, Stockholm [*Proposal for framework and content of process-oriented business descriptions*].

Zachman, John A. (1987) "A framework for Information Systems Architecture." *IBM Systems Journal*, Vol. 26, No 3, pp. 276-292.

# 4

# Process Management in Public Administration: The Social Insurance Office Case

*Jörgen Andersson*

*Establishing a process-oriented view on a business has up to now been carried out mostly in private companies. The following chapter presents how a public authority has proceeded to change its operations towards a process orientation. The Social Insurance Office has among other steps used Total Quality Management and process management to increase quality in its operations at the same time as demands from the government and Parliament to make savings has considerably reduced their economic resources.*

## Operations at the Social Insurance Office

The Social Insurance Office in the county of Östergötland, is one of 25 independent Social Insurance Offices in Sweden. The county is the fifth largest in the country with more than about 400 000 inhabitants. Of these 79 % are registered at the Social Insurance Office. At present the number of employees amounts to more than 700 at about 20 offices/service points. The annual volume of benefit payments is about 11 billion SEK. The Social Insurance Office formulates its business concept in the annual report for 1994/95 as follows:

> *"Through public social insurance we provide financial security during the various phases of a lifetime. We accomplish this by paying benefits to the sick, the handicapped, families with children and senior citizens. We also accomplish it by taking preventative measures against sickness and injuries and also by giving the sick and handicapped the possibility to return to work."*

It is clear from the business concept that the main operations include administration of the benefits people are entitled to from the general social insurance scheme and to take responsibility for rehabilitation of the sick and handicapped.

The National Swedish Social Insurance Board which comes under the Ministry of Health and Social Affairs is the supervisory authority for the country's Social Insurance Offices and the operations at the offices are inspected by the National Audit Bureau.

The offices collaborate with health care officers, employers, social services, labour-market and others to carry out their duties.

During recent years the public sector has been subject to comprehensive changes. Demands to make financial savings have led both to changes in the transfer systems and cut-backs in the administrative budgets of the authorities. Despite this there are increased demands for service and quality in operations. It seems probable that this process of change will continue.

# Background to the changes

Against the background of the increased demands for an efficient administration and the reduced budget frameworks the Social Insurance Office completed a review of its organisation during spring 1993. At the same time work on quality was introduced which involved several activities. The work on quality was carried out in collaboration with the Division of Quality Technology and Management at Linköping University and the aim was:

> *"to start an independently working improvement scheme which is seen as a natural feature of the work carried out at the office. This will be accomplished by raising the competence level, creating positive attitudes and finding methods, ways and routines for working on improvement."* (Annual Report, The Social Insurance Office, 1994-1995)

The starting point for the work on improvement were the principles for the quality concept of "Total Quality Management" (TQM) where the Customer in the centre is one of the corner-stones along with Continuous improvement, Decisions based on facts, Everyone's involvement and a Process view of operations. In addition the involvement of company management is emphasised as well as the overall view (Bergman & Klefsjö, 1994).

Experience from the quality project showed that a high level of engagement is required, both from management and other staff. To create understanding for the work on quality, this also requires clarity in the aims and the visions, good information on ways and methods of working and an overall view where work on quality becomes a natural feature of operations. However, after a time there was a fall in the level of engagement, and management noticed the need for new impulses and ways of thinking. At the same time there were new demands from Parliament to make heavy cut-backs in operations.

The Social Insurance Office decided to introduce a process-oriented way of working where their core business, the operative, would play a central role. Through process orientation the Social Insurance Office saw the opportunity of meeting the demands on increased quality in operations at the same time as the economic framework was reduced as a result of the major demands for savings coming from the central authorities.

One aim, or rather a vision, was formulated which was intended to provide guidance for continuing the work. The vision implied that:

> *"The Social Insurance Office will be renowned for its outgoing business manner with competent, service-minded staff who perform fast and correct assessments."*

This is to be achieved by the staff being competent in their duties, their professional roles being clearly defined and the operative work being organised in self-planning groups as a basis for learning and development. In the vision it has also been determined that the Social Insurance Office is to maintain high quality in all processes and that the work is to be supported by information technology in an efficient way.

This aim implies, within given economic frameworks, generating the largest possible utility for customers by placing the customer, the person insured, in the centre. The Social Insurance Office uses a model of utility for customers which comprises the four components of quality, cost, service and time. Figure 1 below illustrates how the Social Insurance Office makes these components more concrete.

In the first place the Social Insurance Office considers lead time and accessibility to be the components that can provide the greatest improvement for the customers. Maintaining high quality in the decisions that are made is also important, but they judge this as having a better starting-out position.

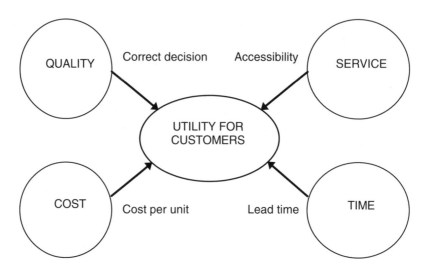

*Figure 1. Expected result of process orientation.*

The concept of customer at the Social Insurance Office is complicated and has also been one of the main points of discussion within the organisation. The Social Insurance Office considers as customers all interested parties they are there for. In the first place it is those who are insured who are also viewed by the Social Insurance Office as being the major customers. Other customers that have been identified are politicians, interest organisations, researchers, employers and others. The Parliament and ministries, which are organs for all citizens, are the employers and the Social Insurance Office is the authority which is to administrate those transfers Parliament decides on. The insured are the recipients of the various benefits and operations are mainly financed by payroll taxes and state subvention. It is thus impossible to directly judge the willingness to pay for the services provided. This also means that the low unit costs which are sought after according to Figure 1 above do not directly come to the advantage of the customer, but on the other hand it is important in the eyes of the general public that operations are run cost-efficiently. They can be said to have indirect positive effects on the customers.

# "Quality in all processes – 97"

The change work was introduced in 1995 during a turbulent period when the demands for savings for the first time in the history of the Social Insurance Office led to staff being made redundant. A model for process orientation was established where the necessity of reducing the administrative superstructure could be seen and also that forces should be gathered for operative business. This starting point meant that there was understanding on the part of the operative staff for the cut-backs that were made. On the other hand the managers at the middle levels who were affected by the decisions were, of course, not as enthusiastic. As notice was being given, the management group, trade union representatives and the Board drew up guidelines for the future process-oriented organisation.

Knowledge about process management was gathered from several sources. Literature was read, seminars given by invited speakers were arranged, consultants were called in and examples were collected from Ericsson, for example. In the winter of 1995 work on producing guidelines for the future organisation began in connection with the presentation of the budget proposals for 95/96.

Management at the Social Insurance Office took major responsibility for the change work and became a driving force, which was appreciated as a strength. In addition a project group was established which as well as a project leader included personnel who knew the methods, development secretaries who have been co-ordinators in the process teams, trade union representatives, IT- and information- specialists and others. The constitution and function of the project group has changed during the project. Much of the work initially focused on training the staff. Since then the work of the project group has progressed from initiating activities to functioning as a co-ordinating group for current projects.

The project was entitled "Quality in All Processes 1997" (KAP-97) and, as the name suggests, the aim was to achieve this during 1997. An action plan was worked out in May 1995 which included the production of a method handbook, decisions on the distribution of responsibility between the line and the process, starting the process teams, information to staff and Board, and training of team members initially and later on the other staff.

# The model of change

The Social Insurance Office has produced a method handbook with guidance for how change is to be introduced. It was considered important to produce a handbook that was adapted to their own operations. Ideas and basic methodology were collected from Ericsson. The method for introducing the whole effort on change consists of five phases:

- *Identification*: In this phase the processes are identified and areas of responsibility for change work are allocated, i.e. process owners and process teams.

- *Analysing*: Process team and process owner acquire the knowledge that is needed to guide and improve the selected processes. In addition the process is given a purpose-oriented form.

- *Realisation*: The improved process is implemented in operations.

- *Stabilisation*: In this phase the ability of the process as far as, for example, quality, time and productivity is stabilised, which is accomplished by following up the results and making corrections.

- *Improvements*: Continued improvements are made to the stabilised process.

In addition it is planned to carry out so-called process revisions where both the work of the process owners and process teams is checked against predetermined goals and current operational goals. Moreover the handbook contains, for instance, general information on TQM, process management and a description of the various roles involved in the work.

The work has been performed to a large extent as described in the method handbook. The Social Insurance Office takes, however, a pragmatic view where methods must be adapted to current circumstances.

# Analysing the processes

The Social Insurance Office has described a process as the set of activities a service passes through from the moment it is initiated until it leaves operations. Process also has a clear focus on the customer as the activities are expected to contribute to the insured party/customer getting the service he or she wants.

When the first processes were to be identified, the management group met at a course centre for two days. The method used was based on brain-storming in groups where sticky labels, flip-charts and whiteboards were used as tools. A schematic process map is shown in Figure 2 below.

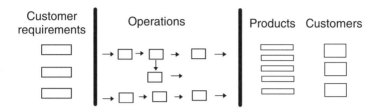

*Figure 2. Schematic process map. Source: Method handbook, Social Insurance Office (1995) (author's adaptation).*

Customer requirements were identified, for example financial security. A number of products such as housing allowance, sickness allowance and rehabilitated customers were discerned. The customers are those who are insured but the self-employed and other actors were identified as customers. The operational processes and the activities they involve were mapped. The activities included, for example, registration, investigations, calculations and serving customers.

Three different types of processes were identified:

- Operative processes
- Management processes
- Support processes

Initially it was the operative processes that were in focus. Here the payment process, the rehabilitation co-ordination process and the preventative process were identified as being core processes. It was noted that the payment process accounted for about 75 % of the operations of the Social Insurance Office and it was divided into several processes. The preventative process which was considered as an operative core process was initially transferred to one of the management processes. The idea is, however, that it should be run as an operative process when it is fully developed.

This finally resulted in four main operative processes: Financial support for families with children and other payments, Sickness and handicap allowance, Allowances for the elderly and for surviving relatives and Rehabilitation co-ordination.

To support a process-oriented organisation characterised by learning and local responsibility as well as a minimised central organisation four important management processes were identified: "Goals/planning/economy", "Knowledge development – insurance", "Supervision/follow-up/assessment – insurance" and "Culture/attitudes". The management processes are to cover overall, strategic issues on goals, control and developing competence.

To meet the demands on resources of the operative processes, support processes were identified such as information/marketing, staff, economy, premises, ADP – running operations and development, office service and other administration.

When the processes were to be refined more closely, this became a task for the process owner and process team. As an example of the method of working in an operative process, the team, aided by consultants, first learned the technique of producing process maps. In connection with this an initial map of the process was made. The team members then visited the local office and there, together with the staff, produced a more thorough map. The team gathered and merged the locally produced maps to a common map. The whole time work was performed with reference to current circumstances, an "is" map. A total goal for the whole process has been formulated and improvements are now under way. The method has been to work through the process from beginning to end, setting up partial goals, and changing and improving activities in the process.

The management processes were not as clear as the operative processes and work on these started later than on the operative processes. Some are of the opinion that work on the management processes should have started earlier and more time should have been allotted to identifying needs and their consequences.

In the beginning there were lively discussions on whether process management was a suitable working method at all for these kinds of operations. The production perspective in TQM was not the easiest to learn. Concepts in the model were considered difficult to relate to the their own operations where, for example, the concept of customer gave rise to much discussion.

Work on the process maps has been found to be very important. First the whole business operation has been analysed, and it has also made people think about their business operations. The maps have also provided an overall view where individuals can see more clearly than before their role in the total operations. Furthermore, the interface between customer needs and business operations, as well as that between the business operations and products/customers, has become clarified (see Figure 2 above).

# Organisation

In connection with the process orientation the Social Insurance Office has performed a reorganisation where the county is now divided into four geographical areas each having a manager (see Figure 3 below). Each manager also became a process owner of one of the main operative processes (which are symbolised by the letters A-B-C-D in the figure).

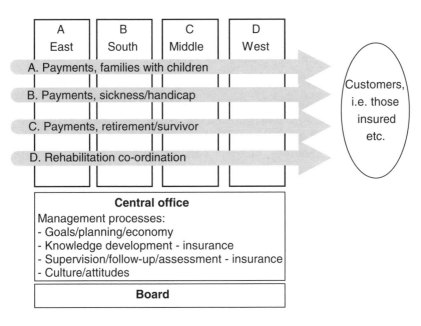

*Figure 3. Organisation plan of the Social Insurance Office.*

The area managers are members of the management group together with the highest officer (the Director) of the Social Insurance Office who is the owner of one of the management processes and also the development managers who have responsibility for the other management processes.

The process owners are continuously responsible for ensuring that the processes stabilise and improve. To their assistance the process owners have a process team which is a consultation organ consisting of several experienced members of the functional organisation. The duties of the team are to analyse the process, follow it up, assess and develop it. In each process team there is a development secretary responsible for the continuing work of the team.

Those responsible for the operative work are the self-planning groups found at each local office. They are part of the functional organisation but have a clear connection to the work on the process. Each group has a certain amount of authorisation to determine its own work. The area manager gives the group a well-defined task and at the same time is responsible for ensuring that the responsibility and authority of the group is made clear to all staff. The aim is for the group to formulate and follow up their own goals, plan their work independently and together with the process team take responsibility for continued work on improvement. The idea of the self-planning groups is to allow for increased responsibility taking and to increase the possibilities for the operative staff to take part in influencing their working situation. It is also hoped that the group should form a basis for learning and development.

During the first phase of change work so-called co-ordinators are selected for each group. The co-ordinator has three main duties. First he/she should function as a bearer of information between the area manager and the group and among various groups. The co-ordinator should also take responsibility for a certain amount of staff reporting. The third and most important duty is to function as a bringer of change, i.e. spreading ideas and understanding of process management and stimulating colleagues to become engaged in the change work. Those who have the role of co-ordinator have been trained, for example via lectures and seminars. The role of co-ordinator is time-limited and will disappear from the organisation. The aim is that the self-planning groups will be so organised that the co-ordinator will no longer be necessary.

Work on the self-planning groups has moved slowly, mainly because it involves a major adjustment for the staff. Managers who were previously available to answer questions, for example, are no longer there, which can sometimes be frustrating. Finding appropriate forms of decision making is important. The size of the group is also significant. Today there are groups of more than 15 people, which the staff feel is too big. Many questions thus remain to be answered before the self-planning groups function satisfactorily. Management at the Social Insurance Office are, however, aware of the problem and have also initiated further actions to support the work of the group by, for instance, providing supervision.

Something that the staff greatly appreciate in the change work is that "insurance" has now been put in the centre, i.e. that priority has been put on the operative work at the expense of administration. In addition it has been possible to reduce the number of managers from 64 to eight. As a consequence of there being fewer managers, certain duties have been assigned to a lower level in the organisation. An example is participation of the Social Insurance Office at regional and national conferences. Now the Social Insurance Office send their case administrators instead of their managers which was previously the case and which is still the case at other offices. The case administrators have sometimes been met by negative attitudes from some of the other offices where managers are used to meeting managers. However, as time has progressed the case administrators' more current and often deeper operative knowledge has made them feel that in many areas they have been able to make significant contributions at the conferences. This has increased the self-confidence of the case administrators and strengthened the opinion of both case administrators and management at the Social Insurance Office that change work is going in the right direction.

What has created major unrest within the organisation is not the organisational change in itself, but rather the fact that staff were to be made redundant. There have been previous threats of redundancies but they have never been put into effect. This time, i.e. spring 1995, it was, however, clear that some people would lose their jobs. The staff were informed about this at an early stage but the decision as to who would be made redundant took quite a long time to arrive. Eventually it turned out that more than 70 employees left or were made redundant. Although the continuous relay of information coming from management was perceived as positive, there were many uneasy months for the staff.

# Process management

Process management is an all-pervading concept in change work. The aim is to leave behind a hierarchical function control and instead introduce more goal- and result-oriented operations where individual employees get more opportunity to exert influence. *What* is to be done is determined within the framework of the processes and *how* it is to be done, i.e. resource issues, were to be determined within the functional organisation.

The overall goals of operations are determined by the government and Parliament. The national goals are often formulated as desired changes in comparison with previous years, e.g. that the number of sick people is to decrease, the average age of retirement is to increase or the number of fathers taking parental leave is to increase. There are also national goals that say that each social insurance office is to set up goals for the time spent on administrating cases. These national goals are broken down into regional and local goals which are to guide operations. The Social Insurance Office has determined two sorts of goals: Operational goals and improvement goals. Operational goals are those which are stipulated by government and Parliament, while improvement goals are those which are set up for each process and which are to be coupled with the operational goals. It is also intended that the self-planning groups are to both determine and follow up their own goals at group level.

As an example we can mention that the rehabilitation process has as its main goal that 95 % of those treated in the process are to once again be available on the labour market. This goal was felt by many to be too high. After discussion and some clarifications the goal was accepted and the first of four sub-goals in the process was formulated. This is where things stand today and measuring the results of the first goal has begun. Feedback has been given to the staff, but there has not yet been time to make a closer assessment.

In general things have not yet progressed so far where measurements in and measuring of the processes are concerned. In general follow-up and assessment of operations should take place on several different levels, from personal reflection on one's own work to formal follow-up through the management processes. The Social Insurance Office have tried to clarify responsibilities and authorisation among various processes, between functional organisation and process, and also among the self-planning group, the process and the functional organisation. This has been done partly by establishing communication paths within the organisation. Networks of experienced case administrators have also been established, which are to support both process team and self-planning groups.

# Information support

To a large extent the Social Insurance Office is dependent on decisions made by the National Swedish Social Insurance Board and has no control of its own over many of the information systems they use. This dependency has been perceived as a major obstruction to change work.

The main production systems within the Social Insurance Offices are developed, run and administrated centrally by the National Swedish Social Insurance Board. The systems are based on an operating system (OS2) which is difficult to integrate with many applications and the character-based interface which is used is felt to be old-fashioned and rigid.

Various attempts have been made by the Social Insurance Office to develop their own computer applications but it happens that the National Swedish Social Insurance Board stops such initiative. Investments of this type are also often too large for the local Social Insurance Office to manage alone.

Another obstruction to efficient IT-usage is that the operations of the Social Insurance Office are of such a kind that in many cases the Swedish Data Inspection Board have prevented various applications, referring to rules for what may be registered in electronic media.

The Social Insurance Office considers that the type of operations run at all social insurance offices in the country could perfectly well benefit from modern information technology. There is a strong interest in this development and there is a will to learn about the possibilities offered by technology and to carry out projects in the area.

Internal TV (U-Link), for example, is used to spread important information to all local offices in the county. Another concrete project using information technology to improve the operative processes is the new county-wide customer service. Previously case administrators answered all phone calls from those who are insured. This has meant that dealing with cases has often been interrupted, with the risk of creating long delays in case administration. The customer service includes a new telephone exchange with a local-call charge where certain so-called one-off cases can be dealt with by using recorded answers. Some cases are administrated by special customer-service staff and for cases that so require, the call is fed through to a case administrator. The new telephone exchange will also facilitate the work of the case administrators.

The spread of internal information via Internet (Intranet) has already begun. It has been planned to develop this further where the aim is partly to change information management from *getting* information to *finding* information. Various types of group software, such as Lotus Notes, are being investigated as well as video conference technology, both individual applications via PC and larger ones such as the TV-studio. The Social Insurance Office is very open to new technology as a means of making its operations more efficient.

# Discussion

Today the Social Insurance Office is right in the middle of the change work where much has been done but where much still remains. Much interesting experience has been gained and some of it is discussed in the following section.

## *Driving forces towards change*

Often changes in the external environment are named as the dominating factor in change work. Increased competition, higher demands from customers and the fast development in information technology mean that companies can no longer be successful by applying their old ways of working. It is true in the case of the Social Insurance Office, too, that there is pressure from the external environment, even though it is not the same as for a commercial company.

The Social Insurance Office does not act on a free market where customers have a choice of distributors. It is thus not possible to assess the efficiency of the work of the Social Insurance Office on the grounds of the customers' willingness to pay. Instead it has been decided to determine the requirements of the customer by means of various customer surveys. Of course, there are differences of opinion within the Social Insurance Office as to the value of such customer questionnaires, but the aim is to base assessments of customer requirements on such surveys rather than guessing what the customer wants.

At the same time there is another kind of pressure from the external environment which is a major reason for their change work. The demands to save money which come from Parliament and the government have forced many public authorities to think in new ways. The demands to save money within public authorities can be likened to a company's aim to make its operations cost-effective. Thus there is pressure from customers and their own striving towards efficiency that can be seen as driving forces both behind private companies and the Social Insurance Office.

## *Engagement*

That management is a driving, visible force in change work is often mentioned as an important factor in implementing change work successfully (Davenport, 1993, p. 167; Rummler & Brache, 1995, p. 128). In the case of the Social Insurance Office management has both initiated and driven forward the change work. The first mapping of processes was done in the management group. The change was grounded in the Board and all members of the management group are also process owners. Models and working methods have also been worked out by management. They have also actively worked towards learning about process management through literature and contacts with the local university.

However, that management is engaged is not sufficient. There is also a need for engagement among the whole staff in the organisation. Work at the Social Insurance Office was introduced during a period characterised by much turbulence and unrest in the organisation, resulting from the decreasing budget frameworks leading to staff redundancies. This turbulence had both good and bad effects on the change work. At the same time that the redundancies and reorganisation created problems in themselves, the willingness towards change possibly increased. Insight into the problem is often given as an important factor in creating motivation for change (IVA, 1995). At the Social Insurance Office expressions such as "creative chaos" are used to reflect some of the circumstances staff found themselves in, which suggests that there was both insight into the problem and motivation when the work started.

The work, however, does not just get completed unaided; it requires continuous nourishment to continue and to grow. An example of this can be seen in that some have the opinion that the change work is going too slowly and that regular impulses are needed to push it forward. There is a risk that a state becomes permanent unless there are driving forces to move forward. Working on the basis of TQM means continually making small improvements. Sometimes more radical changes are required, not least for motivation. Being able to complement the continual improvements with regular "elevations" in development work is a model to strive for.

## Level of process orientation

There is reason to consider how far you want to get with process orientation. What is the ultimate aim? One way of illustrating this is by a ladder where each new level is a step towards an ever more encompassing change (cf. Figure 4 below).

The first step toward a process organisation is that operations are seen in flows. Models are used to describe the flows, usually in the form of process maps. The next step involves defining responsibility for the processes. The processes are to be assessed and measurements and measuring systems must be determined. When the processes completely guide operations and a pure process organisation has been achieved, you have reached the top of the ladder. According to Tolis and Nilsson (1996) there is reason to be thorough in the work at every rung on the ladder in order to facilitate work at the next level.

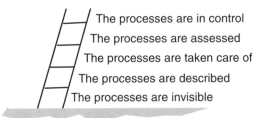

*Figure 4. Levels of process orientation. Source: Tolis & Nilsson, 1996.*

At the Social Insurance Office work is on slightly different levels in different processes. Most have reached the stage where the processes are taken care of, i.e. responsibility for the process has been defined and the process owner and team have been appointed and are functioning. Establishing assessment criteria for the processes is what is just about to be developed. Creating goals and measurements for the various processes is difficult work and the right forms for this have not always been found. Neither is the description technique used for the processes particularly clear when it comes to the in- and out-objects in the processes, which can hinder the development of the measuring system. There are other description techniques which are clearer on this point (see, for example, Tolis & Nilsson, 1996).

The stages above may need to be developed and refined with further steps describing the phases or levels found in work on process orientation, also clarifying the goals of the work, i.e. how far you want to reach. Using the ladder as a model in change work can provide staff with partial goals, which can create even more motivation for the work.

The Social Insurance Office aims to reach high on the ladder, but to go over to a pure process organisation is not the goal at present. The functional organisation in the form of geographical areas is maintained and attempts have been made to clarify the areas of responsibility by saying that the process owner has the strategic functional responsibility while the functional manager has the operative responsibility. The functional manager is also a process owner and all process owners are part of the management group. This organisation is considered capable of handling possible conflicts between function and process. At the Social Insurance Office conflicts are viewed as being "positive" and a means for achieving development.

## Measuring processes

At the Social Insurance Office, Östergötland, providing better customer service is considered to be a significant result of process orientation. A model is used in which four factors are emphasised as criteria (cf. Figure 1).

- Quality
- Time
- Service
- Cost

Quality means that the "right" decision has been made. Legal rights are an important component of this concept. Follow-up and analysis of cases have also shown deficiencies in, for example, the bases on which certain decisions were made. Steps taken to correct this have in a few cases meant that administration of the case was extended by a phase, which conflicts with one of the other criteria for customer utility, namely short administration time.

Measuring case administration time is also carried out regularly. Up to today process orientation has not resulted generally in any major reduction in administration times. However, a clear improvement has been made for some kinds of cases. It is also a fact that it is difficult to compare administration times between different periods as other factors which are not the result of process orientation affect the administration times. One example of this is that inexperienced staff have had to be brought in when the load has become too high. Another is that the flows within a case type have been separated, which has drastically reduced administration times for some cases, while the times for more complex cases have not decreased to the same extent. Higher-level staff at the Social Insurance Office emphasise, however, that changes in working methods will take a long time to compare and that it is still too early to assess the effects of the change.

The Social Insurance Office has interpreted the "service" criterion as accessibility, i.e. it should be easier for the customer to get in touch with the right person at the Social Insurance Office to have his case quickly and correctly handled. One step towards improved accessibility has been to establish the new "customer service", which means that certain cases can be handled by customer service which in turn means that the case administrators are able to spend more effort on the more time-consuming cases. The results from the customer service have been very good and have set a standard for social insurance offices in the country in general.

When it comes to the cost criterion, it is still not the case that the unit price for each case is measured in any more extensive way. However, administration has decreased by a third. The social insurance offices also measure the proportion of time that is used on administrative work and on production work and here the Social Insurance Office has a proportion of 14 % on administrative work compared with the country-wide average of 20,5 %.

How does what has been said above correspond to the subjective perception of customer utility? The Social Insurance Office measures this by means of customer questionnaires and these get quite a high grade even though the customers still find deficiencies in the information provided and that they would also like the staff to be more "service-minded". Another way to get more feedback from the customers are the so-called customer councils which have started in some areas. Just now they have been established for families with children and senior citizens. Experience from these has, for example, provided many important impulses on the design of the forms.

The above-mentioned factors are important for the perceived customer utility, though they may need to be complemented by other assessments as to whether a process is good or not. Mårtensson & Steneskog (1996) mention actor satisfaction as an important factor for a successful process. There are various forms of measures for judging how satisfied staff are. The Social Insurance Office regularly distributes questionnaires to the staff and these show that they are in general positively inclined to the change. However, many feel that the implementation of the change has been somewhat unstructured and that there still remains much work ahead, especially in such areas as control systems and systems of reward. The operative staff have also seen that process thinking has quickly led to simplifications in certain duties, which is considered positive.

Another important judgement criterion mentioned by Mårtensson & Steneskog is flexibility. This criterion involves

> *"the ability to handle changes considering both the environment, circumstances and demands on the process"* (ibid.).

We can judge how flexible a process is by asking questions about what can be changed, what changes can be foreseen and planned for, what risks there are for unplanned and unforeseen changes, and by judging how well the process handles these changes. At the Social Insurance Office there is no clear idea of how the flexibility of the process is to be tested, but as a result of the often recurring and quick changes following from the political decision process, there may be reasons for reflection in this area.

Many agree that an effective measuring system is decisive for a process to be controlled. There are many theoretical guidelines for how this can be done, but practitioners consider this to be a difficult area (IVA, 1995). In the quality movement statistical methods are often commended for measuring and assessing processes. Here quite a large selection of tools for measurement and analysis can be found. Statistical process control (SPC) is an example of a method mentioned (see, for example, Bergman & Klefsjö, 1994).

Rummler & Brache (1995) emphasise the importance of measurements and measurement systems in process orientation. They emphasise the importance of creating a cohesive measurement structure where measurements at a local level, i.e. for an individual member of staff, and measurements on more aggregated levels, such as process or company level, are interconnected and are consistent without goal conflicts.

Measuring and assessing a process are part of a larger context when it comes to judging a company's operations. Traditionally financial measurements have been given much importance in what we call financial control. There is much to support the view that financial accounting in its current form will find it difficult to handle a process-oriented working method. A natural connection to value chains, processes and activities is found in activity-based costing and management (ABC/ABM). There are examples of Swedish companies which have used ABC together with process orientation both for budgeting and accounting (IVA, 1995).

The tendency in today's debate in financial control is that financial measurements are more and more being complemented with non-financial measurements. One example is the "The Balanced Scorecard" (Kaplan & Norton, 1992) where four points of focus are presented. The first is a financial focus where the traditional monetary measurements are used. The second is an internal focus where the company's internal capability is measured, for example by lead times, quality and productivity measurements. The third is a renewal- and learning- focus where the company's ability to develop and continue to create value is assessed. The number of new products can be used as a measurement in this focus. Finally there is a customer focus which involves judging how the customers perceive the company and its products. Market shares and customer surveys are examples of indicators which fall under this focus. The principles for "The Balanced Scorecard" can easily be integrated with the ideas of process management and can provide an overall view on the control of a company's operations.

## Company culture

New ways of working demand new ways of thinking. Valuations and norms must go hand in hand with work tasks and structures, leadership and control systems as well as processes when new work methods are introduced (Hammer & Champy, 1993).

The Social Insurance Office use Hammer and Champy's reasoning above as a basis and try to ensure that, by means of information and training for example, the company culture changes at the same pace as the other changes are made. The Social Insurance Office, like other public authorities, have been strongly characterised by an internal perspective where their own operations have been central. To say that the people insured have been an unpleasant part of the working environment is perhaps to go too far, but there is a drop of truth in the statement. To introduce concepts such as "the customer in the centre" in these circumstances requires much work to become accepted.

The Social Insurance Office is an organisation characterised by a handbook culture, i.e. where rules and regulations govern the work. Changing attitudes and work methods to a business based on goal- and result- control and also personal responsibility can thus be difficult. The project leader expresses this quite drastically when he says:

"It is a matter of destroying the dictatorship of current thinking."

At the Social Insurance Office these questions have been perceived as being so important that a management process, "culture and attitude" has been established.

## Methods for change work

Development work is run in different ways and in different areas within companies. One way to illustrate development work on different levels, which is shown in the general model in Figure 5 below, is to distinguish between development of corporate strategies, business processes, and IS/IT support. The corporate level represents work on developing the company's relation to the external world in the form of strategies and business concepts. The business process level corresponds to work on developing the company's internal operations, usually in terms of some combination of processes and functions. The IS/IT support level can, for example, involve both the company's own application development and purchasing standard application packages.

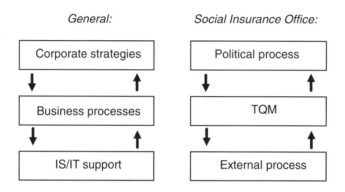

*Figure 5. Development work on three levels (adapted from Tolis & Nilsson, 1996).*

Change work at the Social Insurance Office can best be described as organisational development where it is based on a TQM concept which implies a focus on the business process level (see Figure 5).

What is interesting in the Social Insurance Office case is the lack of autonomy both when it concerns the strategic level and the IS/IT level. The long-term operational goals can be said to be the result of a political process where the goals are set by the Swedish National Insurance Board. The work of the Social Insurance Office is concentrated on how these goals can be achieved and on how to develop an action plan for change in an operational direction which they cannot influence to any major degree.

A similar situation is involved when it comes to information systems. They have no control over the central development of information systems, which is run by the Swedish National Insurance Board, and furthermore it is generally difficult to influence. The Social Insurance Office has a certain possibility to develop systems locally but the freedom here, too, is curtailed both by the Swedish National Insurance Board and limited financial resources.

The efforts that have now been put into applying "Total Quality Management" on operations are being concentrated on the middle level shown in the figure above. On this level there is a relatively large degree of freedom even though obstructions to the work on development have arisen in the form of rules and regulations from central quarters. To keep the work moving forwards it has been necessary to find approaches where the basic concept of development has been retained while taking the limitations into consideration.

To couple organisational development to the national goals which for the Social Insurance Office are given has not been any major problem and the management of the Social Insurance Office agrees with the idea of there being a unity among the country's social insurance offices concerning their relation to those insured, the customers.

The main problem is not being able to take advantage of modern information technology when the new processes were designed. A basic notion in, for example, BPR is that IT is an enabler which facilitates the creation of efficient and competitive processes. In the Social Insurance Office case it is more the fact that they have to talk about IT as a disabler.

A basic conception in our research is that there is often a communication gap between those in charge of organisational development and those responsible for systems development and that this creates problems in the form of information systems which do not sufficiently support operations.

# Conclusion

At the Social Insurance Office there have been a number of discussions on whether the concepts of TQM and process management can actually be applied to the operations of the Social Insurance Office. Concepts and models which are primarily intended for production have sometimes been perceived as being foreign. The Social Insurance Office considers, however, that the discussions on these topics have led to a view where operations can very well be described in these terms. The models must, of course, be adapted to their own operations.

On the basis of the experience gained at the Social Insurance Office there is much to favour the view that process orientation is a possible way to go forward for public authorities, too, in their aim to increase quality in the results of their operations, while at the same time facing reductions in costs.

What distinguishes the Social Insurance Office from most profit-making companies is the lack of a real market, which in the short term means that there is no competition. In the long term, though, it is feasible that the state will find alternative approaches to administrate transfer systems. The Social Insurance Office thus has the goal of being so efficient so as to retain its assignment in the future, too.

The Social Insurance Office is satisfied with how the changes have progressed so far. Their work has attracted attention externally and they have both received visitors from other organisations and have been invited as guests on various occasions where they have shared their experience with others. The dialogue with other actors is also a way of creating impulses towards developing their change work.

The Social Insurance Office will continue this work and challenges facing them in the future include:

- Creating functioning control- and reward- systems which both provide control over operations and which stimulate individual engagement in their work.

- Succeeding in changing the culture within the organisation so that concepts such as customer utility and continuous improvement are actively employed and guide operations.

- Creating efficient information systems which really support the processes and where the connection to the long-term goals is clear.

The Social Insurance Office case, which has been described in this chapter, is part of the ongoing project "Business Modelling". By means of an extended comparative analysis of different organisations we have studied and through future work, we hope to contribute to an empirical advancement of knowledge on connections between business development, processes and information systems.

# Acknowledgement

I would like to thank the staff at the Social Insurance Office in Östergötland for their willingness to provide me with access to their organisation and for their patience in answering all my questions.

The research was funded by NUTEK, the Swedish National Board for Industrial and Technical Development.

# References

Bergman B.& Klefsjö, B. (1994) *Quality – from Customer Needs to Customer Satisfaction*, Studentlitteratur, Lund, Sweden.

Davenport, T.H. (1993) *Process Innovation – Reengineering Work through Information Technology*, Harvard Business School Press, Boston, Massachusetts.

The Social Insurance Office (1995) *Processledning – En metod att organisera, leda och ständigt förbättra en verksamhet*, metodhandbok, internt material, The Social Insurance Office Östergötland, Linköping, Sweden [*Process Management – A Method to Organise, Manage and Continuously Improve an Organisation*, Method Handbook, internal material].

The Social Insurance Office (1994-1995) *Årsredovisning 1994/1995*, The Social Insurance Office Östergötland, Linköping, Sweden [*Annual Report 1994/1995*].

Hammer, M. & Champy J. (1993) *Reengineering the Corporation – A Manifesto for Business Revolution*, Harper Collins Publishers, New York.

IVA (1995) *Nya verksamhetsprocesser – Svenska erfarenheter av verksamhetsförändring i en ny IT-värld*, Ingenjörsvetenskapsakademien IVA, Stockholm [*New Business Processes – Swedish Experiences of Business Change in the New IT-World*, The Royal Swedish Academy of Engineering Sciences].

Kaplan, R.S. & Norton, D.P. (1992) "The Balanced Scorecard – Measures that Drive Performance", *Harvard Business Review*, Jan-Feb, 71-79

Mårtensson, A. & Steneskog, G. (1996) "Business Process Excellence – Some Characteristics", in Lundeberg, M. & Sundgren, B. (eds.) *Advancing Your Business – People and Information Systems in Concert*, The Economic Research Institute, Stockholm School of Economics, Stockholm.

Rummler, G.A. & Brache, A.P. (1995) *Improving Performance: How to Manage the White Space on the Organization Chart*, 2nd ed., Jossey-Bass Publishers, San Francisco.

Tolis, C. & Nilsson, A.G. (1996) "Using Business Models in Process Orientation", in Lundeberg, M. & Sundgren, B. (eds.) *Advancing Your Business – People and Information Systems in Concert*, The Economic Research Institute (EFI), Stockholm School of Economics, Stockholm.

# 5

# Business Modelling in a Historical Perspective: Experiences from Statistics Sweden

## *Bo Sundgren*

*Production and dissemination of statistics is the "business" of Statistics Sweden. There is a long tradition at Statistics Sweden aiming at the integration of systems development and statistical work. How did it start? Which were the obstacles? Was it successful? Which are the plans for the future? This chapter tries to answer these and other questions from a historical perspective, building on experiences from a statistical environment.*

## Introduction

The "business" of a national statistical office is to provide actors in a modern society with relevant, accurate, and timely statistical information, thus enabling them to describe, analyse, understand, make decisions, and act. The actors, i.e. the users of statistics, come from all parts of society: central, regional, and local government, private companies, organisations, universities, schools, and the public at large. Two important roles of official statistics are to facilitate efficient decision-making and to support democratic processes. Statistics Sweden, which is the organisation in focus in this chapter, is highly recognised among statistical offices according to international evaluations (Economist 1991, 1993).

Statistics production was one of the first areas of society to take advantage of computers, and the rapid developments in information technology and information systems methodology have since then been of great significance for statistical work. On the other hand, statistical offices have themselves often been at the forefront in developing and using information system concepts and methodologies. Databases, metainformation, and data warehouses are three examples of important information system concepts that emanate from statistics production. Development methodologies based upon the infological approach and conceptual modelling (data modelling) also have their origin in statistical environments.

# Computerised archives of statistical data – statistical file systems

By the end of the 1960´s most surveys conducted by Statistics Sweden had already become computerised. The "big" mainframe used in those days, an IBM 360/50, was actually much less powerful than the smallest PC today. Computerisation meant rationalisation of resource-consuming manual processes, but it also meant emerging possibilities of making statistical data available to users of statistics in a more flexible way than before. One of the first persons to notice these possibilities was Svein Nordbotten, who was then a deputy director of the Central Bureau of Statistics in Norway, and who became later a professor of Information Systems at the University of Bergen. Already in the middle of the 1960's, Nordbotten (1966) developed the concept of an archive-statistical system, or a statistical file system, as it was also called, a concept with many features in common with the later concepts of databases and data warehouses.

Until Nordbotten launched his seminal ideas, it had more or less been taken for granted that aggregated statistical tables were the natural end-products of statistical surveys. Nordbotten suggested that archives of primary data from statistical surveys, what we nowadays call microdata, would offer significant advantages in terms of flexibility for the users of statistics. First of all, the users could specify their own aggregations on the basis of microdata, rather than being restricted to the classifications and tabulations chosen by the statistics producer. Furthermore, storing primary data from different surveys in one and the same data archive would make it possible to combine data from different subject matter areas, and over time, in new ways that had not been anticipated by the original designers and producers of the respective data sets. In addition to the traditional, preplanned statistical aggregations and tabulations, the concept of an archive-statistical system could offer the users ad hoc processing of statistical microdata.

# The infological approach

Svein Nordbotten's ideas on archive-statistical systems, in combination with the pioneering work of Börje Langefors on information systems, had a great influence on several important development projects conducted by Statistics Sweden in the late 1960's and early 1970's. Among other things an experimental database management system, called ARKDABA, meaning "ARKivstatistisk DAtaBAs" or "Archive-statistical database", was successfully developed. ARKDABA contained statistical microdata from several statistical surveys and administrative registers. It should be noted that this development took place at a time when direct-access storage had just recently become available to application developers, and before software vendors started the marketing of commercial database management systems. In contrast, Nordbotten's concept of an archive-statistical system, had been entirely based upon serial storage technology, i.e. magnetic tapes; in such a system the join operations of a modern relational database had their counterparts in extensive serial file matchings; file transport optimisations like those treated by Langefors (1966) in his Theoretical Analysis of Information Systems were a major concern in those days.

During the development of the archive-statistical concepts and the ARKDABA database management system it became increasingly obvious that there were not only technical problems associated with the new ideas. There were also many conceptual and information contents oriented problems that had to be tackled. Even if it were technically possible to link the records of statistical files to each other, it would not always produce meaningful results. For example, concepts like "company", "household", and "income of person" could be defined in different ways by different statistical surveys, and such differences could make it more or less misleading to combine data from these surveys.

Producers of official statistics have developed a good understanding for the theoretical and practical problems of concept formation. This is particularly true for those statisticians who are involved in the development of standard concepts and classifications to be used in official statistics, e.g. in international overviews and comparisons.

In the beginning of the 1970's Börje Langefors and some of his students, including this author, devoted their attention to the development of an infological theory, a theory of concepts and information contents. Sundgren (1973) developed the OPR(t) framework for so-called infological models, or conceptual models, as they were later called in the international literature. The OPR(t) framework is based upon rigorous analyses of four fundamental concepts: objects, properties, relations (between objects), and time. Langefors' so-called elementary messages, building blocks of information, and other important information constructs and constituents were defined within the OPR(t) framework. It can be noted here that the so-called Entity-Relationship (ER) or Entity-Attribute-Relationship (EAR) approach, which may be regarded as equivalent to a subset of the OPR(t) framework, and which has become internationally (i.e. in the US) better known, was first presented by Chen (1976) only three years after the infological approach had first been published by Sundgren (1973, 1974, 1975).

At Statistics Sweden the infological theory and its conceptual framework were used and further developed in several projects during the early 1970's. One project concerned the development of an integrated conceptual framework for sociodemographic statistics, the so-called System of Socio-Demographic Statistics (SSDS), which was intended to become a counterpart in social statistics to the more established System of National Accounts (SNA), which is used as a conceptual framework for the integration of economic statistics.

Another project aimed at the development of a so-called Catalogue of Variables, a conceptually oriented data dictionary, repository, or meta-database, as we would say today. The catalogue of variables was intended to contain definitions of all important concepts used in the statistical surveys conducted by Statistics Sweden.

Yet another project that was inspired by archive-statistical and infological ideas was the development of the first full-fledged statistical output database of Statistics Sweden. According to the original design, this database was intended to contain three major parts: a microdatabase (partly based upon the above-mentioned ARKDABA prototype), a macrodatabase, containing multidimensional aggregated statistical data, and a meta-database, containing technical and contents-oriented descriptions of the microdata and the macrodata in the two other parts of the database. It is fair to say that this was one of the first data warehouses to become implemented in the world.

The microdata part of this data warehouse system had to be given up at an early stage. This was due to the first privacy debate in Sweden. It was deemed politically impossible to develop a database containing a lot of sensitive statistical data about individual persons (and companies), even though the data were only to be used for statistical purposes, and even though advanced secrecy and security measures were developed to protect the database against disclosures and misuse; actually this work in itself resulted in some early developments in the emerging field of statistical confidentiality; see Rapaport & Sundgren (1975) and Block & Olsson (1976).

However, the macrodatabase and the metadatabase became implemented and were in full operation in 1976. The macrodatabase contained several subsets, e.g. a Time Series Data Base (TSDB) and a Regional Statistical Data Base (RSDB). Both time series data and so-called cross-sectional data were handled by one and the same software system, called AXIS, in-house developed by Statistics Sweden, and all kinds of aggregated statistical data were handled according to the same multidimensional data model, the so-called alfa-beta-gamma ($\alpha\beta\gamma$) model, where the "gamma" variables spanned the dimensions (including time), and where the "beta" variables produced the cell values in the multidimensional structures; the "alfa" property was used to defined the population of objects for which the multidimensional table (or matrix) contained statistical data. Indeed AXIS was a very early tool for On-Line Analytical Processing (OLAP). It has provided on-line statistical services to a wide range of users in Sweden and internationally.

The metadatabase of the AXIS system was an advanced metadata handling system for its time, and it constituted the basis for program/data independence and for a menu-driven, interactive user interface, which did not assume any knowledge on the part of the user as to how the statistical data were physically stored in the database.

The AXIS system is still in operation and was only recently replaced by an SQL-based client/server system, interfacing the users via the Internet and other modern tools.

# Generalised software

The development projects described so far were front-line projects undertaken by the research and development department of Statistics Sweden, and they did not immediately or automatically have an impact on the bulk of application development that took place in the operative statistical work. As late as 1976 the central systems department of Statistics Sweden had some 150 application programmers, most of them tailoring statistics production applications in PL/1.

A national statistical office like Statistics Sweden conducts several hundred regular surveys every year, and for each survey there is one or more computerised applications supporting the statistical work on the survey. This work consists of a flow of typical processes like sampling frame construction and maintenance, sampling, data collection, coding, data entry, data editing (checking and correction of collected data), estimation, tabulation, analysis, presentation, and dissemination. With some oversimplification, one may say that more or less the same processes are repeated over and over again in the hundreds of surveys. Thus the application development should lend itself to rationalisation by generalisation, and, instead of tailoring application software survey by survey, one should be able to design and develop generalised software that can be used by many different surveys.

When academically schooled informaticians entered the arena in the late 1960's and early 1970's they noticed the potential for generalised software in statistics production. At about the same time, some generalised statistical software packages appeared on the market, often originating from statistical and sociological university institutions. These software packages attracted the attention of some statisticians in statistical offices, who wanted to do their own work rather than being dependent on application programmers, whose jargon they did not understand. However, the application programmers themselves showed no interest at all, but rather outright hostility to the idea of (re)using generalised statistical software.

During this phase, the research and development department of Statistics Sweden developed a non-procedural tabulation package, TAB68, aiming at the needs of the subject matter statisticians, who wanted to do their own application development, often in connection with *ad hoc* assignments, where there was no time for a lengthy planning process and traditional application development in PL/1. A TAB68 "program" consisted of a number of commands where the input files and the requested output tables were specified. The tabulation package itself was developed in IBM Assembler Language, an effort which took several years and caused costs of 1-2 million (1970) SEK, a huge amount in those days, equivalent to some 2 million (1996) US dollars. Nevertheless, when at last finalised, the package became extremely popular among subject matter statisticians, and after only one year of operation all development costs had already been recovered, since application development productivity was so much higher with the new tool than with traditional programming. Moreover, development times could be cut from weeks or months to days or hours.

Thus purchasing and/or developing generalised software that could be reused in many applications seemed to be a very promising way of improving efficiency, flexibility, and user-orientation in systems development at Statistics Sweden. The major problem was to convince traditionally trained systems developers and programmers that this was a viable route. Many of them claimed that the systems developed by Statistics Sweden did not lend themselves to use of generalised software, for some reason or other. It was not quite clear what these reasons were, but one characteristic that many systems analysts and programmers pointed to was the complexity and irregularity of data structures, a characteristic that they believed to be inherent in statistical systems. This was a serious problem, because most generalised software products were only able to handle very standardised data structures, typically so-called "flat files", corresponding to relational tables of today.

After some time we found a simple, but rather surprising solution to this problem, a kind of "Columbi egg" solution, as will be discussed in the next section of this chapter.

# The SCB systems development model

In the middle of the 1970's there was a reorganisation of the central systems department, which then consisted of some 150 employees, that is, about 10% of the whole staff of Statistics Sweden. A new policy for systems development work was adopted. Standardised software (commercial or in-house developed) should replace tailor-made programs as much as possible, and the systems development should be based upon the infological approach. The policy was operationalised in a model for systems development, the so-called SCB systems development model.

According to the SCB systems development model, systems development consists of infological, user-oriented tasks and datalogical, technically oriented tasks. The infological tasks concern WHAT the system should be able to do, and the datalogical tasks concern HOW the system should do what it should do. Although the model recognised that systems development work is typically iterative, it stressed that the infological problems should always be treated first, and result in a reasonably complete and precise infological model, before one started to tackle the usually much more resource-consuming datalogical tasks (like programming). The infological model should be systematically transformed into a datalogical model, where data representations and process flows (for manual and interactive as well as automated processes) were specified with appropriate technical details. The infological/datalogical transformations should be as straightforward as possible, leaving out technical optimisations until they were deemed to be absolutely necessary. According to more traditional systems development practices, prevailing at this time, programmers and systems analysts often had the ambition that the system should be as technically efficient as possible, in all its parts; one often neglected to investigate whether it was worthwhile to optimise, i.e. whether it made any significant difference to the overall performance of the system as a whole, whether a certain component was technically optimal or not.

The SCB systems development model was based upon the assumption that most statistical applications consist of a combination of certain typical processes, belonging to three major categories: microdata processes, aggregation processes, and macrodata processes. In the microdata processes the input data to a statistical application are collected and processed until they reach a stage of being "clean microdata", of sufficiently good quality, and stored in a standardised way. The aggregation processes summarise microdata into macrodata, "statistics", which represent estimates of certain statistical characteristics. During the macrodata processes the statistics are further processed, analysed, presented, and disseminated.

The SCB systems development model was database oriented in the sense that it prescribed that microdata, macrodata, and metadata should be stored and accessed in a standardised way. Ideally, the microdata should be stored in a microdatabase, the macrodata should be stored in a macrodatabase, and the metadata should be stored in a metadatabase, and the databases should be handled by database management software. The databases could be unique for a particular application, or they could be common components of several applications; in any case the database orientation and standardisation would facilitate application integration as well as *ad hoc* development of new applications on the basis of existing databases.

In practice, it was not realistic in the middle of the 1970's to make all applications truly database-oriented in a physical and technical sense. Commercial database management systems were still in their infancy and were not suitable for managing statistical data, neither the large volumes of microdata, nor the multidimensional macrodata – not to speak of the metadata. However, Statistics Sweden started to use a relational database management system, called RAPID, developed by Statistics Canada at this time, and it continued to use its own AXIS system for handling multidimensional macrodata and accompanying metadata.

However, for most applications Statistics Sweden started to use a flat file philosophy, which was regarded as a variant of the database-oriented systems architecture prescribed by the SCB systems development model. The flat file philosophy turned out to be the somewhat unexpected answer to the problem of adapting generalised software products to the complex data structures prevailing in the statistical production systems of Statistics Sweden. This problem, which was mentioned above, had for some time frustrated the advocates to the new SCB policy of using standardised software. Many existing systems in those days were based on very complex data structures like files with several record types, variable length records, etc. For some time it was considered to continue the development of existing standard software products, like the above-mentioned tabulation package TAB68, so that they would be able to handle not only flat files (logically equivalent to relations in the sense of the relational data model) but also a range of other common data structures, e.g. so-called "trains", consisting of one "locomotive" (main record type) followed by a number of "wagons" belonging to different categories (sub-record types).

The solution to this problem was found, when the developers of the SCB systems development model shifted their focus from the software to the data. Rather than trying to develop software that could handle all existing data structures, one should first standardise the storage of data by requiring that all data should be stored in relational tables or in flat files that followed the same rules as relational tables (in at least first normal form), although they need not be handled by a relational database management system, but they could be stored and processed as serial files, often still magnetic tape files.

Needless to say, there was an outburst of loud criticism to the proposed policy of permitting flat files only. Many experienced programmers and systems analysts claimed that such a policy would result in unacceptable technical performance losses. The management response to the criticism was to permit exceptional data structures to be used in exceptional cases – but only after the designers had tried to find a solution based upon flat files and could convincingly demonstrate that such a solution would be inappropriate. Actually nobody ever presented such a case, and since then all systems were adapted to the flat file philosophy as soon as they were developed or redeveloped.

During the late 1970's and early 1980's, the TAB68 package became the basis for the development of a whole range of packages supporting other typical processes in statistics production, like sampling, data editing (checking and correcting input data), and computations of different statistical characteristics (estimation). Together these packages constituted a family of related generalised software products for statistics production, "the TAB68 family". All members of the TAB68 family had similar syntax, and the same code was sometimes reused.

In the beginning of the 1980's an international co-operation project between some statistical offices was devoted to the task of developing a statistical base operator algebra, an extension of the relational algebra, and a software system, the so-called Base Operator System (BOS), which implemented the algebra. Every base operator used one, or, e.g. in the case of the JOIN operator, two flat files (or relational tables), together with accompanying metadata, as input, and produced a new flat file (or relational table), with accompanying metadata, as output. The most innovative base operator was one called DEFINE. With this operator it was possible to define new variables, with accompanying metadata, in a very general way, combining arithmetical expressions, Boolean expressions, classifications, and conditional expressions within one and the same definition of a new variable on the basis of one or more existing variables, with their metadata.

In today's terminology, one could say that the Base Operator System constituted a library of reusable software components. Similarly, the TAB68 family of software packages could be seen as a library of reusable components on a more complex level.

In summary the SCB systems development model was based upon the following principles:

1. The systems design process consists of user-oriented, infological tasks and technologically oriented, datalogical tasks. The infological tasks include modelling the universe of discourse (reality modelling or object system modelling) and specifying user-relevant functional requirements. The infological tasks deal with the external properties of the information system, and the results of the infological analyses are summarised in an infological model of the information system to be constructed. The datalogical tasks include a systematic transformation of the infological model into a datalogical model, which also specifies a number of technically oriented, internal properties of the information system to be constructed. For example, the infological model would contain a conceptual model, specifying WHAT information the information system should contain, and the datalogical model would contain a relational data model, or a flat file model, specifying HOW the information should be represented by data. The infological model would specify the functionality of the information

system in terms of user-relevant processes to be supported, and information endproducts to be produced, and the datalogical model would specify how this functionality should be realised by means of software components and data sets (cf. Sundgren, 1984).

2. As a rule, infological design tasks should be executed before datalogical design steps. Iterations between datalogical and infological design tasks should be permitted, and sometimes stimulated, but it should be taken into account that whereas design iterations on the infological level are typically fast and inexpensive, iterations that involve datalogical redesign, and maybe even datalogical reconstruction, are much more resource-consuming. Hence, it is usually rational to make sure that the infological model is thoroughly analysed and stable before extensive datalogical design and construction tasks are started. However, this does not exclude prototyping and experimental systems design, but such design methods should be regarded as instrumental for the design process, and not taken as an excuse for bad design or for unplanned trial and error.

3. An OPR(t) model – ObjectPropertyRelation(time) – is a key element of an infological model of an information system, and it should be one of the first design tasks to elaborate such a model. This design task should be carried out in close co-operation between the system users and the system designers. The OPR(t) model should be regarded as a communication interface between users and designers during the design process, and it is an efficient tool for identifying and solving conceptual problems. Conceptual problems that are not properly identified, and solved, will typically cause difficult problems in construction and operation stages, and during these later stages the problems may not even be properly traced back to their conceptual origin, but they may be mistaken for technical problems.

4. The alfa-beta-gamma-tau ($\alpha\beta\gamma\tau$) multidimensional scheme should be used for analysing the aggregated statistical information, macroinformation, to be produced by a statistical information system. The alfa dimension identifies a population of objects, and it may be based upon several properties, which may in turn be based upon several variables (attributes) of the objects. The gamma dimension is a multidimensional combination of (sub)dimensions, where each sub-dimension is a variable classifying the population of objects defined by the alfa dimension, and where the combination of gamma variables constitute a cross-classification of this population. The beta dimension identifies a number of statistical characteristics that are estimated for the population as a whole, as well as for each subset of objects identified by a combination of values for the

gamma variables, corresponding to a cell in the multidimensional gamma structure. The tau dimension, finally, represents time. The specification of an alfa-beta-gamma structure may contain one or more time parameters. They may be specified in the tau dimension, and referred to in each one of the other dimensions and sub-dimensions.

5. A relational data model, or a flat file model, is a key element of a data-logical model of an information system, and it is the datalogical counter-part of a conceptual OPR(t) model. An OPR(t) model can be systemati-cally transformed into a relational data model, or a flat file model, by means of a small set of relatively simple transformation rules. The result-ing data model will typically (and automatically) be in the so-called third normal form, but this is not regarded as an end in itself.

6. Data and metadata are, at least conceptually, regarded as stored in a statistical database, consisting of three major parts, containing micro-data, macrodata, and metadata, respectively. The microdatabase would typically be represented by a relational database or a collection of flat files, and the macrodata would typically (in the 1980's) be stored in the AXIS database. Now, in the late 1990's, all kinds of data (microdata, macrodata, and formalised metadata) would be stored in relational data-bases; text databases would be used for little structured freetext metadata, and OLAP tools and other specialised software products may become valuable complements.

7. The computerised processes needed to implement the statistics produc-tion functionality of a statistical information system corresponding to a statistical survey should be represented, as far as possible, by standardised software, e.g. commercial packages like SAS, different members of the TAB68 family, or other reusable software components like the Base Operators. Tailor-made programs should be developed only for interfacing standard software, or for system components, where no suitable standard software is available.

8. Application development is supported (in the 1980's) by the CONDUCTOR CASE tool, developed by Statistics Sweden. It supports application development by means of members in the TAB68 family and some popular commercial software products like SAS and EASYTRIEVE, and it supports documentation according to the DOK system, the docu-mentation counterpart of the SCB systems development model.

9. The standardised design procedures prescribed by the SCB systems development model are assumed to result in an information system, which can be run with satisfactory technical efficiency. If this does not turn out

to be the case, due to some exceptional circumstances, but only then, efforts are made to optimise the system from a technical point of view, tailor-programming, if necessary, certain components of the system. The optimisation efforts are limited to situations and components, where they are regarded as unavoidable.

10. Subject matter statisticians are encouraged to make their own application development, using the SCB systems development model and its components, including standardised software packages and the CONDUCTOR tool; today this phenomenon, which occurred at Statistics Sweden in the mid 1970's and onwards, would be labelled as Rapid Application Development (RAD) (cf. Sundgren, 1989).

# Integration of methodologies from statistics and information systems

The SCB systems development model worked reasonably well. The co-operation improved between programmers and systems analysts, on the one hand, and subject matter statisticians, on the other. A new recruitment policy was introduced for the central systems department, whereby subject matter statisticians with an interest in systems development and IT were encouraged to continue their careers within the systems department; some movements in the other direction occurred as well. Step by step, the systems development work became a much more integrated part of the "business" of Statistics Sweden. Employees in the systems department began to appreciate and identify themselves with the goals of Statistics Sweden, rather than seeing themselves just as computer specialists, for whom Statistics Sweden was just one of many different possible working places. On the other hand, many subject matter statisticians – not only those who took the step over to the systems department – found it useful and interesting to be able to develop their own applications, especially in situations, where a statistics user wanted some special product that required *ad hoc* processing of existing data, or even a completely new data collection, and where the user wanted response very quickly.

In the early 1980's this process had gone so far that it became possible to decentralise most application-oriented systems development work at Statistics Sweden to the subject matter departments. Only generalised software development and methodologically oriented work remained in the central systems department.

The decentralisation process was further stimulated at this time by the advent of personal computers (PCs). Like in many other places PCs were first introduced at Statistics Sweden as a tool for office automation, but very soon both systems developers and subject matter statisticians (and the various hybrids of these two categories that now existed) began to realise the potential of the new technology for statistics production as such, that is, for the business of Statistics Sweden. However, this time, too, there was resistance to the novelties, and it came, not surprisingly, from the staff of the computer operations department, whose main responsibility was to look after the mainframe, maintaining the operating system and executing the mainframe applications. These people, of which there were nearly 100, regarded PCs as toys and strongly opposed the emerging development. After a few years of fruitless quarrelling, the problem was solved by outsourcing; the whole computer operations department was sold to DAFA, a government-owned service bureau, which was soon sold again to a multinational company, SEMA Group. The outsourcing took place in 1992, and now, five years later, there has been another call for tender for computer services, which now have a much stronger emphasis on running the PC network; the mainframe will be completely outphased by the year 2000. As a matter of fact, SEMA Group lost the contract, and IBM-owned Responsor will become the new service provider as of July 1 this year; the contract lasts for four years.

The PC technology has "normalised" the role of computers in organisations like Statistics Sweden. Computer technology can now be treated like most other resources that are of vital and strategic importance for the business, and this means that those responsible for the business also have the ultimate responsibility for their IT tools, just like they are responsible for staff and other production factors.

Thus the general development in the IT area has strongly enforced the earlier described development initiated within Statistics Sweden itself, aiming at integration of information systems development and business activities. However, despite the emphasis on the infological, user- and contents-oriented aspects of systems development, it was discovered in the early 1990's that these aspects still did not get the attention that they deserved. The subject matter statisticians had definitely become much more computer literate, and they used generalised software in order to develop their own applications according to the SCB systems development model and with the help of the tools provided in connection with this model. However, the contents experts in the various subject matter fields and the statistical methodologists were still not as engaged in systems development as they should be according to the paradigm. As a result, a typical DOK documentation of the information system corresponding to a statistical survey would often contain only a few introductory pages on the infological aspects of the system, followed by maybe a hundred pages or more of more conventional, datalogically oriented systems documentation. Moreover, key elements of the infological design, like the OPR(t) model, was often reconstructed from existing systems, in a "bottom-up" kind of way, and the reason for this was once again that the real contents experts, who could have designed the model on the basis of more firsthand knowledge, were not sufficiently engaged, or not even at all engaged in the systems development and documentation process. More complex statistical aspects were often neglected altogether, for similar reasons; statistical methodologists were not engaged in the systems design process, and the statistical design was carried out separately from the information systems design.

The director general of Statistics Sweden in those days, professor Sten Johansson, a sociologist, recognised some of these shortcomings. Concretely, he was dissatisfied that he was not able to get a sufficiently complete documentation of certain statistical surveys. He wanted the documentation to be so complete and precise from a contents-oriented (as well as technical) point of view that he would himself be able to analyse the survey microdata, using standardised statistical software with which he was familiar. As a consequence, he asked myself, a professor of information systems, and Bengt Rosén, a professor of statistics, to develop a general documentation system that would satisfy his own needs as well as the needs of many other researchers, who wanted to analyse microdata collected by Statistics Sweden, without having to put a lot of questions to those subject matter experts, who had performed the survey, and who happened to be still around. "You should design a documentation system, which will make it possible for researchers hundreds of years from now to interpret the data from our present surveys", was the message of Sten Johansson to Bengt Rosén and myself. About two years later, the two of us presented a new documentation system for statistical surveys, where contents-oriented, statistical, and information systems oriented aspects were fully integrated; we named it the SCBDOK system; see Rosén & Sundgren (1991).

When we had started the development of the new documentation system, we found rather soon that we had to tackle many fundamental questions. We felt that we had to develop a very general and precise description model of a statistical survey. We started from the beginning and worked ourselves through all the typical steps of a statistical survey. We were careful to define all concepts that we encountered on our way in such a way that both of us could understand and accept the definitions, regardless of whether it was a statistical concept, an information system concept, or some kind of combined concept. We focused on concepts rather than terms; many terms could be allowed as synonyms for the same concept. The need for such an approach became even more evident, when we tried different concepts and terms on our colleagues. The choice between different terms often provokes strong emotions, whereas concepts are easier to agree upon, once they have been properly analysed.

Since we chose to introduce and define all concepts (and alternative terms) in their natural context, rather than by means of some list or dictionary, we ended up by producing a document, which could be seen as a kind of tutorial on statistical surveys and statistical information systems. Having done this, it was a relatively simple task to summarise the description model in the form of a documentation template, containing sections, items, and sub-items corresponding to the phases, tasks, and steps in the planning and execution of a statistical survey.

Table 1 shows the present version of the documentation template, SCBDOK 2.0, which is now a formally approved internal standard of Statistics Sweden, and which has influenced similar work in other countries.

The template reflects the process of designing and executing a statistical survey in the following way. When designing a survey, one first has to define the purpose and contents of the survey and its main expected outputs. This is reflected in chapter 1, *Summary*, of the documentation template, and it corresponds to early infological tasks in a traditional systems development model. The next logical step in the planning of a statistical survey is to specify the procedures for obtaining input data: designing the survey frame (e.g. a register containing references to the objects of interest) and the frame procedures associated with the frame, sampling procedures, measurement instrument (e.g. a questionnaire), data collection procedures, and data preparation procedures (coding, editing, etc.). These are major statistical design tasks, and they are reflected in chapter 2, *Data collection*, of the documentation template.

When the input data have been collected and prepared, they are to be organised in an observation register, a register of "clean" microdata with accompanying metadata, which can be used as a basis for many different estimation and analysis processes, immediately, as well as in the more or less distant future. Thus the observation register has to be carefully documented, and this is done in chapter 3, *Observation register*, of the documentation. It should be noted that the documentation contains two kinds of metainformation: on the one hand information resulting from design decisions, and on the other hand information resulting from the actual execution of the survey, e.g. response rates. When a survey has been executed in the sense that a final observation register has been produced, and chapter 3 in the documentation has been completed, the observation register is "frozen", and a "snapshot" copy is taken of the documentation at this stage to accompany the observation register into the archives for future users and usages.

| **0 Administrative information** | **1 Summary** |
|---|---|
| 0.1 Survey name | 1.1 The survey plan |
| 0.2 Branch of statistics | 1.2 Contents: statistical characteristics |
| 0.3 Responsible organisation, person | 1.3 Output: statistics and microdata |
| 0.4 Approximate cost of the survey | 1.4 Time frame |
| 0.5 Purpose and history of the survey | 1.5 Documentation |
| 0.6 Users and usages | |
| 0.7 Voluntary/mandatory response | |
| 0.8 Confidentiality | |
| 0.9 EU regulations and requirements | |
| **2 Data collection** | **3 Observation register** |
| 2.1 Frame and frame procedures | 3.1 Target and observation objects |
| 2.2 Sampling procedures | 3.2 Variable lists |
| 2.3 Measurement instrument | 3.3 Physical organisation |
| 2.4 Data collection procedures | 3.4 Experiences from last survey cycle |
| 2.5 Data preparation: coding, editing, etc. | |
| **4 Statistical processing and presentation** | **5 Data processing system** |
| 4.1 Estimates: assumptions and computation formulas | 5.1 System summary and system flow |
| 4.2 Presentation and dissemination procedures | 5.2 Processing |
| | 5.3 Database models |
| | 5.4 Database tables |
| | 5.5 Database accessories |
| | 5.6 Reports |
| | 5.7 Other data sets |
| **6 The log-book** | |

*Table 1. Documentation template for a statistical survey and its production system.*

Chapter 4, *Statistical processing and presentation*, in the documentation registers how the "first-time" estimation processes were designed and executed by the original statistics producer. Future (re)users of the collected data may of course make other assumptions and choices, which will result in other statistical estimates on the basis of the same data. However, for most users of an observation register, it will be useful and interesting to know the assumptions and choices made by the original statistics producer in connection with the first-time processing of the data.

Chapter 5, *Data processing system*, contains such detailed and technical information about the production processes, which is not necessary to have for interpreting' and processing a final observation register from a survey. This part of the documentation will typically have the flavour of a more traditional, datalogically oriented system documentation. It should be useful for those who are responsible for the execution and maintenance of the production processes, as long as the production system is "alive", but for the end-users of the final observation registers produced by the production system, it should be of little significance. All metainformation that is significant for present and future end-users of observation registers should be in the other chapters of the documentation, i.e. those parts which are contained in the "snapshot" that accompanies the observation register.

Finally, chapter 6, *The log-book*, is a place, where one should always make a note, as soon as the design of the survey is changed in some way or another. The log-book serves two important purposes. First, it makes it easy and simple to register all design changes, even if one should not have time or motivation to update the proper items and sub-items in other parts of the documentation. Second, it is sometimes important for users to get an overview of all changes in the design of a (repetitive) survey that have taken place over the years. This is particularly relevant for users of time series data.

In summary, the philosophy of the documentation template is that it should stimulate and facilitate a documentation process, which is closely synchronised and co-ordinated with the underlying design and execution processes. Ideally, the latter processes should almost automatically "generate" the metadata contained in the chapters, sections, and items of the documentation. On the other hand, the documentation template could also serve the purpose of being a "checklist" for the tasks to be carried out at some stage in the design and execution of a statistical survey. Even though the template is structured to reflect the major flow of the design and execution processes, these processes naturally need not slavically follow the structure of the template. However, it is important that all design decisions are made consciously (and not by default) at some stage, and that whenever a design decision is taken, formally or informally, the full meaning of the design decision is captured in the accompanying documentation and metadata.

The SCBDOK model for describing a statistical survey is described in several reports from Statistics Sweden; see Rosén & Sundgren (1991), Sundgren (1992, 1993). There is also a handbook on how to use the documentation template, which is an integral part of the description model.

# The future: integrated data and metadata management

At present the generalised information systems development work of Statistics Sweden is very much focused on the needs of external users of statistics, i.e. it is focused on the core business of a national statistical office. Some requirements that many statistics users have in common are that

- users stress availability aspects of the information, including the availability of high-quality documentation and metadata, so that they can interpret and analyse the statistical data correctly and on their own, independently of the producers at Statistics Sweden;

- users want to be able to transfer data in electronic form to their own computers, where they want to process the data further, using software products of their own choice;

- users often need to combine statistical data from different surveys, handled by different organisational units at Statistics Sweden, and sometimes the users also need to combine official statistics with their own statistical or non-statistical data.

Although different users of statistics have certain typical requirements in common, it is maybe even more characteristic for them to have quite different requirements. What is top priority for one user maybe of little or no significance for another one, and vice versa.

It is a non-trivial task to satisfy the many-faceted, and sometimes even contradictory needs of different categories of users of statistical data. Making compromises between user demands will often result in all users being completely dissatisfied rather than (half) satisfied. Better solutions can be found by aiming at the production and dissemination systems of a national statistical office to become a flexible data and metadata infrastructure, which is open for further processing by the users themselves. Particularly important features of such an infrastructure are that

- the primary data (microdata) are of good statistical quality and are completely and precisely described by accompanying metadata;

- data and metadata are electronically stored according to standard formats;

- data are defined and stored in such a way that they are easy to combine, from a contents-oriented as well as from a technical point of view;

- systems and subsystems can easily exchange data and metadata with each other, and with the human users and their computerised systems through standard interfaces;

- systems and subsystems obtain their functionality by means of generalised, standard, reusable software components that communicate with one another through well-defined, standard interfaces;

- systems and subsystems are open-ended, so that new useful software components can easily be "plugged in", as they become available;

- all data and metadata processes in the infrastructure are streamlined and synchronised in such a way that they can be routinely operated and monitored with a minimum of human efforts; data and metadata should be entered manually at most once, and, ideally, as direct and automatic side-effects of the object system events where the data occur naturally for the first time; after that, data and metadata should be systematically and automatically transformed throughout the flow of processes, rather than being manually reconstructed and re-entered.

Statistics Sweden has just launched a new dissemination system for statistical data (macrodata and microdata) and accompanying metadata. It is based upon the principles stated above for a flexible infrastructure. Standard relational databases are used for storing statistical data and formalised metadata describing the statistical data in a structured way. Freetext metadata are stored by a standard text management system. There are several different user interfaces, corresponding to different user needs. Some of them are based upon the Internet and Internet-related, standard tools. The relational databases can be accessed by all software products that support the SQL standard.

The feeding of the statistical dissemination databases with data and metadata is not yet as streamlined and synchronised with the underlying production system as prescribed by the principles stated above. However, all production systems supporting the surveys and statistical information systems of Statistics Sweden are now being moved from the old mainframe platform to a new platform based upon networked client/server systems, running on PCs. The databases are relational databases conforming to the SQL interface. Moving the production systems from the mainframe to the new PC-based platform involves a complete re-engineering process. According to present plans this process will be finalised by the year 2000.

The detailed design of the client/server architecture used by the new, re-engineered production systems is still under discussion. There is a proposal to use a so-called 3-tier client/server architecture, consisting of

- a personal client level for user interactions and single-user applications
- a data management server level for shared databases
- a business logic server level for multi-user applications

The introduction of a separate level, or tier, for business logic has several advantages. In a conventional, 2-tier client/server architecture, it is not clear where the application software should belong. If it is placed on the clients, it will lead to maintenance problems, if there are several clients running the same application. On the other hand, if the application software is integrated with the database management, e.g. by means of so-called stored procedures, there is an obvious risk that data/program independence is lost. Moreover, stored procedures are not very good at handling complex business logic. A separate business logic level solves both these problems and is clearly in line with infological principles as well as object orientation. The business logic server (which need not necessarily be a physically separate server) will house reusable software components supporting the business logic, i.e. reusable software components, or objects, corresponding to generalised software packages and standard software components in earlier generation application systems.

At the end of this development, one may see a flexible production and dissemination infrastructure that will finally implement, in full scale, the early vision of Nordbotten concerning an archive-statistical system. Actually the implementation could have occurred much earlier, using technology available then, but the rapid technical development, which is now taking place, makes it almost impossible to avoid implementing the vision, which is so attractive for the users of statistics. If statistical offices will not do it, probably somebody else will; cf. Guteland & Malmborg (1996), Rauch (1997).

# References

Block, H. & Olsson, L. (1976) "Backwards Identification of Person Information", *Statistisk Tidskrift – Statistical Review*, Vol. 14, No. 2.

Chen P. (1976) "The Entity-Relationship Model – Toward a Unified View of Data", *ACM Transactions on Database Systems*, Vol. 1, No. 1.

Economist (1991) "Official Numbers – The Good Statistics Guide", *The Economist*, September 7th, 1991, p. 84

Economist (1993) "Economics Brief – The Good Statistics Guide", *The Economist*, September 11th, 1993, p. 63

Guteland, G. & Malmborg, E. (1996) *Our legacy to future generations – using databases for better availability and documentation*, Statistics Sweden, Stockholm.

Langefors, B. (1966) *Theoretical Analysis of Information Systems*, Studentlitteratur, Lund, Sweden [Also published 1973 by Auerbach, Philadelphia].

Malmborg, E. (1982) *The OPREM-approach – An extension of an OPR-approach to include dynamics and classification*, Statistics Sweden, Stockholm.

Nordbotten, S. (1966) "A statistical file system", *Statistisk Tidskrift – Statistical Review*, Vol. 4, No.2.

Rapaport, E. & Sundgren, B. (1975) "Output Protection in Statistical Data Bases" *Conference of the International Statistical Institute*, Warsaw.

Rauch, L. (1997) *The rapid change of new information technologies – a growing challenge for the development of a statistical information system*, Statistics Sweden, Stockholm.

Rosén, B. & Sundgren, B. (1991) *Dokumentation för återanvändning av mikromaterial från SCBs undersökningar*, Statistics Sweden, Stockholm [*Documentation for reuse of microdata from the surveys carried out by Statistics Sweden*; English translation available].

Sundgren, B. (1973) *An Infological Approach to Data Bases*, Statistics Sweden and University of Stockholm, Stockholm.

Sundgren, B. (1974) "Conceptual foundation of the infological approach to data bases" In Klimbie, J. W. & Koffeman, K. L. (eds), *Data Base Management*, North-Holland, Amsterdam.

Sundgren, B. (1975) *Theory of Data Bases*, Petrocelli/Charter, New York.

Sundgren, B. (1984) *Conceptual Design of Data Bases and Information Systems* Statistics Sweden, Stockholm.

Sundgren, B. (1989) "Conceptual Modelling as an Instrument for Formal Specification of Statistical Information Systems" *47th Session of the International Statistical Institute, Paris.*

Sundgren, B. (1992) *Organizing the Metainformation Systems of a Statistical Office*, Statistics Sweden, Stockholm.

Sundgren, B. (1993) *Guidelines on the Design and Implementation of Statistical Metainformation Systems*, Statistics Sweden, Stockholm.

# 6

# Business Process Development and Information Technology in Small and Medium-sized Companies

*Jörgen Andersson*

*Computer maturity is at a high level in Swedish companies! This claim can be established after a study made on smaller and medium-sized Swedish manufacturing companies. The companies are prepared to take a new step in development from having concentrated computerisation on making internal routines more efficient to supporting the company's communication with the external world using new technology. There is, however, still a certain lack of competence in the area of information technology, particularly in the planning of information systems.*

## Is information technology used in smaller companies?

The rapid development of computer technology has made the costs of computer systems sufficiently low to enable even small companies to invest in their own computerised information systems. The question, then, is to what degree computers and information technology are actually used in smaller and medium-sized companies.

During 1996 a questionnaire survey of Swedish companies was carried out within the framework of an EU project (COMPETE) amongst other things on their use of information technology. The questionnaire covered 509 manufacturing companies with between 20 and 200 employees. On the basis of the answers received from the questionnaire 40 companies were singled out for a more extensive follow-up interview. The selection was based on several different criteria such as size, region, branch and so on.

(Results from the interviews are also presented in Stymne & SWECOMPETE Group, 1997.)

COMPETE is an EU project involving collaboration between Italy, France and Sweden with the aim of strengthening the competition factor of small companies, in particular the role information technology plays in this context. Project leader is Patrizia Fariselli of the NOMISMA research institute, Bologna. The Swedish part of the project is led by Professor Bengt Stymne at the Institute for Management of Innovation and Technology (IMIT). The universities taking part are Stockholm School of Economics, Chalmers Technical University in Gothenburg, Linköping University and the Swedish Agricultural University in Uppsala. The French part is carried out by LEREP, Toulouse and INTEGRAI, Bordeaux.

The results of the questionnaire show that a relatively high proportion of the Swedish companies use information technology in their operations (for a more extensive report, see Stymne et al, 1997). In Figure 1 below it can be seen that as many as 98% of them use PCs and 67% have a local network. The proportion of companies using Internet, e-mail and EDI is significantly smaller. In addition to the use of PCs it seems that in general the larger companies have got further as far as computerisation is concerned.

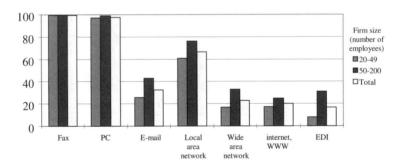

*Figure 1. Information technology used (%) (adapted from Stymne et al, 1997).*

If we compare these results with previous studies, we can see that the extent of computerisation has increased. Raymond & Magnenat-Thalmann (1982) studied the use and advantages of computerised information systems in 218 smaller and medium-sized companies in Canada. The study showed that about 60% of the companies used some form of information system. Of these about 75% had their own computer while the rest employed service bureaus. About one third had software they had developed themselves, while the rest used standard application packages.

Other studies in USA, England and Canada during the period 1986-1991 show highly varying results for computerisation in smaller companies. The lowest figure noted was 27% while the highest was 79%. However, what the results have in common is that larger companies have a higher level of computerisation than smaller ones (Chen & Williams, 1993).

The interviews in the COMPETE project also show a consistently high level of computerisation where PC-based systems or client/server set-ups with minicomputers or workstations as servers are used in most companies. What is of most interest for many companies at the moment is Internet and EDI. Many companies are testing the new technology and are trying to gain an understanding of whether World Wide Web, for example, is a medium for increased contact in the market. Replacing paper-based communication between companies and their vendors/customers is also high on their list of priorities.

## Computerised functions

When considering the functions that are at least partially supported by computerised information systems, it can be seen that accounting and personnel administration are the functions that show the highest level of computerisation (see Figure 2). Apart from accounting it is also the case that there is a significant difference between the larger and the smaller companies.

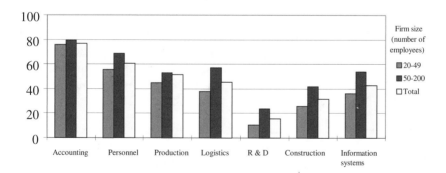

*Figure 2. Computerised functions (%) (adapted from Stymne et al, 1997).*

The result agrees well with previous studies where it has been shown that the first to be computerised are the financial routines. (see, for example, Raymond & Magnenat-Thalmann, 1982; Baker, 1987; Chen & Williams, 1993).

The results from the interviews show that for a longer period many companies have had support for the routine type of transaction-based functions such as accounting, payroll and manufacturing planning and control. In these areas there are many companies which are facing the generation shift where out-of-date systems are being replaced by new ones. In general a higher degree of integration is being sought for and those who are considering acquiring a new system are also the ones who are most interested in integrated standard application packages.

Among the functions that are still not computerised to any greater extent we find purchasing, sales, marketing and construction. Within purchasing and sales it is mainly in communication with external partners where the companies want to computerise. Several companies would also like to introduce sales support systems where, for example, they could use to their advantage mobile computer communication in supporting salesmen out in the field. There is also a need for systems for information on the market and on competitors.

In construction there is a higher degree of integration between construction and other systems which is being sought for, both internally within the company and externally in relations with customers, vendors and consultants. Functions where just now there does not seem to be any greater need of computer support for include research and development (R & D) and also personnel systems with the exception of payroll systems.

## Degree of specialisation

In the questionnaire companies were also asked to state the extent to which personnel were specially grouped for different functions. Of the companies in the study about half had specialists in the IT function. This is a significantly lower proportion than, for example, accounting, manufacturing or logistics (see Figure 3).

The interviews also show that to the extent they have IT specialists these often have the role of operations personnel, while very few companies have personnel who are specialised in analysis of information needs, requirements specification or strategic IT issues. This is of particular interest as previous studies have shown that the availability of IT competence in the company increases the chances of development and the introduction of information systems being successful (see, for example, Lees, 1987; Montazemi, 1988; Schleich et al, 1990). The importance of competence in information systems planning, information requirements analysis and evaluation is also pointed out in these studies. As the companies lack competence in these areas, it means that they are often dependent on the system vendors. The quality of the system vendors then becomes decisive for the quality of the information systems.

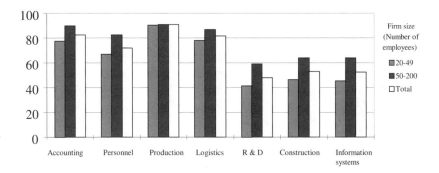

*Figure 3. Companies with specialised staff (%) (adapted from Stymne et al, 1997).*

It is also the case that the IT function is the one which to the largest degree is left to an external vendor even though generally only a low proportion of the companies use external services for their functions (see Figure 4).

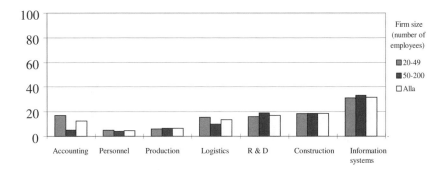

*Figure 4. Outsourcing (%) (adapted from Stymne et al, 1997).*

The differences between the larger and smaller companies in the selection are not as great in this respect as in previous results. However, a significantly larger proportion of the smaller companies use external services for accounting.

The impression gained from the interviews is that there is generally a certain reluctance against handing over responsibility for the company's functions to external companies. Furthermore several companies would like to reduce their dependence on, for example, system vendors. On the other hand there is an open-hearted attitude towards various actors in the refinement process where customers and vendors are seen as partners where advantages can be gained for all partners through collaboration.

## *Advice-giving services*

The proportion of companies which use external competence from universities, research institutes or public technical advisors is relatively small. On the other hand many companies use private consultants when they themselves lack competence within the company. The locally active consultants are the ones employed first of all. In Figure 5 below you can see that about half of the companies use these consultants.

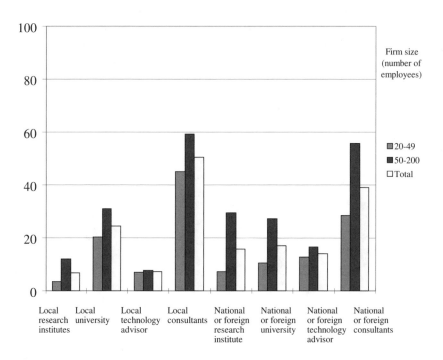

*Figure 5. Co-operation with technology advisors (%) (adapted from Stymne et al, 1997).*

Here, too, it is the larger companies that use external competence to a greater degree, which can seem somewhat surprising as it is the smaller companies that are most often assumed to lack competence in several areas. According to the interview material it is often in connection with work on quality and certification that companies hire consultants, but organisational change and construction issues can give rise to the need for external advice. When it comes to IT issues, it does not seem as though independent consultants are used to any greater degree. Even if companies use various consultancy services to a large degree, there is, however, a somewhat reserved attitude towards consultants mainly due to the highly varying quality of their work.

## Business process development

The extent to which companies put effort into business process development can be seen in Figure 6 below. The results show that during recent years changes have been introduced to a relatively large degree and it is above all the manufacturing process and organisation that have been the subject of the change.

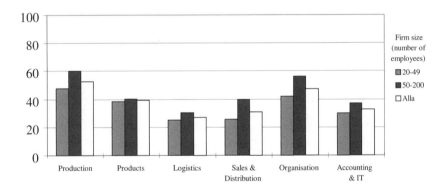

*Figure 6. Major changes 1993-1995 (%) (adapted from Stymne et al, 1997).*

In the interviews the company managers state that it is both external forces in the form of customers and competitors as well as internal requirements to improve efficiency in the organisation that are the driving forces behind the changes.

About one third of the companies have changed their information systems. The impression the interviews give, however, is that IT issues are in focus for most of the companies and many companies are at present involved in making major changes in their information systems. There may be many reasons behind the need for changes in the information systems. Changes in business operations may, of course, require changes in information systems, but the rapid development in the IT area also provides possibilities for increased computerisation. New applications and new computerised approaches can influence the company's way of working. It is difficult to determine whether it is the operational requirements or the possibilities the technology provides that is driving development forward.

When companies have made larger changes in the production process and organisation, the quality issues are largely the basis for change. In the study this is reflected by the methods the companies use in business process development. This is shown in Figure 7 below.

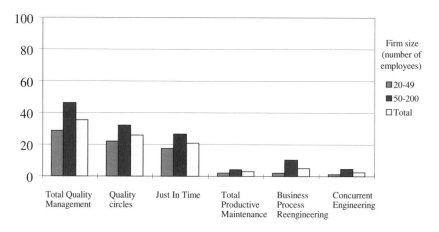

*Figure 7. Methods for improvement (%) (adapted from Stymne et al, 1997).*

In general, formal methods for business process development are used to a rather limited extent. In this context the questionnaire also contained an open question as a complement to the fixed alternative answers above. Here companies could specify other methods which were used for business process development. Most of the companies specified no other methods, and of those which specified any method ISO 9000 was by far the most common reply. Otherwise a few companies mentioned methods such as 'unlimited flow organisation' or 'kanban'.

The interviews strengthen the impression that formal methods are not used and knowledge of available methods does not seem to be especially widespread; few company managers, for example, know what 'Business Process Reengineering' stands for.

Explanations for why smaller companies seldom use formal methods can be found in previous studies on decision making in smaller companies. Several studies have shown that company management and decision making in smaller companies differ from the larger ones. Cohn & Lindberg (1972) are among those who consider that small companies are essentially different from large ones and this means that management at small companies must differ largely from management at large companies.

Even if information is just as important for small companies as for large ones, many managers at small companies consider that intuition, the feeling of how the company is doing, is at least as good as actual information. This leads to many small-company managers not bothering to acquire information and thus, according to the authors, they always lack relevant decision information. Above all there is a lack of information about factors outside the company. Even though they have good control over personnel costs, product prices, orders, etc., they nevertheless do not have information about customer requirements, their own market share, competitors' prices and so on. Furthermore, the authors find that decisions made at small companies are more often based on information in the form of numbers or through recommendations made by other people than the decision maker.

Beckérus & Roos (1985) find that when a decision is to be made, what "feels right" is more important than maximising profit. This means that even if there is time to collect more information, the decision will be made intuitively. The businessman "feels" rather than "considers" the decision. The very strong psychological connection between the company manager/owner and the company/business provides a good explanation for why managers at small companies can oppose change, unwilling to take risks and in other ways not behaving in a "rational" way.

Rice & Hamilton (1979) show that the company manager has vague or undefined aims which are mainly short-term and pragmatic. Furthermore, the authors find that the company managers have an incomplete understanding of the external world's influence on the company. They can thus neither identify nor thoroughly assess the alternative forms of action that are available. The conclusion is that company managers seek pragmatic, satisfying solutions to their problems. Decision making is an incremental process where each new step takes place on the basis of experience and is aimed at a vaguely perceived optimal situation.

Many of the results on intuitive decision making are also confirmed by Andersson (1995). There it is shown, however, that there can be large variations among managers at smaller companies both as far as conception of goals, decision processes and use of formal methods are concerned. So it may be dangerous to generalise too far on small companies as a group.

# Implementation of information technology in small companies

The results above thus show that formal methods are not so common in smaller companies. Hence it may be of interest to ask what effects this has when implementing new information systems in these companies.

Various factors which influence the success of a system have been presented by different authors. Many are common factors, but there are differences, too. Results show that in those cases where users participate in the process, the system will be more successful than otherwise (Montazemi, 1988; Evans & Nesary, 1991). The participation of company management is at least as important as that of the users (Lees, 1987).

As far as availability of expert knowledge is concerned, studies show that satisfaction increases if the expertise is found within the company, but there can even be negative connection between using external consultants and the satisfaction of the users (Lees, 1987). Computer vendors were also shown to be a critical factor. In the cases where there was trust in and close collaboration with the vendor, the users were more satisfied with the system. Montazemi (1988) also shows that more formal planning and thorough analysis of information requirements produce a better result.

Experience from the COMPETE project shows that in the companies studied there is a lack of the competence that the above authors maintain is important. The companies thus become dependent on the system vendors and their quality becomes decisive for the success of the system. Despite this, very few of the companies interviewed are dissatisfied with their information systems.

In previous studies the results are somewhat contradictory as to the effect which a longer term use of computers in the company might have on the success of a system. One study shows a clearly positive effect (Lees,

1987) while another (Montezemi, 1988) can not show any effect at all. However, the results are unambiguous in that individual computer experience has a positive effect. The size of the company is significant as to the extent to which the systems are used, though not as far as satisfaction is concerned. According to Montazemi (1988) the users are also more satisfied if the company has a decentralised organisation.

The interviews in COMPETE show that in certain cases it can be difficult to reach full usage of a system's capacity owing to lack of knowledge on behalf of the users. This might also be due to a generation issue where older people may find it more difficult to get to grips with the new technology. Some few companies have also tried to encourage individual computer usage by arranging the purchase of personal computers for private use for their employees. In this was management hope to increase computer experience and thus efficiency in the company.

Many authors point to various factors which make the implementation of information systems into small companies difficult (see, for example, Kieckhaefer & Inderrieden, 1987; Raymond, 1989; Schleich et al, 1990; Geisler, 1992). Factors mentioned are:

- The rapid development of technology.
- The large variety of vendors and the lack of confidence in them.
- Insufficient analysis and evaluation of system alternatives.
- Incomplete analysis of information requirements and poor planning of the system.
- A lack of knowledge and experience of new technology.
- A lack of support from external expertise.
- Individual-related problems.

The result of our study also indicates that company management feel a certain uncertainty when it comes to the rapid development of technology, which is expressed in the uncertainty about which systems should be selected for introduction into the company. There are also examples where the analysis of different alternatives is not made with sufficient thoroughness, but reliance is put into a vendor instead. However, it is generally the case that the companies studied are rather satisfied with their systems and also with their vendors. Several of the companies interviewed are, however, uncertain about the costs of the information systems and neither do they have a clear picture of what the total costs of the systems are.

Various authors provide their view of how you ought to proceed in order to successfully implement an information system into small companies. The main emphasis is on the planning of information systems. This involves the activities that should precede the purchase of an information system. Such activities include the design of the aims and strategies of the information systems, the analysis of information requirements and determining critical factors for success in the company (see, for example, Bergeron & Raymond, 1992).

# Summary

What do the results of the COMPETE project tell us? First of all it can be established that in a historical perspective it is clear that the level of computerisation has increased in this type of company. The impression gained from the interviews, however, is that the level of maturity is higher than we expected. Many companies are following information technology developments very closely and are making an effort to acquire knowledge in the area. Many also feel a competitive pressure to keep abreast of developments and it has become a requirement that the companies' information systems work in a modern and efficient way.

It is also the case that most companies are aiming for a higher level of computerisation and are prepared to come to grips with the new technology in many new areas. Another clear tendency is that the companies have come a relatively long way as far as information systems which support their internal business operations are concerned and now they are looking for technical approaches to communication with the external world. Internet and EDI are important approaches here.

It is also clear that even though the level of computer maturity is high, there is still a lack of competence within the companies, with the result that they are dependent on external services, which is not really what the companies want. Generally it appears that the companies want as high a level of competence within the company as possible. Whether this is a good attitude or not is more difficult to determine. It is also the case that many companies consider training personnel in using the systems is an important question as far as gaining efficient use of the systems is concerned.

Generally companies seem highly inclined to change, which is shown in many companies having made thorough changes in several areas. This highly contradicts other studies which claim that this group of companies is unwilling to change. That results from different studies vary may depend on which size groups have been compared. The COMPETE material indicates that the smaller companies are generally less inclined to change than the larger ones.

The results also show that there are general differences between the smaller and the larger companies in the group under study. In all variables except the use of external services the smaller companies show a lower percentage value. For many of the variables this is hardly surprising but there are points worth noting. For example, the smaller companies are less inclined to use external advice-giving services. This can, of course, be explained by the fact that economic reasons prevent smaller companies from using consultants. There may be reason to consider how, for example, universities and public technology advisors can better reach this group of companies.

The final analysis of the COMPETE study has not yet been done why the discussion is somewhat hypothetical concerning the result from the COMPETE study. Hopefully further analysis can give a deeper understanding for the role of information systems in this type of companies.

# Acknowledgements

This chapter is based on work carried out within the European Commission's DG III Esprit Project no 21865 "COMPETE."

The research was funded by NUTEK, the Swedish National Board for Industrial and Technical Development.

# References

Andersson, J. (1995) *Bilder av småföretagares ekonomistyrning*, Licentiate thesis, Department of Computer and Information Science, Linköping University, Linköping, Sweden [*Images of Management Control in Small Companies*].

Baker, W.H. (1987) "Status of Information Management in Small Businesses", *Journal of Systems Management*, Vol. 38, No. 4, pp. 10-15.

Beckérus, Å. & Roos, B. (1985) *Affärer som livsstil*, Liber, Stockholm [*Business as a Lifestyle*].

Bergeron, F. & Raymond, L. (1992) "Planning of Information Systems to Gain a Competitive Edge", *Journal of Small Business Management*, Vol. 30, No. 1 pp. 21-26.

Chen, J.-C. & Williams, B.C. (1993) "The Impact of Microcomputer Systems on Small Businesses: England, 10 years later", *Journal of Small Business Management*, July, pp. 96-102.

Cohn, T. & Lindberg, R.A. (1972) *How Management is Different in Small Companies: an AMA management briefing*, American Management Association, New York.

Evans, G. & Nesary, M. (1991) "Computerizing Small Business", *Montana Business Quarterly*, Vol. 29, No. 3, pp. 2-7.

Geisler, E. (1992) "Managing Information Technologies in Small Business: Some Practical Lessons and Guidelines", *Journal of General Management*; Vol. 18, No. 1, pp. 74-81.

Kieckhaefer, G.V. & Inderrieden, E.J. (1987) "Planning Information Systems for the Growing Business", *Business*, Vol. 37, No. 4, pp. 18-24.

Lees, J.D. (1987) "Successful Development of Small Business Information Systems", *Journal of Systems Management*, Vol. 38, No. 9, pp. 32-39.

Montazemi, A.R. (1988) "Factors Affecting Information Satisfaction in the Context of Small Business Environment, *MIS Quarterly*, Vol. 12, No. 2, pp. 239-256.

Raymond, L. & Magnenat-Thalman, N. (1982) "Information Systems in Small Business: Are They Used in Managerial Decisions?", *American Journal of Small Business*, Vol. VI, No. 4, pp. 20-26.

Raymond, L. (1989) "Management Information Systems: Problems and Opportunities", *International Small Business Journal*, Vol. 7, No. 4, pp. 44-53.

Rice, G.H. & Hamilton, R.E. (1979) "Decision Theory and the Small Businessman", *American Journal of Small Business*, Vol. 4, No. 1, pp. 1-9.

Schleich, J.F., Corney, W.J. & Boe, W.J. (1990) "Pitfalls in Microcomputer System Implementation in Small Businesses", *Journal of Systems Management*, Vol. 41, No. 6, pp. 7-10.

Stymne, B., Tunälv, C., Eriksson, M. & Barrientos, D. (1997) *Informationsteknik och affärsstödjande processer i mindre företag – Rapport från en undersökning våren 1996*, Report, Compete 1, IMIT, Stockholm School of Economics, Stockholm [*Information Technology and Business Processes in Smaller Companies – Report from a Survey Spring 1996*].

Stymne, B. & SWECOMPETE Group (1997) *The Use of Information Technology in Swedish SME´s – Progress Report from 40 Field Visits*, Report, Compete 4, IMIT, Stockholm School of Economics, Stockholm.

# Part II:

# Exploration of Different
# Points of View

# 7

# Facilitating Understanding and Change: The Role of Business Models in Development Work

*Christofer Tolis*

*Models are commonly used by people engaged in understanding and changing organisations. Despite benefits resulting from this type of model work, there are a number of difficulties experienced. Instead of facilitating it, the development work is often hindered by people's different preferences and the multitude of different model types available. A conceptual framework of model work is presented in this chapter, drawing on theories of signs, learning, and knowledge. The framework highlights differences and alternatives within three areas: model artefacts, model activities, and model assumptions. It is suggested that recognising and exploring a larger part of the framework will facilitate the development work.*

## Working with models in development work

Much development work in organisations involves working with models in order to facilitate understanding and change. Based on earlier work (Tolis, 1996 a and 1996 b), this chapter argues that many perceived problems and neglected opportunities result from a lack of awareness of certain differences related to model work. Instead of facilitating development work, these differences often hinder it.

### Development work and the going concern

The core characteristic of development work is that it is directed towards another activity, a "going concern" to use a term from the field of accounting, an activity that it tries to understand and change. This going concern is viewed as an ongoing activity in contrast to the development work, which is often more delimited in time. For example, the work of developing an information system is more delimited than the business activities that the system is to support. Development work can be seen as an attempt to influence the going concern in some way, while at the same time being influenced by it. When people in the going concern also engage in development work, this might represent a shift in their learning process towards "deutero-learning" (Bateson, 1972): in addition to their "normal" learning about their environment, they are also learning about their own learning.

In many cases, the distinction between going concern and development work is vague. Most people in a company face a trade-off between the two and find themselves continuously changing focus – either consciously or not. Although time spent on development work means less time for the going concern of today, the going concern of tomorrow will hopefully benefit. The going concern can thus be said to "work for today", whereas the development work can be said to "work for tomorrow". This situation can be viewed as a struggle between the two forces of tradition and transcendence (Ehn 1988, p. 161), or, from another perspective, between the anxiety to change and the anxiety *not* to change (Schein, 1993).

Development work within companies takes many different directions. The type of problem perceived and the type of solution available (they are often interrelated) are two main reasons for the diversity of directions. However, some directions are more common than others; for example, many companies do engage in some kind of organisational development.

People might not participate in the going concern that their development work focuses on. Especially in large companies, there are often different people engaged in these activities, leading to a communication gap. The specialisation that takes place is partly a result of differences in knowledge and experience required, e.g. familiarity with certain solutions. Moreover, specialisation often leads to the formalisation of development work, for example by initiating explicit projects that are more or less separated from the going concern. The balance between development work and the going concern is important in this respect. In the context of information systems, this means different emphasis being placed on *developing* systems and *using* them (cf. Ehn, 1988; Göranzon, 1993).

As Figure 1 illustrates, several types of development work are often in progress more or less simultaneously – e.g. strategic, organisational, and systems development. They are often initiated and undertaken by different people and groups, both within and outside the company. While, for example, the development of information systems might involve the IS department, strategic development might be the task of the company's top management.

*Figure 1. Paths of influence between the going concern and three common types of development work.*

The division of labour between the going concern and various directions of development work has obvious consequences with regard to communication and co-operation. Background, prior experiences, goals and behaviour of people differ to greater or lesser extent. For example, a business manager's work in a going concern is quite different from a system expert's development work. Problems may arise in both directions, i.e. regarding the requirements for development work as well as its implementation. These issues are complex and often problematic, as witnessed by research areas such as requirements engineering and implementation studies.

## Model work in the development context

A central feature of development work is the use of models. Model work is a recurring activity, not only in the special context of information systems but also in design in general (cf. Schön, 1988). Common examples of models include drawings of the company's organisational structure, descriptions of the handling of incoming orders, stepwise instructions on how to run a project, and descriptions of causes and effects in a problematic situation.

Some models are specific to a certain company and situation, while others are intended for more general applicability, e.g. as the basis of methodologies and conceptual frameworks. A specific model might capture the particular company's information structure used in their databases, whereas a general model might deal with a common procedure for developing information systems. Furthermore, some models use novel ways of expression, while others are instances of already established model types. A novel model in this sense contains new symbols and rules for interpretation, whereas an established model type is made up by a certain standardised notation or language agreed upon (cf. Sällström, 1991).

Whatever the specifics of the models in question, their actual use varies depending on the situation and the people involved. For an individual, models might aid the thought process and provide a basis for action. As development work deals with ideas for the future, it is useful having tools that enable the representation and exploration of ideas. For a group there is an added dimension, as issues of communication, co-operation, and potential conflict become more salient. Consequently, the use of models for those purposes increases in importance.

## *People's different preferences*

People's preferences regarding model work can differ in many ways. Each preference, whether explicitly stated or implicitly acted upon, is a case of delimitation in respect to other alternatives. Each preference emphasises certain issues, suggesting that these are especially important and should be dealt with, if not exclusively then at least primarily or initially. Six examples of common preferences emphasise:

- Detailed, preferably formalised, descriptions
- Objects and conceptual structures
- Analytic work and articulate knowledge
- Preparation and planning
- True descriptions of reality as it is
- Unifying descriptions for shared understanding

Many of the problems and opportunities associated with using models in development work stem from the great diversity of the activity. People with different background bring with them their own preferences, ways of working, and ways of using models. Furthermore, even without counting all the novel models, an almost endless number of established model types are available.

Important differences might both hinder and facilitate the development work. Differences might hinder when they are not recognised and dealt with properly. They can lead to chaos and confusion – making it harder, for example, to see important similarities, discriminate between relevant issues, make useful comparisons, choose appropriate alternatives, appreciate current focus, and see an overall picture. On the other hand, differences might facilitate the work when they are recognised and dealt with properly. They can lead to cross-fertilisation and mutual learning – making it easier, for example, to find new alternatives, avoid unnecessary distractions, develop a clear orientation, understand other perspectives, and improve communication.

## *A conceptual framework of model work*

To benefit from model work, and to avoid the pitfalls, it is necessary to deal with perceived differences. In the following, a conceptual framework is presented, which highlights important differences within the context of development work. The framework is an attempt to provide a basis for understanding and changing model use in development work, drawing on theories of signs (semiotics), learning, and knowledge. As shown in Figure 2, the framework explores differences within three areas: model artefacts, model activities, and model assumptions.

*Figure 2. The framework's three areas of model work.*

Within each area, differences are discussed in terms of two dimensions. Each dimension is made up of two opposing concepts. Rather than representing clear-cut categories, the dimensions are continuums where various artefacts, activities, and assumptions have different emphasis.

# Different model artefacts

The first of the framework's three areas concerns model artefacts and how they differ. A *model artefact* is an artefact that is used instead of something else. This notion is inspired by the concept of *sign* used in semiotics, the theory of signs (cf. Peirce, 1893-1910, p. 5). As will become evident below, the term artefact is used in a wide sense, including all results of human activity – also more "processual" ones. In a computer simulation, for example, not only the computer and the software can be considered artefacts – but also the simulation process itself, when the computer is running the software.

The framework divides artefacts using two dimensions, with varying focus between representation-manifestation and content-process (see Figure 3).

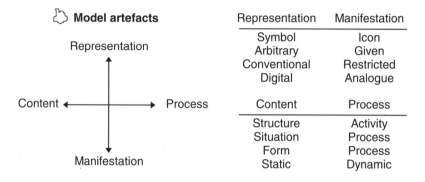

*Figure 3. Two dimensions of artefacts explored in the framework.*

## Representation and manifestation artefacts

The first dimension of artefacts is based on the two concepts *representation* and *manifestation*. Drawing on the semiotic concepts of symbol and icon (cf., e.g. Peirce, 1893-1910, p. 8), it deals with the question of what leads the artefact to be perceived as a model; how the artefact emphasises what it does.

- A *representation* artefact is characterised by convention. It is relevant as a symbol, i.e. for what it is representing. Its form is mainly arbitrary.

- A *manifestation* artefact is characterised by restriction. It is relevant as an icon, i.e. for what it is manifesting. Its form is mainly given.

Another illustration is the distinction between an artefact and its medium. This is clear in case of a representation artefact (e.g. between a text and the ink that it is written with), but less clear in the case of a manifestation artefact (e.g. between a toy car and the material it is made of). Examples of the dimension can be found in clocks and other measuring instruments: digital displays are more representational, analogue ones are more manifestational. The same also applies to user interfaces in the area of human-computer interaction: key words are more representational; graphical icons are more manifestational.

## Content and process artefacts

The second dimension of artefacts is based on the two concepts *content* and *process* (cf. Tolis, 1994, pp. 8-9). It concerns what the model emphases.

- A *content* artefact is characterised by a focus on what is (or might be). It emphasises structures and non-temporal relationships.

- A *process* artefact is characterised by a focus on what happens (or might happen). It emphasises change and temporal relationships.

The work of two Greek philosophers from around 500 BC can be used to illustrate the dimension's long tradition. *Parmenides* emphasised content, arguing that being is everything; all becoming (change) is an illusion (Lübcke, 1988, p. 418). *Herakleitos*, on the other hand, emphasised process. He argued that change and motion is all there is: you cannot step into the same river twice (ibid., p. 225).

Other related concepts include Structure vs. Activity, Situation vs. Process (Lundeberg, 1993, p. 4), Form vs. Process (Bateson, 1979, pp. 209-219), and Static vs. Dynamic.

## Examples of model artefacts

The models used in development work clearly differ in many ways. Using the first area of the framework (cf. Figure 3, above), four main types of model artefacts emerge. As the two types of representation models contain a large number of established model types, e.g. from the field of information systems, they have been subdivided into two perspectives each (cf. Tolis, 1994, pp. 8-9; Tolis & Nilsson, 1996).

- *Content representations.* These models can be further divided into two perspectives: category models (e.g. entity-relationship diagrams and semantic networks) and factor models (e.g. causal networks and problem maps). When aiming for more general applicability, content representations often form the basis of conceptual frameworks.

- *Process representations.* These models can be further divided into two perspectives: transformation models (e.g. dataflow diagrams and process graphs) and behaviour models (e.g. flow charts and state transition diagrams). When aiming for more general applicability, process representations often form the basis of methodologies.

- *Content manifestations.* A carved piece of wood resembling a real boat and a physical model of a car used for aerodynamic testing are two examples of content manifestations. This type of model, in the form of mock-ups, has also been used in the development of information systems (e.g. Ehn, 1988, pp. 335-339).

- *Process manifestations.* A simulation running on a computer and a role-play performed by people in the organisation are two examples of process manifestations. Compared to a content manifestation, it is the process itself – rather than the structure of the things or people involved – that comprises the model.

# Different model activities

The second of the framework's areas concerns model activities and how they differ. A *model activity* is an activity that involves models. An activity is something that someone engages in; it can be viewed as behaviour in the widest sense, not limited to externally observable actions.

Kolb (1984) – inspired by the work of Piaget, Dewey, and Lewin – argues that a central feature of all human activity is learning. Drawing on his theory of experiential learning, the framework divides activities using two dimensions, with varying focus between abstract-concrete and reflective-active (see Figure 4; cf. Tolis, 1994, pp. 5-7).

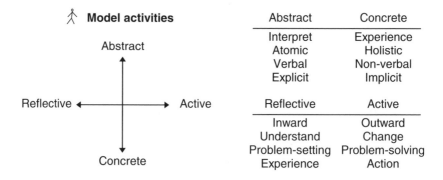

*Figure 4. Two dimensions of activities explored in the framework (adapted from Kolb, 1984, p. 42).*

## *Abstract and concrete activities*

The first dimension of activities is based on the two concepts *abstract* and *concrete*. It differentiates between two ways of relating to the world.

- An *abstract* activity is characterised by a focus on something for what it stands for. Interpretation, reasoning and the verbal aspect of communication are salient.

- A *concrete* activity is characterised by a focus on something for what it is in itself. Direct experience, using an overall feeling rather than explicit guidelines, and the non-verbal aspect of communication are salient.

Greater familiarity – a higher level of expertise – is coupled with an increased concrete focus. The frame of mind shifts from atomic, analytical, and rational to holistic and 'a-rational' (Dreyfus & Dreyfus, 1986, p. 36). As experts, a driver and a computer user navigate without deliberate decisions; they use their tools (steering wheel, gearshift, mouse, desktop, etc.) in a direct and intuitive manner. In terms of knowledge, the dimension parallels the difference between explicit and tacit knowing (Polanyi, 1958; cf. Johannessen, 1988).

## *Reflective and active activities*

The second dimension of activities is based on the two concepts *reflective* and *active*. It differentiates between two ways of transforming one's grasp of the world.

- A *reflective* activity is characterised by a focus on "inward" behaviour. It aims towards observing, understanding and making sense.

- An *active* activity is characterised by a focus on "outward" behaviour. It aims towards experimentation, change and control.

Other notions of the dimension are problem-setting vs. problem-solving (Schön, 1979, p. 255) and experience vs. action (Checkland & Scholes, 1990, p. 3).

## *Examples of model activities*

Characterising an activity in terms of the framework consists of establishing its focus in terms of the dimensions. As a result, four main types of model activities emerge (cf. Figure 4, above):

- *Abstract reflection.* Explicitly analysing key figures in a product report is an example of this kind of activity. Models and other representations are used as a means to achieve understanding. Interpreting and creating models to gain insight are other examples of activities that share this focus.

- *Abstract action.* Presenting a monthly work-plan is an activity of this kind. Models and other representations are used to achieve change. Examples include using models to aid communication and to guide work, e.g. by using existing frameworks and methodologies.

- *Concrete action.* Skilfully assembling the parts of a product is an example of this kind of activity. The activity is not guided by explicit decisions, e.g. following the steps of a methodology, but rather by experience acquired over a long period of time. Models are acted upon not as abstract symbols, but rather as concrete icons.

- *Concrete reflection.* Appreciating a product's finish is an example of this focus. The activity makes use of an overall feeling rather than explicit guidelines. Models are perceived not as abstract symbols, but rather as concrete icons.

# Different model assumptions

The third and final area of the framework concerns model assumptions and how they differ. A *model assumption* is an assumption regarding model work. An assumption is an underlying belief that is attributed to people or their constructs, e.g. statements and theories (cf. Burrell & Morgan, 1979, pp. viii-xii). They can be more or less explicit; often they are taken for granted and not reflected upon. In the case of explicit assumptions, the attribution is one's own; otherwise it is someone else's.

Building on Burrell & Morgan (1979), the framework divides assumptions using two dimensions, with varying focus between objective-subjective and consensus-conflict (see Figure 5). The ideas developed by Burrell & Morgan (1979) have been applied in different contexts, e.g. information systems development (Hirschheim & Klein, 1989). Other classifications of basic assumptions have taken the form of clusters where similar theories are grouped together, for example in organisational theory (Morgan, 1980, 1986; Bolman & Deal, 1984, 1991) and in knowledge theory and research methods (Pepper, 1948; Alvesson & Sköldberg, 1994).

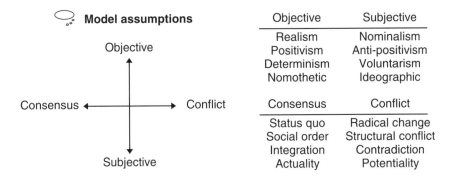

| Model assumptions | Objective | Subjective |
|---|---|---|
| | Realism | Nominalism |
| | Positivism | Anti-positivism |
| | Determinism | Voluntarism |
| | Nomothetic | Ideographic |
| | Consensus | Conflict |
| | Status quo | Radical change |
| | Social order | Structural conflict |
| | Integration | Contradiction |
| | Actuality | Potentiality |

*Figure 5. Two dimensions of assumptions explored in the framework (adapted from Burrell & Morgan, 1979, p. 22).*

## Objective and subjective assumptions

The first dimension of assumptions is based on the two concepts *objective* and *subjective*. It differentiates between two views of the nature of the social world and the way it may be investigated. In model terms, the dimension concerns the relation between the model and what is modelled.

- An *objective* assumption is characterised by a focus on structures in the world. Models are viewed as expressions of facts, not influencing what is modelled. They are valued in terms of correspondence.

- A *subjective* assumption is characterised by a focus on structures in the human mind. Models are viewed as expressions of values, influencing what is modelled. They are valued in terms of beauty (e.g. simplicity, elegance).

The dimension is linked to different views regarding ontology (what exists), epistemology (how to gain knowledge), human nature, and methodology. Objective assumptions focus on realism, positivism, determinism, and a nomothetic interest. Subjective assumptions instead focus on nominalism, anti-positivism, voluntarism, and an ideographic interest (Burrell & Morgan, 1979, p. 3).

## Consensus and conflict assumptions

The second dimension of assumptions is based on the two concepts *consensus* and *conflict*. It differentiates between two views of the nature of society and has consequences for how the purpose of a model is viewed.

- A *consensus* assumption is characterised by a focus on agreement, unity, and order. Models are viewed as a means for understanding and consensus. They are valued in terms of meaningfulness.

- A *conflict* assumption is characterised by a focus on disagreement, contradiction, and chaos. Models are viewed as a means for change, influence, and power. They are valued in terms of usefulness.

Consensus assumptions focus on the status quo, social order, social integration and cohesion, solidarity, need satisfaction, and actuality. Conflict assumptions, on the other hand, focus on radical change, structural conflict, contradiction, emancipation, deprivation, and potentiality (Burrell & Morgan, 1979, p. 18). The dimension can be characterised by the two complementary questions "Why is it like it is?" and "Why isn't it like it isn't?" While the first question indicates an interest in the way things are (focus on consensus), the second one indicates an interest in the way things could be (focus on conflict).

## *Examples of model assumptions*

Using the two dimensions described, four types of model assumptions emerge (see Figure 5, above). Each combination represents a certain type of basic assumption in relation to model work, i.e. model artefacts and model activities.

- *Objective consensus.* In this perspective, working with models is geared towards understanding the way things are. Models are seen as meaningful facts. Modelling becomes a rational activity that results in correct models without affecting what is being modelled. Change is primarily viewed as a means for understanding.

- *Objective conflict.* As in the previous perspective, models are seen as representing an independent reality. However, the focus on conflict means an emphasis on different perspectives. While a particular model might be advantageous to some people, it might be disadvantageous to others. Models are viewed as useful facts and modelling as an opportunity to gain and exercise power. Understanding is primarily viewed as a means for change.

- *Subjective conflict.* This perspective shares the assumptions about models as useful tools for change. However, in contrast to the previous perspective, models are viewed as representing useful subjective values rather than an external and objective world. As a consequence, modelling is a way to bring about personal emancipation and change.

- *Subjective consensus.* The subjective focus of this perspective is common to the previous one. However, it shares the focus of consensus with the first perspective. This means that models are viewed as meaningful values, and tools for understanding more than change. Modelling thus becomes a means to achieve consensus and shared understanding.

# Putting the framework to use

How can this conceptual framework of model work be of help for people engaged in development work? Of what use can the dimensions describing model artefacts, activities, and assumptions be? The overall aim of using the framework is to increase the likelihood that differences encountered in the work will facilitate rather than hinder it. Two particular reasons for using the framework are discussed below: to aid understanding and to aid change.

## *Understanding model use in development work*

The first reason for using the framework is to aid in the understanding of model work. This includes understanding one's own focus as well as the focus of others. The earlier examples, of people's different preferences regarding model work, can be re-stated in terms of the framework. Each preference indicates a certain focus within the framework:

- Detailed, preferably formalised, descriptions: focus on *representation artefacts*
- Objects and conceptual structures: focus on *content artefacts*
- Analytic work and articulate knowledge: focus on *abstract activities*
- Preparation and planning: focus on *reflective activities*
- True descriptions of reality as it is: focus on *objective assumptions*
- Unifying descriptions for shared understanding: focus on *consensus assumptions*

Figure 6 illustrates the preferences in terms of the framework. As shown, they represent a focus on certain parts of the framework. For the area of model artefacts, the focus is on content representations; for model activities it is on abstract reflection; and for model assumptions it is on objective consensus. Although there might be common patterns of focus between the three areas, every combination is possible. For example, a person may use all types of artefacts in a certain type of activity and may engage in all types of activities from a certain type of assumption.

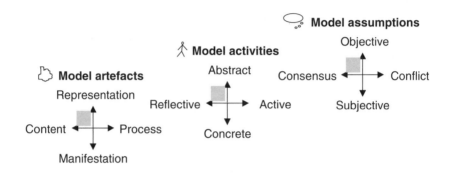

*Figure 6. Example of current focus (shaded) of model work in terms of the framework.*

Seeing patterns in one's own model work and that of others is an important way to better understand different situations. The framework might provide a tool for analysing and discussing questions such as: Where is the current focus? What types of artefacts, activities, and assumptions are now being emphasised? Do people within the group have similar or different focus? How are they different? Is the focus for the group as a whole narrow or more dispersed? Has the focus changed in any way during the development work?

A further illustration of the use of the framework to aid understanding is to make sense of differient opinions regarding the benefits of model work. In this matter, people in organisations express everything from overwhelming enthusiasm to serious doubts. However, an alternative way of framing the issue, is that the opinions expressed may well concern a particular view of model work. In the field of information systems, the traditional view is perhaps not far from the earlier example of preferences. The framework shows that this view is only one alternative among many others.

## Changing model use in development work

The second reason to use the framework is to help promote changes in model work. Although the framework in itself does not prescribe any particular course of action (like a methodology might do), it provides a "playground" that allows for different strategies and combinations. However, from the perspective of improvement, what is currently *not* covered is perhaps even more interesting than what is. One important use of the framework is to help identify alternatives within each area; it enables a search for "blank spots," i.e. parts of the framework that are not currently covered. Figure 7 shows the "blank spots" in the earlier example of preferences regarding model work.

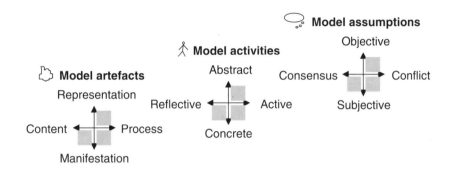

*Figure 7. Example of alternative focuses (shaded) of model work in terms of the framework.*

In relation to the framework as a whole, it becomes obvious that any specific view of model work might easily become too narrow. Instead of trying to find one 'best' combination – like the example of preferences mentioned earlier – it could be more advantageous to think in terms of repertoire. The larger parts of the framework one is familiar with, the better the chances of finding an appropriate solution in a specific situation.

When using the framework as a tool for change, alternatives to the current focus can be dealt with in two ways: either the people involved try to cover a larger part of the framework themselves, or they bring in other people who have the desired focus. Changing focus in the three areas can be more or less difficult. Switching from one type of model artefact to another, e.g. from *content representations* to *process manifestations*, is probably much easier than a corresponding change in model assumptions, i.e. from *objective consensus* to *subjective conflict*.

The framework might also be useful when new workgroups are being formed. Being aware of the differences, there is the advantage of together having a broader focus of model work. In co-operative work, the team hopefully covers larger parts of the framework than the people do individually.

# Facilitating understanding and change

To conclude, this chapter has tried to illustrate some of the complexity associated with the use of models in development work. Whether involving one or several people, the dependencies between development work and the going concern provide a context in which a large number of more or less important differences become apparant. The aim of the proposed framework is to support the activities of understanding and change by an increased awareness of certain differences. As summarised in Figure 8, this means recognising and exploring differences among various model artefacts, model activities, and model assumptions.

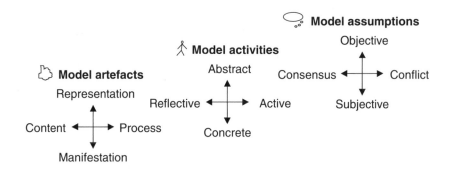

*Figure 8. The framework's three areas and six dimensions.*

Making sense of differences encountered, as well as taking advantage of them, is hopefully facilitated by the use of this framework. Whether this is done in order to establish a common frame of reference or to strengthen the position of certain interests, is itself an issue that can be discussed in terms of the framework: do we have a focus on consensus or conflict?

# Acknowledgements

The research was funded by NUTEK, the Swedish National Board for Industrial and Technical Development.

# References

Alvesson, M. & Sköldberg, K. (1994) *Tolkning och reflektion. Vetenskapsfilosofi och kvalitativ metod*, Studentlitteratur, Lund, Sweden [*Interpretation and reflection. Philosophy of science and qualitative method*].

Bateson, G. (1972) "Social Planning and the Concept of Deutero-Learning," in *Steps to an Ecology of Mind*, Ballantine Books, New York.

Bateson, G. (1979) *Mind and Nature – A Necessary Unity*, E.P. Dutton, New York.

Bolman, L.G. & Deal, T.E. (1984) *Modern Approaches to Understanding and Managing Organizations*, Jossey-Bass Publishers, San Francisco.

Bolman, L.G. & Deal, T.E. (1991) *Reframing Organizations. Artistry, Choice, and Leadership*, Jossey-Bass Publishers, San Francisco.

Burrell, G. & Morgan, G. (1979) *Sociological Paradigms and Organisational Analysis – Elements of the Sociology of Corporate Life*, Heinemann, London.

Checkland, P.B. & Scholes, J. (1990) *Soft Systems Methodology in Action*, John Wiley & Sons, Chichester, England.

Dreyfus, H.L. & Dreyfus, S.E. (1986) *Mind over Machine – The Power of Human Intuition and Expertise in the Era of the Computer*, The Free Press, New York.

Ehn, P. (1988) *Work-Oriented Design of Computer Artifacts*, Arbetslivscentrum, Stockholm.

Göranzon, B. (1993) *The Practical Intellect: Computers and Skill*, Springer Verlag, London.

Hirschheim, R.A. & Klein, H.K. (1989) "Four Paradigms of Information Systems Development," *Communications of the ACM*, Vol. 32, No. 10, pp. 1199-1216.

Johannessen, K.S. (1988) "Tankar om tyst kunskap," *Dialoger*, Nr 6/88 ["Thoughts about tacit knowledge", *Dialogues*].

Kolb, D.A. (1984) *Experiential Learning. Experience as The Source of Learning and Development*, Prentice-Hall, Englewood Cliffs, New Jersey.

Lundeberg, M. (1993) *Handling Change Processes – A Systems Approach*, Studentlitteratur, Lund, Sweden.

Lübcke, P. (ed.) (1988) *Filosofilexikonet*, Bokförlaget Forum, Stockholm [*The encyclopaedia of Philosophy*].

Morgan, G. (1980) "Paradigms, Metaphors, and Puzzle Solving in Organization Theory," *Administrative Science Quarterly*, Vol. 25, No. 4, pp. 605-622.

Morgan, G. (1986) *Images of Organization*, Sage, Newbury Park, California.

Peirce, C.S. (1893-1910) "Logic as Semiotic: The Theory of Signs," in Innis, R.E. (ed.) (1985) *Semiotics, An Introductory Anthology*, Indiana University Press, Bloomington, Indiana.

Pepper, S.C. (1948) *World Hypotheses. A Study in Evidence*, University of California Press, Berkeley, California.

Polanyi, M. (1958) *Personal Knowledge*, Routledge & Kegan Paul, London.

Schein, E.H. (1993) "How Can Organizations Learn Faster? The Challenge of Entering the Green Room," *Sloan Management Review*, Winter, pp. 85-92.

Schön, D.A. (1979) "Generative Metaphor: A Perspective on Problem-Setting in Social Policy," in Ortony, A. (ed.) (1979) *Metaphor and Thought*, Cambridge University Press, Cambridge, Massachusetts, pp. 254-283.

Schön, D.A. (1988) "Designing: Rules, types and worlds," *Design Studies*, Vol. 9 No 3.

Sällström, P. (1991) *Tecken att tänka med. Om symbolisk notation inom musik, dans, kartografi, matematik, fysik, kemi, teknologi, arkitektur, färglära och bildkonst*, Carlssons, Stockholm [*Signs to think with. About symbolic notation in music, dance, chart-making, mathematics, physics, chemistry, technology, architecture, colour theory and visual art*].

Tolis, C. (1994) *Reframing Business Modelling – Exploring the Relation to Personal Learning by Creating and Applying a Conceptual Framework*, M.Sc. thesis, Dept. of Information Management, Stockholm School of Economics, Stockholm.

Tolis, C. (1996 a) "Business Modelling for Understanding and Change: A Conceptual Framework of Model Work", in Schreinemakers, J.F. (ed.) *Knowledge Management: Organization, Competence and Methodology, Proceedings of the Fourth International ISMICK Symposium*, Ergon Verlag, Würzburg, Germany, pp. 81-92.

Tolis, C. (1996 b) "Working With Models in Development Work: Differences that Hinder or Facilitate", in Keen, C.D., Urquhart, C. & Lamp, J. (eds.) *Proceedings of the 7th Australasian Conference on Information Systems (ACIS'96)*, University of Tasmania, Hobart, Australia, pp. 735-745.

Tolis, C. & Nilsson, A.G. (1996) "Using Business Models in Process Orientation", in Lundeberg, M. & Sundgren, B. (eds.) *Advancing Your Business – People and Information Systems in Concert*, The Economic Research Institute (EFI), Stockholm School of Economics, Stockholm.

# 8

# Lessons Learned from Applying Business Modelling: Exploring Opportunities and Avoiding Pitfalls

## Claes-Göran Lindström

*In applying Business Modelling, what issues have proved to be the most relevant ones? Where have we succeeded, what pitfalls could be noted and why did they probably occur? After a brief review of some practical implications of basic infological concepts the often discussed issue of simple vs. sophisticated models is commented upon from the practitioner's viewpoint. A "multiple simple model" strategy is advocated. Confluence from business style, participativeness and group dynamics is brought into the picture. The effects of recent trends like Business Process Management and Object Orientation are discussed. Finally, some comments are given concerning the need for tools for model documentation and communication. We need to accomplish the "dynamic documentation state" to take full advantage of Business Modelling as a major vehicle for business development.*

## Foundations review

Business Modelling deals with *models* and *information*. Both these widely used words are given numerous more or less disparate interpretations. This being the case, I consider it appropriate to start with a declaration of how I would like the terms to be understood in this context.

### *What are models for?*

The concept of "Business Model" is given a very wide interpretation in this chapter. A "model" is a simplified (and usually graphic) description of some aspect of a business. A "business" is any usage of a limited set of resources intended to create/increase customer-perceived value.

The main objective of any business model is to be a vehicle for communication of the human thought, facilitating the mutual perception and understanding of some aspect of a common business reality. Business models in the format of organisation charts are used to communicate the distribution of responsibilities within a company. Business process models are used to describe to the various (and sometimes numerous) actors of a particular activity chain how the activity architecture should be set up in order to generate maximal customer satisfaction. Conceptual models are frequently used to establish definitions of important business building-blocks clear-cut enough to make business-internal communication unambiguous and thus efficient. And so on with other types of business models.

Business modelling in this broad sense is by no means anything new. We have "always" done it in various forms. Julius Caesar, Lord Wellington, Cecil Rhodes and Henry Ford certainly applied "business models" to their reality in order to make appropriate operative decisions. However, it could be argued that the usage of Business Modelling has increased very substantially within the Western World (and especially in Scandinavia) through the last two decades. The main reason for this is undoubtedly the development in information technology (IT). With the rapid automation of business message handling, the need for continuously improved "interpretation filters" has become obvious. And recently, the increasingly popular concept of Data Warehousing has demonstrated once again how useless even hecatombs of data are – if they do not relate to manageable, i.e. understandable, business concepts.

## Information

The term "information" is used in very many senses. To take a somewhat extreme view, it could be said that information can only exist in a human brain as the "insight about how something is". In this sense, information is created by two "agents". One is perceptual data: messages brought to the brain by the human's senses; the other is this person's "frame of reference": his/her "model of the adjoining world", filtering any message that the senses are bringing in.

This "two-agent perception" of the information concept was pointed out already by Börje Langefors more than 30 years ago (e.g. in Langefors, 1966). Through the following decades of increasingly swift IT-development we have become more and more aware of the importance of the frame of reference, the "mental model", in the information generating process. In many awkward ways we have proven that sophisticated IT support for unified message handling is of limited use for the business – as long as we do not also ascertain a comparatively unified interpretation of the messages by co-ordinating the frames of reference involved.

However, this problem still does not seem to be fully recognised by all IT professionals. Even today, too many development projects spend the bulk of their budget on data handling issues, i. e. message transportation, while quality assurance of the message interpretation into *information* is next to neglected.

Fortunately, the increasing use of Business Modelling through recent years is effectively improving this situation. With or without documentation, Business Modelling leads to increased awareness of existing mental models – and their subject-matter importance – for all parties involved.

# Sophisticated or simple models?

It is debated whether the model types used should be very simple or more sophisticated, rich and detailed. There seems to be no generally true answer to this question. Rumour has it that Einstein formulated the sentence: "Everything should be done as simple as possible – but no simpler than that". And this is, I think, very relevant also for modelling.

Working with a modelling method comprising a rich and expressive model syntax is of course advantageous in many situations – if the parties involved are *very* well trained to use this method. In Business Modelling in general this is, however, not the case. The specialists involved need to be specialists in their business. One could rarely expect them to also be experienced specialists in structural description according to the modelling method XYZ. The tool to teach them in order to help them express their first-hand knowledge of the business must not be a hinder in itself – it has to be as self-evident and as easy to learn and apply as ever possible. Which, indeed, speaks for the use of very simple modelling techniques, that unfortunately cannot pick up all fine nuances and details. Details that, for instance in later phases of IT systems design, are badly needed in order to understand how the technical formalisation should be done for the IT tool to best serve the business specialists (commonly called users).

Imposing sophisticated – and thus more expressive – modelling methods on the business specialists usually does not solve this problem, according to my experience. The problems with teaching – and learning – a complicated modelling technique become overwhelming, shadowing the *real* problems, i.e. the business problems that should be explored by the modelling in the first place.

Instead, a different approach has proven to be successful: The conscious combination of two or more "simple" modelling techniques. A three-dimensional thing, for instance a house, may be sufficiently described by a *set* of three two-dimensional drawings (front view, side view, top view). Applying the same principle, people's multi-dimensional mental models of some specific part of the N-dimensional reality may be better described by a *set* of simple, "few-dimensional" models than by one sophisticated (but still not very multi-dimensional) model. This is the core of the modelling concept MALDIV (Modelling Applying Linked Dimensions to Improve Versatility). By applying a *concepts* model, a *flows* model, an *objectives* model and sometimes also an *events* model to the same "reality slice" – in combination (cf. Figure 1). The "linkage" between the simple models consists of successive references from one model to another, similar to what you have in mathematics when you want the derivative of a function of many variables and use the partial derivatives in combination.

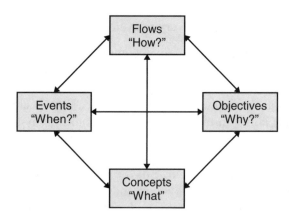

*Figure 1. The MALDIV principle of combining simple models to illustrate a multi-dimensional reality.*

Sophisticated model types may of course be very helpful in later stages of formalisation, for instance in IT systems development – but preferably in the hands of IT-technicians rather than business specialists. IT systems always are (and will remain?) strictly formalised few-dimensional representations of a much more multi-dimensional reality. Preliminary IT systems analysis and design therefore appears to be the relevant realm of sophisticated methods for dimension-reduction, generating the blueprints for practical systems design and development.

Thus: The initial question of *either* sophistication *or* simplicity is a little naïvely put. Rather than "either-or", the answer is "both-and" – well considering the situational context and purpose.

# The impact of business style

Having had the opportunity to do business modelling with groups in a variety of cultural environments, a few observations might be of interest. Being born into the country, I got my first experience of modelling within the Swedish business environment quite a few years ago. However cold and dark Sweden may appear from a meteorological point of view, its modelling climate was advantageous already in those days – and it has even improved over the years. One favourable characteristic is that most organisations offer a rather permissive mental atmosphere to its employees. At events like modelling seminars, it is usually accepted to speak out possible criticism, without risking neither dismissal nor future bad attitudes from superiors. Also, people tend to take a solemn interest in their work and its meaningfulness, both for the organisation and for themselves – it is not often looked upon only as something you have to do to get paid by the end of the month.

Organisations where entrepreneur-spirit is actively promoted certainly offer the best conditions for business modelling. People tend to be responsible, involved, used to "long leash management" and they usually have a holistic view of the organisation, seeing further than to their immediate functional neighbourhood. In such environments it is also easy to get an understanding for the positive qualities of heterogeneous competence in the modelling groups – it is advantageous for the modelling result if the economist has to explain his view in such terms that the engineer understands and vice versa (although it takes time).

The level of "freedom" and general self-appreciation in the organisation is very decisive for the successfulness of business modelling together with the employees – at all levels. Accordingly, modelling is a rather dubious tool in utterly hierarchical organisations, where no one subordinate dares to give his opinion until his boss has said something, thereby taken position. Then the subordinate may consent (but often no more). When this is the case, business modelling is hardly possible – at least it will probably not be appreciated by the organisation. It is likely to be perceived as meaningless for the organisation as it is scaring to the participants. It usually does not help much even to pick all the seminar participants from the same organisational level – the internal competition will prevail in the seminar group, anything said and suggested will immediately be criticised by the contenders.

Through the years, successively collected and combined pieces of experience among Swedish modelling practitioners have merged into a "standard recipe" for Business Modelling that generally works well. Main ingredients are:

- establish the modelling objective clearly

- form a small (seven people or less) modelling team with heterogeneous subject-matter competence

- prepare and motivate each team member by personal interviews

- do the modelling in seminar form, using wall-graph technique

- work out and distribute the seminar documentation as quickly as possible

- execute follow-ups and establish action plans based on the modelling result

This recipe has been successfully applied also outside Sweden. However, the (Swedish) modelling facilitator applying the recipe abroad needs to take some extra care. It is a challenge to work in another cultural environment. There are "dos" and "don'ts" that do not exist at home. And there is always, to some extent, a language problem. In most countries, English is by far the most frequently used vehicle for international communication but it has not yet become everybody's second mother tongue. Misunderstandings may occur, especially when neither the team members nor the facilitator are native in the language used for communication.

To my experience, modelling abroad calls for even better preparations than are needed in Sweden. The "atmosphere" has to be gauged properly, the seminar participants chosen with even more care than at home (ranks are usually vital to observe), pre-seminar interviews done, preferably not by phone (considered sloppy by some) but eye-to-eye. It is very important to well establish the purpose of the modelling, how the results will be presented, who are going to have access to the documentation, etc. No fuss, no Kindergarten-playing-around in work hours!

Even if some Americans tend to love over-simplifying and some Latinos love to debate details for hours, it is my experience that Business Modelling "the Swedish way" has usually been appreciated very well when tried abroad. The confusion in the beginning may last a little longer than among Swedish participants but soon enough creativity starts to emanate. But, as already mentioned, it is essential to "gauge the atmosphere" beforehand – and take the proper cautions. When signs of "the Boss is always right, also when he is not" are perceived, one has to be especially careful.

Modelling in a public service environment is sometimes rather different from doing the same within a profit-oriented business. The main reason seems to be that the over-all objective – and the complying sub-goals – are usually easier to communicate the more market-driven the business is. The general commercial idea is rather easy to grasp. There are seldom doubts about who is really the customer and what do we do to make him happy enough to keep ourselves alive also in the future. Usually, all employees on all levels are more or less aware of these facts.

In a public service organisation, on the other hand, the main objective is more often than not manifold (even implying contradictory top level objectives sometimes), the customer concept is often vague (if recognised at all), and the external effects of the work (products, services) are not always really realised by the people that produce them. Asking "Who is actually the customer of this department's efforts?" might be perceived as an insult. A different language may have to be applied (beneficiary instead of customer, maybe) and it usually takes longer to stretch out organisational and functional question-marks. One has simply to realise, that utterly few Public Service bodies do operate under conditions equal to those of the private-owned, market-driven, profit-oriented organisations – even if it has been popular for decades to try to import management principles from the latter into the former. Which, as such, may not at all be wrong as long as the conceptual and environmental differences are recognised and duly respected.

# Participativeness and the power of the group

In this chapter, Business Modelling is tacitly understood to be interactive modelling with groups in a seminar environment. A few remarks might be relevant concerning the major Critical Success Factors (CSF) of such events.

In my opinion, the far most important CSF is *participativeness*. This seems to be agreed upon by practitioners like myself as well as by researchers of the field. Enid Mumford was one of the earliest to stress the vital importance of participativeness, thus having the term "participativeness" closely linked to her researcher's profile (see e.g. Mumford & Weir, 1979).

A modelling team is usually set up ad hoc, with little or no possibility to "grow into a group" before the modelling is to take place. Still, every member's participativeness is vital to the success of the team. In order to accomplish that, *each* member has to:

- *understand* the objective of the modelling

- *agree* upon the importance of this objective

- feel personally *capable* to contribute to a positive result

- *be comfortable* with the rest of the team (including the modelling facilitator)

Therefore, *modelling seminars should be prepared* (by the facilitator, mostly) through personal interviews with each of the intended team-members. At least by a phone-call, preferably eye-to-eye, for about a half to one hour. This personal preparation is more important the less the organisation/environment is "used to" Business Modelling. And – of course – the interviews should aim at leaving the intended participant comfortable with the above four points.

The longer your experience as a modelling-facilitator, the more you realise the necessity of performing preparations like the above described. Of course you *may* be able to run a successful modelling session without previous interviews – but your odds are bad! *With* interviews – *accordingly acted upon* – you have a far better chance of success.

I have myself since long refused to accept assignments as modelling facilitator unless I get the opportunity to interview the seminar participants beforehand. I usually also claim the right to question the choice of participants, having made the interviews. Dragging a non-participative person to a modelling session is by all means wrong and contra-productive – and also an offence to the person in question.

The second-most important CSF is to *use the group concept efficiently*. Experience shows that a modelling group should:

- not be too large (max. 6-7 people; otherwise you will need a chairman, which would be contra-productive to group creativity)

- be as heterogeneous as possible with respect to organisational position, subject-matter competence, business experience, age, gender, personal character etc.

"The power of the group" is likely to show clearer the more heterogeneous the group is – provided each member is working towards the unanimous ideal of consensus. No team member should be apt to resign to his mates until he is convinced that it is really a *common as well as an individual* advantage that he changes his view of the subject under modelling and aligns it to that of his comrades.

For further details on the composition of modelling teams, please see chapter 15 by Willars.

# Influence by trends: Process Management and Object Orientation

The last few years the Object Orientation (OO) concept has matured and become popular, more generally demanded and believed in even by board members. In parallel, the Process Management (PM) wave has hit the Western World, mainly labelled BPR (Business Process Reengineering) (see e.g. Davenport, 1993; Hammer & Champy, 1993).

The PM and OO concepts have certainly affected Business Modelling substantially – for better and for worse. Since around 1990, I have myself spent weeks and months modelling process flow structures together with business representatives of various companies, often within the Ericsson Group. And as soon as IT support seems to be the ultimate goal of a modelling event, OO strategy is what is asked for in these days.

## *Process Management*

Process Modelling is a variant of business flow modelling. A Process is (to my apprehension) nothing more – and nothing less – than a "recipe" for how an intended increase of customer-perceived value should be achieved with controlled effectiveness and efficiency. Primarily, interface objects and their qualities are focused; secondly the internal structures of the processes (cf. Rummler & Brache, 1995).

In my opinion, the process orientation trend has been extremely advantageous to Business Modelling as a discipline. It has become realised by many (even executives and board members) that Business Modelling really could be the leverage of business development rather than some fancy academic play-around with the employees stealing time from their real work. In many cases, process modelling has become the entrance gate to more thorough business analyses employing also other types of Business Modelling than those dealing with flows – for instance business objectives analysis. Another effect is that graphic as well as verbal documentation of process structures has been spread and discussed widely within companies and organisations, thus making the people more apt to think and communicate in modelling terms. The pure pedagogical effects of process modelling may in the long run prove to be even more important than the efficiency increases that might have been accomplished in the short run.

Backlashes of process modelling have also occurred. Those who expected that Process Management, BPR in particular, itself should solve all the problems of the company and guarantee its prosperous future have become disappointed more often than not. Reactions have sometimes been "to shoot the messenger", i.e. blaming the process modelling activities (and/or the involved consultants) for the "failure". It may take several years before Business Modelling will be an accepted tool in such companies.

## *Object Orientation*

While Process Management could be said to have entered the business environment via the board-rooms, Object Orientation (OO) has taken the back door, being introduced by technicians and programmers. Accordingly, the OO concept has difficulties in becoming understood, accepted and applied by company management. In some organisations, however – like for instance the engineer-driven Ericsson Group – the basic OO ideas were adopted by management very early. This company's success cash cow through the last decades, the AXE telecom switching system, was conceptually founded on OO principles (see Jacobson et al, 1993).

For many years, I have felt a conflict between OO principles and Business Modelling. I do appreciate the logical clarity and consistence of the OO concept – it seems to be an excellent paradigm for *design* in the case where you start with nothing but a clean workroom and want to – for instance – create a maintainable telecommunication switch system. Of course it should be built according to OO principles with self-containing building blocks with very distinct and well-documented interfaces. That would be engineering at its best.

However, Business Modelling works the other way round: There *is* an already existing reality out there, a business, that you want to understand and describe. Could you really presume that this reality is in fact generically object oriented in itself? Even to the extent that you would base your *analysis* paradigm on OO principles? Is there not a risk that if you do adopt the OO paradigm, you will *not* get a model of the reality but rather a model of what this reality "should" be like, had its creators been aware of the superiority of the OO concept?

Having said that, I would be the first to confess that Business Modelling has benefited a lot from impulses from the OO world. For one thing, the OO development has influenced and speeded up the development of modelling languages. Elements of these languages have been successfully applied also within Business Modelling that is not primarily OO. And many practitioners (I for one) have found themselves to have grown more skilful as modelling facilitators as they have struggled to understand and put together the sometimes contradictory bits and pieces of OO theory that have come from numerous sources through the years when the OO concept has gradually matured.

However, it has been – and is still – difficult to apply the full set of OO methodology to "ordinary" Business Modelling. To IT laymen and non-specialists, OO appears cumbersome and hard to really grasp without considerable effort. But this might change for the better. By the launching of UML (Unified Modeling Language), the OMG (Object Management Group) has taken a big step towards both unifying the various flavours of OO methodology and simplifying the OO cornerstones to modelling practitioners – facilitators as well as ordinary modelling team members.

A recent book, "UML distilled" by Fowler and Scott (1997), gives an excellent and easy-to-read presentation of the latest UML version.

## Tools for Business Modelling

Business Modelling needs two categories of tools: Firstly "groupware" to use at the modelling seminars, secondly tools to condense, maintain, store and distribute the modelling results.

## *"Groupware"*

Tools to help the modelling team to build their common model must – first and last – be easy to learn and simple to use. Blackboards, whiteboards, flipcharts have those qualities – but also some drawbacks, poor mobility being one. The most modern tool used for group modelling – a wall-large, computer operated, back-projection screen – is also very stationary. And it needs a "pilot" to operate it, thus putting some restrictions on the spontaneous creativity that modellers usually develop.

Maybe the "plastic sheet and adhesive patches tool" comes closest to the ideal here. Primitive as it may appear, it is very flexible, very versatile and very mobile. You can even perform modelling outdoors, should you prefer that.

The main advantage with back-projection screen tools is of course that they are computerised "from the beginning", thus taking away most of the tedious documentation work that inevitably follows the use of any "manual" tool. And development goes on. With even better software and more luminant video projectors it might be possible to create a modelling environment that is user-friendly enough not to discourage even the anti-technical modelling team member.

## *Tools for final documentation and broadcasting*

The most primitive tools applied here are drawing aids, making it possible to refine and condense the graphs created as wall-graphs at the modelling seminars. For years, we have put up with products like Mac Draw, Meta Design and ABC Flowcharter – and done quite well as we thought. However, when Business Modelling grows within an organisation, when tens, hundreds and thousands of models should be maintained and spread, more sophisticated tools are needed. A general experience is that paper is not sufficient as a basis for the documentation – primarily because it is almost impossible to maintain and update a documentation that is spread in numerous binders over a large geographical area. At the present state of IT development, when most organisations have local networks with Internet and Intranet, it is natural to demand documentation tools that allow everybody with access to the network to also get access to the results from Business Modelling. There are a few products on the market that allow for this, and probably many more to come.

With general access to currently updated Business Models – process flows, conceptual charts, objective structures, etc. – the organisation will finally have reached one of the ultimate goals of Business Modelling: The models have become efficient vehicles for a more unambiguous communication of human thought – all over the organisation, world-wide if necessary.

# Conclusions

One important driver for the development of Business Modelling is the very large step of formalisation that has to be taken when we want to create computer-based data representations of business realities in order to facilitate our business decisions. We have gradually learned that this is not an easy problem to solve. The gap between the perceived business reality and what can be represented by digits in files is usually both wider and deeper than we initially thought. And, trying to build a bridge by applying Business Modelling, we have often found that the abutment on the business side of the gap is unstable – we simply do not have a correct understanding of what the business is like. Which calls for more and even better Business Modelling. There is a lot of development to be made here.

Another major development driver, probably increasingly important in the future, is business competition. Any business has to improve its external effectiveness and internal efficiency continuously, should it be able to survive and prosper. Customer satisfaction should be maximised and all forms of waste eliminated. To be able to do that, better and still better business information is needed. Business Modelling is a way to improve the self-insight – and also to efficiently communicate the information to the relevant business operators.

"Everything should be done as simple as possible – but no simpler than that". Business Modelling certainly has a great future.

# References

Davenport, T.H. (1993) *Process Innovation – Reengineering Work through Information Technology*, Harvard Business School Press, Boston, Massachusetts.

Fowler, M. & Scott, K. (1997) *UML distilled: Applying the Standard Object Modeling Language*, Addison-Wesley, Reading, Massachusetts.

Hammer, M. & Champy, J. (1993) *Reengineering the Corporation – A Manifesto for Business Revolution*, Harper Collins Publishers, New York.

Jacobson, I., Christerson, M., Jonsson, P. & Övergaard, G. (1993) *Object-Oriented Software Engineering – A Use Case Driven Approach*, revised fourth printing, Addison-Wesley, Wokingham, England.

Langefors, B. (1966) *Theoretical Analysis of Information Systems*, Studentlitteratur, Lund, Sweden [Also published 1973 by Auerbach, Philadelphia].

Mumford, E. & Weir, M. (1979) *Computer Systems in Work Design – The ETHICS Method*, Associated Business Press, London.

Rummler, G.A. & Brache, A.P. (1995) *Improving Performance – How to Manage the White Space on the Organization Chart*, second edition, Jossey-Bass Inc. Publishers, San Francisco.

# 9

# Business Process Models Revised: Challenging the Physical Metaphor

## Gösta Steneskog

*Present business process concepts and modelling techniques have shown severe shortcomings in handling such processes as order processes, development processes, control processes and most types of computerised business processes. In this chapter the author claims that behind today's process models there are implicit concepts inherited from the physical world view. This heritage prevents us from creating models supporting us to fully utilise the potentials of the virtual (digital, electronic and computerised) world. The conclusion is that the present ways of modelling business processes will have to be radically changed if we really want to realise the potentials of the present development of information technology.*

## Introduction

Process modelling is one way of describing an enterprise. However, there are a number of slightly different ways of defining what a business process is, and hence how it can be modelled (Davenport, 1993; Hammer & Champy, 1993). In CEBUSNET (ESPRIT No. 21776), a research project where six business schools in Europe are co-operating, we use the following definition (cf. Figure 1).

A business process is:

- a course of *activities*

- structured to create an *output* which is predefined and has *customer value*

- *transforming/adding value* to (main) input objects while consuming input material to create the wanted customer value

- having a well-defined start and stop

- executed repetitively

- executed by *actors*: people (with tools), belonging to different organisational units, and/or machines (e.g. computer-based programs)

- utilising a platform of resources

- meeting enterprise objectives

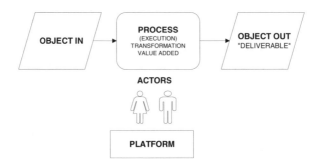

*Figure 1. The basic components of a business process.*

Based on this definition, which emphasises the important role of the business object, we also developed a way to graphically describe business processes (Steneskog et al, 1996).

If we apply these principles to a part of the production process for the famous wooden horses from Dalarna, Sweden, it could look like Figure 2:

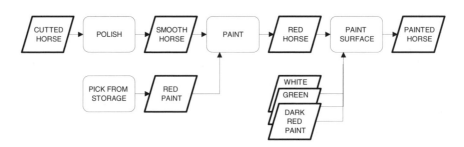

*Figure 2. The value chain of painting a wooden horse.*

The business object is transformed (value-added) step-by-step from being a roughly cut piece of wood, a smoothly cut one, a polished one, a red-painted one, to a complete well-painted wooden horse ready for sale. This type of description put emphasis on the process (courses of activities) as most process notation methods do, but also on the business objects which is not that common (e.g. Rummler & Brache, 1995, does not).

Here we are using an example where the transformed business object (the piece of wood) is a monolithic, psychical one. It makes it relatively easy for the reader to grasp the concept of business processes. The first modelling principles were developed when trying to model processes in the physical world, i.e. with physical business objects. For a physical object, the value-adding process is primarily sequential. The object is owned by one sub-process at a time and it is in a certain well-defined state when being passed between the sub-processes. Still, those principles are (implicitly or explicitly) underlying most business process models.

Rayport and Sviokla (1995) presents an interesting concept about two different worlds under the title "Exploiting the Virtual Value Chain":

"Every business today competes in two worlds: a physical one of resources that managers can see and touch and a virtual world of information.

But the processes for creating value are not the same in the two worlds."

My thesis is that if we use these modelling techniques – based on the laws of the physical world – on processes in the virtual world, we will not be able to effectively describe the processes in the virtual world and hence not be able to fully realise the potential of that world.

This has given rise to the questions:

* How do you define these two worlds?

* What are the basic differences between objects and processes in these worlds?

* How do you model your business processes in these different worlds in order to fully utilise the capabilities of each world?

Why is it so important to improve our abilities to master the development of processes in the virtual world? There are a number of reasons:

* More and more business objects are chunks of information in virtual form instead of physical objects

- The development and use of IT for computing, communication and networking (e.g. Internet) will further a rapid development of the business processes in the virtual world.

- During the last decades more and more business processes have been moved into the virtual world.

## The physical world and the virtual world

First, we have the physical world of resources that managers (and everybody else) can see and touch. This is our normal, real and concrete world. We know that one quite well.

Second, there is some world of information Rayport & Sviokla (ibid.) has identified. However, information and data appear in many different forms and worlds, so I have found it useful to distinguish between the different forms information objects can have.

Physical form: the information is "glued" on a physical carrier, e.g. written on a paper, carved on a rune-stone, etc. You cannot move the chunk of information without moving the physical carrier. We are in the physical world.

Virtual form: the information is computerised, digitised and in electronic form. For a chunk of information to be in the virtual world is synonymous with being in the computer world. The properties of these chunks of information are very different from the properties of physical objects. Also the properties for the processes for creation/development, recreation/production and transportation are very different for those types of objects.

So, we have these two worlds. Now, let us have some examples on how objects and processes appear in those worlds and how they have been moved from the physical to the virtual world. During the last decades the number of processes in the virtual world have increased dramatically (cf. Negroponte, 1995).

## Process mirroring

In the beginning everything was physical. So, let us return to our simple wooden-horse example. We modelled that process according to our modelling principles. But, why did we model the process at all? There are some common purposes for doing business modelling.

- To understand the process, which increases our ability to handle problems ad hoc.

- To improve, or even re-engineer, the process, to change it to the better.

- To control the process by using the model as a base for collection of relevant data about the process, decision-making and interventions in the process

So, we model the physical process in order to manage it and to improve it and we implement the model in the virtual world to control and co-ordinate its executions (cf. Figure 3).

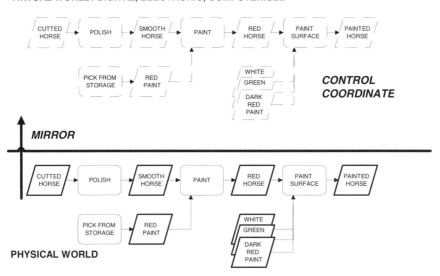

*Figure 3. Example of process mirroring.*

A well-known example is the Frito-Lay case. They carefully modelled the production and distribution process, implemented a series of ways to collect data about the status of the process, made calculations, decided upon what to do, and ordered what to do. The physical process itself what not really changed, but the way it was controlled.

In this case the process is modelled and mirrored in the virtual world – in the computer.

*Process mirroring is modelling a business process and implementing that model in the virtual world in order to co-ordinate and control the process in the physical world.*

The physical process does still exist in the physical world, the value is added to the physical objects by the process in the physical world.

Another example is Federal Express. Each parcel – the physical object in the physical world – is mirrored in the virtual world, it has a corresponding virtual object. The physical object is the business object itself, the virtual object is a chunk of relevant information about the physical object which makes it possible for Federal Express to keep track of all their parcels.

The virtual process is then mirroring the physical process and it gives us a clear picture of the state of the latter so we can co-ordinate and control it.

One major problem is to have relevant, up-to-date information in the virtual world about the physical world. It is often difficult to capture information in the physical world and to convert it into a virtual form. There are may ways to do that, e.g. the use of bar-code reading as in the Federal Express case.

In many cases mirroring is done without having an explicit process model. You just collect what you think is relevant information, process it and distribute it. However, not having a process model gives you a worse foundation for controlling and monitoring the mirrored process.

# Process migration

Now it is time for the next step. In a number of processes the business object which is transformed is an information object, i.e. a chunk of information. Let us take a part of a bond-selling process as an example (cf. Figure 4).

These processes might be executed in the physical world: the transformed business object is a chunk of information on a document and that chunk (not the paper) is added value to along the process.

If we model that process and implement it in the virtual world (i.e. we computerise it) we find that the original physical process disappears. If we move a process with informational objects to the virtual world there is usually no reason for keeping it in the physical world as the informational objects are migrated to the virtual world.

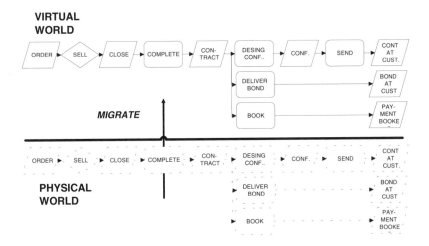

*Figure 4. Example of process migration.*

*Process migration is modelling a business process with informational objects and implementing that model in the virtual world leading to the disappearance of the process in the physical world.*

For an order process this means that all physical handling of documents etc. could disappear.

It is not only administrative processes that might be migrated but also production and delivery processes where the business object is an information object (a chunk), e.g. an invoice, a payment, a computer program, a novel, a piece of music, etc.

Some months ago, I was searching for a new program for creating mindmaps (cf. Figure 5):

- I started by searching on the Internet and found four possible alternatives.

- I read the descriptions (virtual distribution of "brochures").

- I down-loaded a test version of the most interesting one (virtual (re)production and distribution of the product/object itself).

- After having tested it, I decided to order and mailed my order for the complete product (virtual ordering).

- Then the company e-mailed my license number to me (virtual distribution).

- Finally I opened the test version again, entered my license number and got access to all program functions!

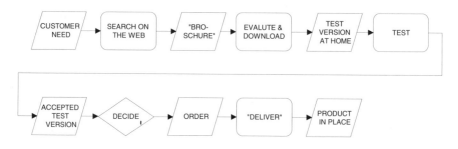

*Figure 5. Illustration of the process of getting a program via the Internet.*

This is an example of how all the objects and processes have been migrated to the virtual world and the whole set of processes was completed in a few hours (if we exclude my testing days).

In this case IT is not just supporting these processes, IT is the machinery running them.

## *Car construction*

Another example is the car construction process.

In the beginning the construction process took place in the physical world filled with drawing-boards, blue-prints etc.

With the entry of CAD this process was migrated to the virtual world and parts of the previous physical process disappeared into the virtual world.

Of course, there are parts of the construction process where you really have to build the physical car. As long as the final product is a physical one sooner or later you have to return to the physical world.

# Process simulation

Now, we come to the concept of process simulation. When you simulate a process you model it and move it (objects and processes) into the virtual world. The physical object is mirrored in the virtual world, the transformation process is simulated and the resulting information object is (hopefully) a mirror of what would have been the object out if the corresponding physical process had been executed.

Boeing did that for their wind-tunnel tests many years ago (cf. Rayport & Sviokla, ibid.).

In the first stage they used just physical simulation. A physical model of the wing was tested in a wind-tunnel and all the different values were physically measured.

Then the physical wing was replaced by a virtual wing in the virtual world. The process was also moved into the virtual world. After having tested different designs of the wing by executing the simulated process, the tests were verified by returning the test to the physical world.

Why did they do it? Because the properties of the objects and the processes in the virtual world made it very advantageous to mirror and simulate the physical process in the virtual world. Often, such a move is more advantageous than expected, because we cannot foresee all changes that will occur.

## Orders of change

The Boeing case exemplifies the different types of changes that do occur also when moving to the virtual world.

- Changes of first order – changes we directly create: Objects (wings) and processes (windtunneling and measuring) are moved to the virtual world. We do the same thing as before but faster and cheaper.

- Changes of second order – short term reactions created by the process actors' reactions upon the changes of first order: The design and test process changed to a more trial-and-error approach due to the fact that it was easier and cheaper than before to run a wind-tunnel test. The amount of analysis and design before testing was reduced and the number of test shots increased. This led to testing of more radical wing designs which in turn led to much better solutions than ever before.

- Changes of third order – long term changes created by investments and desinvestments in the process. In this case it could lead to reduction in as well analysis competence as resources for physical wind-tunnel tests.

# Physical and virtual – two different worlds

After having described how physical business objects and processes may be mirrored or migrated to the virtual world it is time to investigate how the physical world and the virtual world provide different conditions for business processes. The next question will be if the same principles are suitable for modelling of business process in both worlds or if a new approach is needed for the virtual world.

## *Object properties*

We perceive physical objects as hard, i.e. they are either monolithic or consists of a number of monolithic parts. Virtual objects (chunks of information) are soft, i.e. they are composed of a very large number of information parts and those parts may be successively improved.

We also perceive physical objects as hard to change. To change a physical object may require hard work or replacement. Virtual objects are principally easy to change but it may be more difficult to know what may be the right change (cf. Table 1).

|  | Form<br><br>how the object exists in the world | Softness<br><br>how easy it may be modified | Stability<br><br>how controlled changes are | Visibility<br><br>how easy it is to see and understand it |
|---|---|---|---|---|
| Virtual object | electronic digitalised computerised | easily modified | changed only on request | invisible |
| Physical object | physical or attached to a physical carrier | hard to modify | very stable (usually) | visible, easy to review |

*Table 1. Properties of virtual and physical objects.*

## *Process properties*

Moving a process to the virtual world not only changes the properties of the business object but also makes it possible for the process to use computer and telecommunication technologies in the execution of the transformation processes. In Table 2 and Table 3, I have tried to compare some characteristics for different types of business processes in the two worlds.

| Process | Physical world | Virtual world |
|---|---|---|
| Marketing | | Parts of marketing may done early by involvement of clients. |
| Sales and Order | | Parts of sales may be done during beta-test where clients may participate. Parts of the ordering process may be in the virtual world |
| Production | Every individual product must be produced one-by-one | Easy to copy existing object. Tailoring may be more difficult |
| Distribution | Has to be physically distributed | Electronically distributed. |
| Maintenance/ repair and upgrade | Physical products are subject to wearing. Repair and upgrade has to be done locally. Which parts are going to be changeable has to be defined in advance. | No wearing. Diagnose, repair and up-grading can be done remote. Each "bit" is possible to delete or replace. |
| After Sales | | Upgrades are easy to sell and install. |

*Table 2. The sales, production and delivery processes.*

This explains why it is more easy to identify and describe processes acting on physical objects – the flow of objects is easy to see and follow. Also the different object states are easy to define.

Processes for virtual objects are much more difficult to identify – you cannot "see" the flow of objects, the scope of the objects are harder to define and the objects are changing in small bit-steps so it is difficult to find well-defined states of the objects. One usual way to cope with this problem is to visualise the virtual object as a "document" and to define the scope by defining the expected content of the document at that state, i.e. to make it "physical".

| Process | Physical world | Virtual world |
|---------|----------------|---------------|
| Analysis | Extensive analysis in order to define customer needs due to the high up-front costs for construction. | The initial analysis to create the architecture must be done carefully. The further analysis can be done incrementally in co-operation with clients/users in order to interactively define user processes and the Business Object. |
| Design | The design must be completed before construction starts due to the high costs of construction. | The basic design = architecture must be carefully developed. Detailed design can be done during the iterative construction and testing in co-operation with customers and production partners |
| Construction | Time-consuming, expensive to create prototypes | Can be built in an iterative manner due to ease of adding, modifying and testing |
| Test | Extensive testing of finished products due to costs of update/replace in the field. | Successive testing during iterative construction. Update/ replace in the field is easier but still expensive. |
| Implementation of processes | Extensive efforts in building the pre-production and testing. Major investments may be needed for (sales and) physical delivery. | Minor capital investments in building the development. Low entry costs for Sales and Delivery processes (see below) |

*Table 3. The product development processes.*

In order to be able to take advantage of the development of IT and especially networking, it is necessary to analyse one's physical processes for production and delivery and to improve their control processes.

For the processes handling virtual objects the changes will be more radical for production and delivery as well as for development. Today many of these processes are based on experiences of corresponding processes for physical objects. The radical improvements will occur first when we take the next step and design them based on the principles of the virtual world.

# Consequences for Business Modelling

Let us return to the beginning of this chapter, where we presented one example of a physical business process: the creation of a wooden horse (cf. Figure 6).

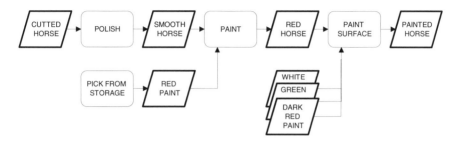

*Figure 6: The value chain of painting a wooden horse.*

The object is transformed in a linear, stepwise fashion in an order which is almost impossible to change (you cannot paint before polishing). The process is performed in functionally oriented steps (polishing, painting etc.). The steps are sequential. After each step the object has a certain well-defined status. The object may be in only one process at a time.

If we take one process from the virtual world e.g. writing an article there are a number of differences (cf. Figure 7).

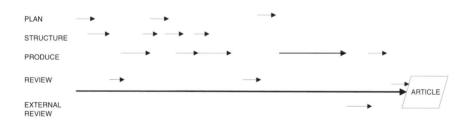

*Figure 7. The process of writing an article.*

The object is transformed in an organic growing fashion where different parts may develop in different order from article to article. The process is performed in short functionally oriented steps. These steps are often overlapping, re-occurring and "pushing" the object to its end state in an organic way. The object and even the same parts of the object may be worked with in different processes at the same time.

These examples are in no way complete but give an example of how different processes in the two worlds really are.

## Modelling the software development process

An interesting process is the process of developing information systems, a process which was among the first processes to be migrated into the virtual world. The first process models were based on the physical metaphor which led to the now depreciated "water-fall" methods. They were really a true result of trying to apply the principles of a physical process for a virtual process and not taking into consideration the softness of the virtual objects and the characteristics of processes based on computers and telecommunication. Software is treated as a form of hardware! Or, in my words, virtual objects are treated as physical objects.

In practice, however, these models are not closely followed by most projects as the dogmatic practising of the model leads to obviously unproductive behaviour.

The present object-oriented movement is also getting inspiration from the hardware world, and software objects are compared to integrated circuits. A critical question is how much this hardware metaphor is influencing the object-oriented paradigm, and thus making it as old-fashioned as the water-fall thinking.

A break-through in software development may only be possible by abandoning the physical metaphor and designing new process based on a new virtual paradigm. In my further research I plan to review some of the new methods presented in the last years to see in what degree this "virtual" thinking is emerging.

## Conclusions

Today, business process modelling is based on our experience of the physical world and this metaphor has pervaded our thinking and our models for business modelling.

This concept is less useful when applied to processes in the virtual world. To model processes according to the physical paradigm based on the physical metaphor is useful for processes in the physical world but not sufficient for processes in the virtual world. To use the physical paradigm is not useless because it creates an overall understanding also of the virtual processes and is probably a useful first step in the development of business process modelling. However, the present common definition creates problem when modelling virtual processes, e.g. for iterative processes, for parallel processing etc. This is probably the reason behind the problems we presently have in modelling development and control processes.

It also means that we do not have the right thinking for utilising the potential benefits of today's rapid development of computer and telecommunication technologies.

We need to create new definitions for virtual business processes and new ways of process modelling. We have to revise the Business Process concept and the techniques for business process modelling to take into consideration the possibilities the virtual world is presenting.

This is of increasing importance for all processes having informational objects such as product development processes (especially when developing virtual products, e.g. software) and processes on the Internet.

# References

Davenport, T.H. (1993) *Process Innovation – Reengineering Work through Information Technology*, Harvard Business School Press, Boston, Massachusetts.

Hammer, M & Champy, J. (1993) *Reengineering the Corporation*, Harper Collins Publishers, New York.

Negroponte, N. (1995) *Being Digital*, Vintage Books, New York.

Rayport, J.F. & Sviokla J.J. (1995) "Exploiting the Virtual Value Chain", *Harvard Business Review*, Nov-Dec.

Rummler, G.A. & Brache, A.P. (1995) *Improving Performance: How to Manage the White Space on the Organization Chart*, 2nd ed., Jossey-Bass Publishers, San Francisco.

Steneskog, G., Mårtensson, A. & van der Heijden, H. (1996) *Modelling Business Processes: The P-graph Notation*, Management report series no. 279, Faculteit Bedrijfskunde, Erasmus Universiteit/Rotterdam School of Management, Rotterdam, The Netherlands.

# 10

# Principal-Agent and Transaction Cost Theories in Business Modelling

*Birger Rapp*

*New models are introduced, used and they disappear. Many of them are launched as the final model that will overcome all obstacles with existing models. However, in a long-term perspective we can see that the models are not as good as promised and that they do not solve the problems or questions they were aimed to solve. This chapter aims to show how two theories, the principal-agent theory and the transaction cost theory can broaden the perspective on model building. As an introduction I give an overview of the two theories. Then I suggest some modifications and finally I stress the possible applications of these theories in Business Modelling.*

## The Principal-Agent theory

Relations are a part of our world. They have influence on both our private and professional lives in a significant way. Principal-agent theory is about relations between a principal and one or several agents. (In Rapp & Thorstenson, 1994, this is described in more detail. See also Eisenhardt, 1989). There are, for example, similarities between hiring a lawyer in a dispute, buying a car, consulting a dentist, lending money to a company, delegating the system management group the responsibility to carry out the work of the computer system, or controlling a department or the behaviour of an individual. All these examples are relations that deal with an agreement between parties.

### Asymmetric information

In most cases it is possible to distinguish between a principal and an agent where the principal wants to delegate a task to an agent. Based on today's knowledge an agreement is set up. But the outcome is in the future and is thus uncertain. The future will not always be as expected. Furthermore, if the principal and the agent have different background knowledge or different pieces of relevant information at the time of agreement, it becomes obvious that contracts are always incomplete.

The principal wants to work out the agreement in such a way that he will have a good result despite lack of relevant information or knowledge. This is not an easy task. For example, how shall an agreement between a patient (principal) and a dentist (agent) be designed? The dentist has the superior knowledge of the patient's teeth. You can in most cases only check what your dentist has done through your own well-being. Based on this it is easy to understand the Chinese phrase that you shall only pay your doctor when you are well and not when you are ill.

The same types of questions arise when an agreement between the system owner (principal) and the system manager (agent) is designed. The principal cannot know all details. However, he will get some information through the end users' reactions. It is also likely that the two parties have asymmetric information and different attitudes to risks.

When describing a department it is easy to disregard the fact that different staff members interpret given information differently. Instead it is often assumed that all members will act according to the instructions.

## Basic assumptions

The principal-agent theory provides a frame of reference for the relation between two parties, the principal and the agent. The idea behind the theory is that the agreement between the principal and the agent reflects the relation between the available information and the risk. The investigated unit is the contract. The agreement is here synonymous with the metaphor contract. The agent has bounded rationality and acts according to his own interest, which is expressed in the utility function. Different principals and agents might have different utility functions. Finally, the theory regards information as a production factor. It is possible to get information, but it may cost something to get it. We have thus a situation where we shall balance the cost for more information with the consequences of a decision based on the information we have.

The theory illustrates different assumptions and problems when designing a contract and its observance of the contract. The direct application of the theory has been questioned. However it gives a frame of references that is directly applicable to areas such as risk sharing, incentives, observability, moral hazard, adverse selection, signalling and the ratchet effect. These concepts will be described briefly in the following sections.

## Risk sharing

A contract can be designed in many ways. One way is that the principal or the agent take the whole risk, that is the consequences of future outcome. Pure risk sharing is a situation when none of the parties can influence the outcome of the project. In most cases both the principal and the agent are risk avert, which means that they treat risks with caution. But if one of them is risk neutral, he will take the whole risk. If the principal is risk neutral, he will take the whole profit except for a fixed amount to the agent. If a principal is risk neutral and wants to outsource the computer department, then the outcome of this activity is random. Thus he must take the whole risk and give a fixed fee to the agent. However it is more likely that both the principal and the agent are risk avert and that the agent's activities influence the outcome. The contract must then be designed in such a way that it stimulates work that improves the outcome.

The theory assumes that through the contract the principal can influence one or several agents to behave in line with his preferences. When all information is available, it is possible for the principal to judge the agent's activities and link them to the derived outcome. Even if the outcome is random he can always judge the agent's activities. However, the principal has to pay for this information as a piece of information is not without cost. He can now balance the cost for further information or additional incentives to get the agent to do the job well.

## Different designs of contracts

In principle, there exist two different types of contracts, behaviour-oriented and output-oriented. Behaviour-oriented contracts are based on your behaviour and they reward you for what you do. For example, you are paid for your presence and not for the work you are carrying out. You pay a programmer for the time he is writing a programme. In order to be sure, the principal needs additional information about the agent's working time, (e.g. time clock). In order to use output-oriented contracts some measurable output variables must be known. You may pay the programmer by the number of programmes he has written or by the number of lines in the programme. There are also contracts where the agent is paid if the programme runs correctly and where he gets nothing if it does not function.

## *Observability*

If there exists a person who can play roulette via the telephone, I am sure that there are several persons who would accept to run this game. Thus it is important that some information is available to both the agent and the principal. Observability is a fundamental concept in a principal-agent relationship. However, complete information is a matter of money. Either you pay for more information or you pay the agent through the contract to behave as if you had complete information. Some pieces of information are always important for both parties. In the basic principal-agent theory you assume that the outcome is observable for both parties and that they interpret it in the same way.

In an agreement the principal can require a certain behaviour from the agent. For example, a back-up must be taken every day. If the computer crash occurs the agent must show that he has taken back-ups correctly as this limits the costs to get back into operation again. Cost is here used in a broad sense, implying that revenues are regarded as negative costs.

## *Moral hazard*

If the principal does not have complete relevant information, (observability), moral hazard can occur. This means that the agent can behave in an unpreferable way. Sometimes this is called hidden action. A long time ago it was possible to take a personal insurance on others' properties. Then it could happen that a ship was over-insured by several persons and the insurance company could not explain why this ship was wrecked. Today it is not possible to insure something over its value or to take a life insurance on another human being's life.

The theory provides different solutions to decrease moral hazard. One way is that the agent has to pay some amount of the total cost. One example is an insurance where the holder has to pay the excess. Another example is that a borrower has to give a personal guarantee to get a loan. The principal can also require a certain behaviour from the agent, which can be observed ex post or ex ante. Some insurance companies reduce the premium if a certain type of lock or alarm is used. Ex ante, the policy holder has to prove that he has installed the lock or alarm. Ex post, after a burglary the policy holder has to prove that his additional protection was in operation.

## Incentives

A real contract is often a mixture between behaviour and output-oriented contracts. It is then important to observe that they are sometimes based on different incentives. You may choose an agent based on aspects of behaviour and his personality. However, later on you then introduce an output-oriented reward system which might stimulate other behaviours. We also know that an agent may behave differently in a given situation. For instance, a manager's behaviour can radically change if there is a risk for bankruptcy.

All contracts are incomplete and one should not try to achieve complete contracts. Simple contracts can be motivated from the point of view of efficiency. Human beings have a limited capacity and they can rarely consider, simultaneously, more than 3 to 5 factors. Thus contracts must be simple in order to be able to motivate the agent and communicate the right measure to the agent. This is also an argument for using one-dimensional contracts. However, what you want to achieve with the contract must be measurable, that is identifiable and quantifiable.

Applying simple contracts does not mean that the principal need not follow up the relation with the agents. There are many examples where companies have outsourced their computer departments and after a while they have not followed up how the total costs for all the computer services have developed.

A contract lasts over a period. The length can vary. The future is uncertain, and thus there cannot be any complete contract. Choosing short contracts means that both the principal and the agent have to be aware of the other party's interest. If an agent is discontented in a long contract, he will try to avoid doing things that the principal cannot observe.

Shall a contract include terms of randomness? Heath & Tversky (1991) have shown that human beings prefer to base their decisions on their own judgements rather than games, if the probability for a correct answer is high. On the other hand, if the probability is low, a human being will choose games. An interpretation of this is that if an agent looks upon himself as highly competent, he will accept a contract with random terms. The agent will then explain a good outcome by his high competence and a bad outcome by bad luck. However, if the agent has low competence in an area, a success is worth less as it will be explained by luck. A bad outcome will, however, be explained by lack of competence. In this case the agent will prefer a contract with less randomness.

In model-building, it is important to have an holistic view. You have to understand the agent's view, too. Limiting the problem-area can give wrong signals to the agent. In the following we present some examples.

- During the 1970s a company wanted to stimulate their staff's attendance. They introduced a bonus for those who had worked a whole month. However, the effect was the reverse of what was expected. The staff reported the higher salary to the national insurance office and could then be away some more days and were paid as before.

- The doctor was paid according to his efficiency in treating the patient. The efficiency (strictly speaking, productivity) was measured as the throughput time per patient. However, empirical studies have shown that if the patient received a short term of treatment, he/she would come back for a new treatment. A thorough treatment took more time, but the patient did not come back. Taking the whole hospital into consideration this was a more efficient treatment.

- If a principal states after which dimensions future evaluation will be set, all agents will move along these dimensions. For instance, one CEO said that he wanted details of the energy consumption each month in the future from all factories within the concern. Immediately, consumption decreased for all units.

If you want to change an employee's behaviour, there exist, in principal, three different ways of action, namely threat, reward and persuasion. In applications they often appear in combination. Persuasion (education) is the only way that has a long-lasting effect. One can say that human beings are clever and that they quickly learn how to avoid the threat, receive the reward and behave as before. This means that it is important to thoroughly go through the structure of the incentives in order to obtain the behaviour of the agents that you really want.

## Adverse selection

When a principal has to choose between several agents and cannot observe the agents' relevant qualifications, such a situation is called adverse selection. One famous example is Akerlof's (1970) example from the car trade. It is assumed that the buyer (principal) only knows the average quality and cannot see the difference in quality for each make of car. Let us suppose that there only exist good or bad cars. The salesmen (agents) know the difference, but not the buyers. The price level on the market will now be influenced by the average quality estimation of the buyers. Cars of higher quality than the average will leave the market. However, there exists a solution. By signalling, the car dealer can show that his cars are of higher quality. For instance, he can design a guarantee in such a way that car dealers selling bad cars cannot afford to give such a guarantee.

A bank offered the possibility of obtaining loans by telephone. The idea was to attract busy financially sound people to apply for loans. But the result turned out differently. More borrowers than estimated later became insolvent. The financially sound borrowers were aware of their own financial situation. They took the time they needed to go to a bank and get good loan conditions. Another bank (principal) succeeded in attracting the sound clients. Before this bank would offer any advantages, the clients (agents) had to signal that they were the right clients. Each bank client that set up an account with a certain amount got "his own bank-man". This attracted financially sound clients. However, not all of them used the service they had the right to use. They were satisfied in knowing that the possibility existed. In total this was profitable for the bank. They got financially sound clients who did not use the service they had the right to use.

The same types of problems exist when a principal wants to choose the right system operator or computer supplier. The principal can have a feeling that everything is OK before signing the contract. The problems arise later. Then the principal thinks that the agent has promised too much. It is clear that some of the problems can be avoided by good contracts. In my opinion one should consider contracts that give the agents a reward when they are running well and some additional costs if any undesirable situation occurs. It is also wise to look into risk-sharing possibilities.

## Costs

The original principal-agent theory distinguishes between three types of costs. Jensen & Meckling (1976) call them agency costs. They are costs of incentives, opportunity costs, and monitoring costs.

The costs of incentives are the costs (rewards) that the principal includes in the contract in order to stimulate the agent's behaviour. The opportunity costs include the costs that occur when the agent performs the task in a way other than intended. The monitoring costs are all costs related to choose the right agent, initiate the relation and to control it.

Some of the criticism against this theory is that the costs are not easy to express operationally. In the next section other ways to look at costs will be discussed.

## *Summing up*

It has thus been shown that in processes where human beings are actors, it is important to consider the effects of incomplete information and the incentive structure. It is important to map the risk situation in order to understand who is taking the risk in the agreement. Short contracts are attractive as you cannot foresee the future and the interpretations of concepts and instructions change as time goes.

# Transaction cost theory

Transaction cost theory has grown during the last decades. It will be mentioned here as it gives us the possibility to introduce a broad view on changes. (Main references are Williamson, 1975 and 1979, but the theory has it roots in Robertson, 1923, and Coase, 1937).

Transaction cost theory attempts to explain why some economic activities are co-ordinated through the market and some within the company or organisation. According to this theory, the existence of companies is to some extent explained by market failure. This is due to human factors such as bounded rationality and opportunism. Other factors are environmental factors such as complexity/uncertainty and the "small number of exchange" (asset specificity). These factors give three types of costs when using the market.

- *ex ante* costs for ascertaining relevant prices *(searching costs)*,

- *ex ante* costs for negotiating and formulating contracts *(contracting costs)*,

- *ex post* costs for following up contracts and enforcing legal rights *(monitoring and legal enforcement costs)*.

The transaction costs are determined by the asset specificity, the degree of complexity/uncertainty and the frequency of a given transaction. When the transaction costs are too high in the market, the transaction will be carried out within the company.

Transaction cost theory has been criticised by several authors. The critique can be summarised by three main points. It is a theoretical construction and it is not possible to define the costs operationally. The theory is built for manufacturing companies and perhaps other types of companies need to highlight other types of costs. In next section other types of costs will be discussed. Psychologists often claim that human beings behave in the way they are expected to behave. When you introduce opportunism in the theory, the agents' opportunism will be even more outspoken and they will behave in unexpected ways.

## Generalised transaction costs

In the original transaction cost theory it is possible to discuss how the organisational form is changed when costs are changed. A need to modify the described theories is necessary when paying special attention to the effect of introducing new information systems. Lindström & Rapp (1996) discuss how this can be done. Six different types of internal costs will be introduced in order to make it possible to discuss the effects of new information systems in an organisation. It is also possible to introduce the same type of external costs.

Here communication, coordination and information costs will be distinguished. Communication is a wide and important concept. Some authors claim that "one cannot *not* communicate" (see, for instance, Rapp, 1993, for further discussion). This means that everything a human being does involves communication. Authors like Trevino et al (1990) claim that managers often spend about 80% of their time communicating. Conrad (1985) gives a more specific definition. He distinguishes among three communication functions: the command function, the relation function and the ambiguity-management function. The command function involves giving and taking orders for instructions or control. It is often formal communication. In many cases it is vertical within the organisation. Introducing information systems creates new ways to communicate. Coordination is closely related to this type of communication. Here Conrad's first type of communication will be included in our definition of coordination. In it, costs associated with project leadership will be included, which is not necessarily a command function.

Communication classified as the relation function covers the creation and maintenance of business-like personal acquaintanceships and relations. For instance, it might be possible to locate part of the company close to an important supplier or customer, who will lower these types of costs. This is particularly true when the organisation is geographically dispersed.

The third type of communication deals with ambiguity in decision making. Here it is included in the information cost. This concept includes both searching for information for decisions as well as handling remaining ambiguity. They will here be called information costs.

When changing the organisational form this can affect the way of producing and/or moving some unit to another place. They are here called the specific costs and they include changes in location and production costs that can occur.

So far, annual (i.e., variable) costs have been discussed. It is also necessary to consider investment cost when changing from one form of organisation to another. These costs appear once, for instance when introducing a new information system. These costs will here be called investment costs.

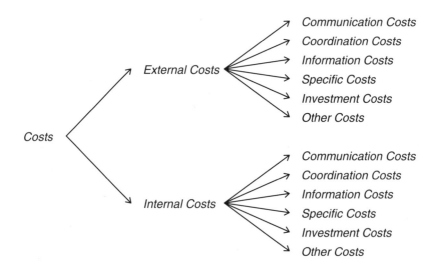

*Figure 1. Cost structure for internal and external costs.*

This classification is not exhaustive. Other costs can be the costs for staff's learning or comfort. They are here called other costs. The costs are summarised in Figure 1. In a specific situation it is not likely that all external and internal costs need to be considered. In Lindström & Rapp (1996) not more than one external cost is considered, but all six internal costs.

In next section the model will be illustrated by an example from Lindström & Rapp (1996).

## *An example*

Company A performs opinion polls, market research, surveys, telemarketing and related activities. In this field, companies compete on the basis of quality and price of services. Information flow is simple. A qualified project leader who can give the customer what he needs and an efficient field research that can keep down costs are needed. Here we discuss the cost changes when company A creates a detached unit.

The main information flow from customers to the company is simple and can be divided into four steps.

- The customers need to have qualified contacts with the company because the customers often need help in identifying and defining a project in order to obtain desired results. Several project leaders are responsible to customers for projects. Sometimes a project leader has only one large, important, customer. However, the project leaders often have several customers/projects and some projects are small.

- The project leader transforms the customer's wishes to tasks in an operational plan. The plan must then be interpreted for those who will carry out the investigation. After defining a project together with the customer, the project leader instructs the field research staff about the project and how it should be carried out. Instructions can be quite complicated, as there are many parameters to be considered.

- A "field research group" performs the tasks and reports the results to the project leader.

- The project leader accepts the project results or asks for a revision. Upon acceptance, the project leader presents the report to the customer. The customer can also ask for additional work to be done.

Before the reorganisation in Company A, the project leader and the field research department were situated in the same building. It was then an easy task for the project leader to have access to the ongoing work at the field research department. Some of the contacts were rather informal and the project leader could modify his instructions as the investigation progressed. In sum, it was not clear how to allocate costs to projects.

The investigators need modern telephone equipment to contact people. They also have to be cost efficient. Before they moved to the rural district, their equipment was technically out-of-date. Furthermore it was rather difficult to hire people who were motivated for this kind of work in the urban districts.

These factors resulted in the decision to move the field research to a rural district. After the move, Company A was geographically detached along line a-a shown in Figure 2. Figure 2 is simplified to show only one customer, $C_i$ and one project leader, $P_j$.

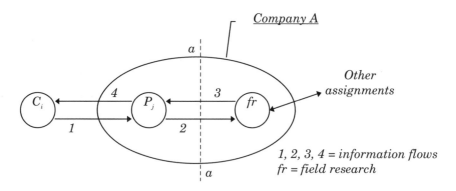

*Figure 2. Company A after the reorganisation.*

The reorganisation meant that the basic tasks and activities remained largely unchanged. What was new was a geographical separation between the project leaders and the field research group. As a result, the activity/task of information transfer from the project leader to field research changed. For the costs in our model, we can see that the marketing costs for the client were not changed, since the project leaders remained at the old location. The internal coordination costs, however, increased mostly because the project leader travelled between the rural and urban offices to give "face-to-face" instructions. The communication costs probably changed in pattern but not necessarily in amount because the kind of communication included in our communication cost concept did not take place between the project leaders and the field research group to any larger extent before the reorganisation. The information costs probably increased for reasons of ambiguity in information transfer when the project leaders chose not to travel but to use the telephone or some other technique for transferring instructions to the field research group.

The investment costs went up as a result of buying new equipment. However, a large part of these investment costs was covered by government grants. It was possible to receive these types of grants when one of the departments of the company moved from an urban district to a rural one. The company also received grants to train the new staff in the rural district. The location costs and production costs went down. The staff were more motivated and the turnover was low. The salaries were lower and the additional costs for new office space were also paid by grants. The operating costs for office space were slightly lower. Therefore, the field research group's production costs decreased. The field research group was also allowed to sell other types of simple services of its own. Existing regular work was to some extent used to smooth out the utilisation of staff. However, this arrangement led to unintended consequences. As the work load of the department went up, when using an opportunity cost approach the set-up costs (time costs for instructions) increased. This result implied that small projects did not benefit from the lower specific location costs and production costs. However, the large projects did.

The reorganisation has also meant that the field research became a profit centre, implying better control of the total costs of the projects. Most of the employees were hired and paid for a certain time-period. Some of the agents were also guaranteed a certain amount of hours a week. As a result of the new telephone equipment it is possible to determine the efficiency of different employees. For example, it is possible to measure the contact time the employee has with different persons. These data are not used to introduce output-oriented contracts. The staff are still paid with behaviour-oriented contracts. But those who turned out to act inefficiently were not rehired.

The project leader's task of giving instructions to the field research group has always been performed face-to-face. The company continued this procedure. However, project leaders spent a day flying to the new district to give instructions. Coordination costs, therefore, went up. For large projects this was compensated by lower production costs. However, for small projects this was not the case. Before the move of the field research group the project leader often based the small projects on informal contacts. The project leader has now formalised the instructions of the projects as he has to control the number of contacts. It became obvious that the project leader could not visit the field research group for special instruction on the small projects. The project leader then tried to give telephone instructions. This sometimes failed. The project leader did not succeed in transferring complicated messages by phone. The company also tried sending instructions by videotape, but without success. It is now considering moving part of the field research group back to the urban office.

In conclusion, the most important gain of the reorganisation was high productivity in the field research. The staff utilisation rate also went up. New services were offered and labour costs decreased because the staff in the rural district were more loyal and more enthusiastic. Sometimes the staff felt that this type of work gave them contact with the outside world. However, for small projects, the increases in coordination and information costs were not covered by these positive effects. Table 1 sums up the discussion.

| Type of costs | Change of costs for large projects | Change of costs for small projects |
|---|---|---|
| marketing costs | constant | constant |
| communication costs | no significant change | no significant change |
| coordination costs | up | up |
| information costs | slightly up | slightly up |
| specific location costs and production costs | down | down a little |
| other costs | not considered | not considered |
| investment costs | usually up but not this time due to grants | usually up but not this time due to grants |
| Sum of total changed costs after reorganisation | down | up |

*Table 1. Company costs.*

In Table 1 the total costs increase for small projects but not for large ones, even though the direction of change is the same in both cases, because the increase in coordination costs is a larger fraction of the total for small projects.

# Final comments

In this chapter I have briefly introduced two different theories, the principal-agent and the transaction cost theory. I have also discussed a modification of these theories in order to make them more applicable to situations where you introduce information systems and perform reorganisations. The example above shows this. Further examples are found in the literature.

Authors such as Bergvall & Welander (1996) stress the importance of clear responsibility in system management. They believe that the different actors must sign contracts in order to clarify the responsibility. They see the computer department as a supplier and the users as clients /buyers. In the framework of principal-agent theory the users are the principals and the suppliers are the agents.

If the principal is in business operation, he wants to buy good computer services and has often the possibilities to choose between different agents (suppliers). An agent can be the "in-house computer department supplier " or an external supplier. The principal has now the possibility to use a contract that discriminates between the agents.

Suppose that you as the principal regard a project where you know that a certain ability (competence) is required. However, it is not possible to know the different agents' abilities. If you also know that a lack of competence will lead to certain consequences in the project, you can design the contract in such a way that it will be too costly for an agent to claim that he has a certain ability and then fail. Thus only those agents who know that they have the specific ability will make a bid for the project.

An awareness of the importance of a good contract will hopefully change the focus in this type of purchasing, from lowest bid to the design of contracts.

In work flow theories there has been a shift from regarding everything as physically well-defined and well-behaved entities to include human beings as independent interpreting units. Speech act theories have shown the importance of communication between the actors. However, the broader understanding of these theories has shown that it is possible to discuss in terms of costs or efficiency. Here generalised transaction costs might help to structure the problem. The main advantage of this approach is that it helps you to identify the different flows of activities and information. It therefore makes it easy to understand or to explain the different outcomes.

The generalised transaction cost approach has similarities with Business Process Reengineering (BPR). Renzhog (1996), for example, claims that the process view has three different approaches. Firstly you can create a management structure. Secondly you can improve the performance of the process and thirdly you can make the staff process-oriented in their daily work. The first approach adding the staff's way of working provides the generalised transaction cost approach.

# References

Akerlof, G. (1970), "The Market for Lemons: Qualitative Uncertainty and the Market Mechanism." *Quarterly Journal of Economics*, Vol. 84, pp. 488-500.

Bervall, M. & Welander, T. (1996) *Affärsmässig systemförvaltning*, Student-litteratur, Lund, Sweden [*Business-Driven Systems Maintenance*].

Coase, R.H. (1937) "The Nature of the Firm," *Economica*, Vol. 4, pp. 386-405.

Conrad, C. (1985) *Strategic Organizational Communication: Cultures, Situations and Adaptation*, Holt, Rinehart and Winston, New York.

Eisenhardt, K. (1989) "Agency Theory: Assessment and Review", *Academy of Management Review*, Vol. 14, No. 1, pp. 57-74.

Heath, C., & Tversky, A. (1991) "Preference and Belief: Ambiguity and Competence in Choice under Uncertainty", *Journal of Risk and Uncertainty*, Vol. 4, pp. 5-28.

Jensen, M. & Meckling, W. (1976) "Theory of the firm: Managerial Behavior, Agency Costs and Capital Structure", *Journal of Financial Economics*, Vol. 3, pp. 305-360.

Lindström, J. & Rapp, B. (1996) "On Costs in Teleworking", *International Transaction in Operational Research*, Vol. 3, No 1 pp. 51-63.

Rapp, B. (1993) "Informationshantering på individ- och organisationsnivå", in Ingelstam, L. & Sturesson, L. (eds.) *Brus över landet – Om informations-överflödet, kunskapen och människan*, Carlsson Bokförlag, Stockholm ["Treatment of Information on a Personal and an Organizational Level", in *Noise over the Country*].

Rapp, B. & Thorstenson, A. (1994) *Vem skall ta risken?* Studentlitteratur, Lund, Sweden [*Who Should Take the Risk?*].

Renzhog, O. (1996) *Core process management*, Licentiate thesis, LiU-Tek-Lic-1996:07, Linköping University, Linköping, Sweden.

Robertson, D. (1923) *The Control of Industry*, Nisbet, London.

Trevino, L.K., Daft, R.L. & Lengel, R.H. (1990) "Understanding Managers' Media Choices: A Symbolic Interactionist Perspective", in Fulk, J. & Stein-field, C. (eds.) *Organizations and Communication Technology,* Sage Publications, Newbury Park, California.

Williamson, O. (1975) *Markets and Hierarchies: Analysis and Antitrust Implications*, The Free Press, New York.

Williamson, O. (1979) "Transaction-Cost Economics: The Governance of Contractual Relations", *Journal of Law and Economics*, Vol. 22, No. 2, pp. 233-261.

# 11

# Business and Systems Development: Opportunities for an Integrated Way-of-Working

*Christer Nellborn*

*One of the problems with information system requirements engineering is that of traceability and validation. Validation of design against requirements is fairly well understood by researchers and practitioners today, but validation of requirements against stakeholder needs is still a comparatively unknown area. One of the reasons for this is that requirements validation is a cross-disciplinary topic. It involves both information system developers and business developers and has much to do with communicational problems. The competitive situation for many companies today with short product life cycles, rapid changes and demands for flexibility calls for an integrated business development and information systems development. A framework for classifying methodologies according to their ability to cover the span from strategic planning to information systems design is presented and discussed with some examples.*

## Introduction

To characterise the problem addressed in this chapter, let us start with an often-quoted field study by Curtis and Krasner (1988). Some years have passed since this field study, but it can be argued that the findings are of a general nature and that the conclusions in the Curtis' field study are still relevant today.

In a field study (Curtis & Krasner, 1988) of the software design process for large software development projects, the three most salient problems found, in terms of the additional effort or mistakes attributed to them, were:

- the lack, or scarceness of application domain knowledge
- fluctuating and conflicting requirements
- communication and co-ordination breakdowns between the participants in the projects

The problem with the thin spread of application domain knowledge in software development staffs manifested itself on an individual level as there were only few people who really understood the problem and the application domain well enough. On a project level this had as a result that substantial design effort was spent on co-ordinating a common understanding among the staff of both the application domain and how the system should perform within it. The conclusion pointing to the importance of managing learning, especially of the application domain, as a major factor in productivity, quality and costs.

It was found that the problem with fluctuating and conflicting requirements had many sources, but were usually the result of market factors such as differing needs among customers, the changing needs of a single customer, changes in underlying technologies of competitors' products and from misunderstanding the application domain. Other sources for requirements problems were company internal, such as marketing and corporate politics. The requirements were not the stable reference for implementation that they were intended to be. The communication and co-ordination processes within a project became crucial to coping with the fluctuation and conflict among requirements.

The third problem, communication and co-ordination breakdowns, is about the difficulties communicating within and between groups and organisations. Organisational boundaries hindered understanding the requirements and temporal boundaries buried the design rationale. The complexity of the customer interface hindered the establishment of stable requirements and increased the communication and negotiation costs.

In the report of the case studies, three issues are suggested for improving software productivity and quality:

- Increase the amount of application domain knowledge across the entire software development staff.

- Software development tools and methods must accommodate change as an ordinary process and support the representation of uncertain design decisions. Change management and propagation is crucial throughout the design and development process.

• The software development environment must become a medium of communication to integrate people, tools and information.

## *A communication problem*

In the field study of Curtis and Krasner, poor communication was identified as one of the main problems. This problem has several interesting dimensions, for example:

• a social dimension concerning how individuals communicate and develop common understandings

• a contextual dimension concerning how individuals and groups interpret and describe the world around them

• a intentionality dimension concerning differences in intention, ambition, scope, purpose, planning etc.

• a time dimension concerning how context and interpretations change over time

In this chapter, based on Nellborn (1996), the focus is on the contextual and intentionality dimensions and in particular on how methodologies for business and information systems development address this communication problem.

## *The "Berlin wall" dilemma*

Business developers and information systems developers have for many years worked side-by-side on opposite sides of a communicational equivalent of the Berlin wall. Both living in the same place but with very different frames of reference and value systems and knowing very little about what life is like on the other side. They have communicated mainly by throwing things over the wall, such as requirement specifications, data models, prototypes, policy documents, design models, test procedures, QA-documents etc. Both sides making assumptions about the knowledge, needs and context of the other side.

On the business development side, the ability to handle changes in customer requirements is often a high priority. Today, many organisations experience that customer requirements change more rapidly now than only a few years ago. Also markets change rapidly thus sometimes making it necessary to make changes even before they become customer demands, in order to remain in the market.

The role of information systems and information technology is more central to the business now than a few years ago. The telecom industry is a good example of this. Telecom companies compete with new and more flexible services. Interviews with product developers and product managers in telecom companies has shown that new services typically have to be available within 12-18 months from the first idea or detected need and will have a life cycle of perhaps 3-5 years. Many of these services are completely automated information handling. From this point of view, it is obvious that the development of information system and the development of the business are opposite sides of a coin and have to be performed simultaneously and that the information systems development process must be able to handle uncertainty, rapid changes and conflicting requirements.

On the information system development side on the other hand, stability and persistence are key issues. Requirements on the new information services should be clear, precise, consistent and preferably valid for a long time period. Given a well-defined, unambiguous, consistent and stable set of requirements, the task is to analyse the requirements and design a system that fulfil the requirements. From this point of view, it is obvious that the "erratic" behaviour of stakeholders continuously changing the requirements will cause problems.


## Approaches to solving the dilemma

Each project facing the above-described dilemma have to choose a strategy to handle it. From discussions with business developers and information systems developers the different approaches can largely be classified as follows:

- More formal specifications: Stabilising the requirements by using formal methods, descriptions and languages. The idea is that there exists a well-defined, unambiguous, consistent set of requirements that is free from contradictions. The cause for the dilemma is that requirements are too "fuzzy" i.e. not described formally. By using formal specifications a consistent, provable set of requirements can be defined.

- Fragmentation of development projects: Divide-and-conquer approach. Repeatedly splitting up large development projects in a number of small, manageable pieces until the set of requirements for each piece becomes consistent. The cause for the dilemma is the size of the planned system. It is impossible and unnecessary to get a complete, consistent set of requirements.

- Standard application packages: No in-house development. Developing systems in-house is too expensive and also unnecessary. The idea is to integrate standard components bought off the shelf into a complete system. The dilemma is caused by too much freedom in formulating requirements. The business processes and the information system components can both be adjusted to form a working system.

- Integrated way-of-working: Integration of methodologies and techniques for business development and information systems development. The cause for the dilemma is a communication problem which stems from the fact that business development and information systems development are seen as separate issues performed by different people and not as two components of the same solution to a problem. By integrating methodologies, techniques, tools and way-of-working for the two, the communication problem is reduced and the development approach becomes more holistic and the development cycle becomes (ideally) seamless.

In this chapter we explore the last approach.

# The relation between enterprise and information system

The relation between the enterprise and its information systems is complex and has many aspects. It can be argued that it is difficult to separate the information system of an enterprise from the enterprise itself. It is an integrated part of the enterprise, whether manual or computerised. Thus it is not unreasonable to argue that the development of the enterprise (the business) and the information system are interconnected and are equally difficult to separate. We will use the requirements engineering process as a starting point for the discussion since it is in that process that the problems with the relation between business development and information system development often become obvious.

In an ideal requirements engineering case, the requirements on the information system form a set of non-contradicting, well defined needs in a consistent and well understood enterprise with a homogeneous group of users and requirement holders. Figure 1 illustrates this.

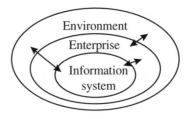

*Figure 1. An ideal requirements analysis situation.*

In this case, requirements on the information system come from the enterprise itself and from the environment around the enterprise. Both the enterprise and the environment have requirements on the new system either directly or indirectly through requirements that the environment have on the enterprise. The new information system may also have requirements (restrictions) on how to interact with it. Under the assumption that requirements are well known, well structured without contradictions and consistent over time, the requirements analysis process is very simple and straightforward.

In most cases, however, the situation is much more complex. Requirements originate from different enterprises and/or organisational units within the enterprise and from stakeholders and users with different views and ideas about the purpose of the new information system (see Figure 2). These requirements are often contradicting and may change more or less rapidly over time.

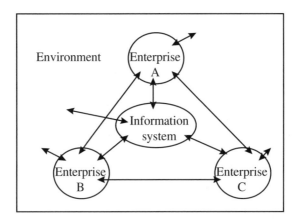

*Figure 2. A more complex environment to the information system. Conflicting requirements are likely to appear.*

In situations like this, the picture you get when bringing all requirements together is often confusing. The requirements engineer is the one experiencing the problem but it is a problem for the enterprise as a whole and not a problem just for the systems developer. In fact, contradicting requirements on the IS support systems can indicate more general problems within the enterprise and/or between stakeholders.

It is not uncommon that projects that start off as pure information system development projects after some time have expanded to include business development activities.

## Integrated business development – a framework

To describe how we view the interaction and dependencies between the enterprise and the information systems we put the purpose of the information systems in the perspective of the purpose of the enterprise for which it is being developed, see Figure 3.

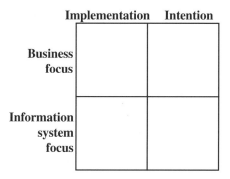

*Figure 3. Four areas of interest for the development process.*

The business focus (the top two squares) refers to issues relating to the business itself.

- The implementational aspect of the business focus (the top left square) refers to the structures of the business or enterprise. Concepts related to this square are for example business objects, business processes, product descriptions, product structures and organisational structures. This part of the framework relates to descriptions of the current state of the enterprise. Business rules may be found here since they can be of various degrees of precision and intentionality.

- The intentionality aspect of the business focus (the top right square) refers to the rational for the business. Concepts related to this square are for example business goals, vision, mission and strategy. Things used for guiding and directing an enterprise. The intentionality aspects describe the future either as achievable states for the business or as the direction in which it should go. Related concepts are opportunities (future states that may be chosen as goals), problems and threats (possible problems). Scenarios are also related. Closer to the top left quadrant (Business/Implementation) we find strategies, tactics and business rules.

The information system focus (the two squares at the bottom) refers to issues regarding the information system.

- The implementational aspect of the information system (the bottom left square) refers to the structures of the information system. Concepts related to this square are for example data structures, system architecture, database structures, and program design. Manual routines for administrating the information system belong here.

- The intentionality aspect of the information system (the bottom right square) refers to the purpose of the information system support to the business. The goals and visions for the information system support. What do we want with the information system support? What is the IT-strategy? But also the perhaps more interesting question about the information usage strategy.

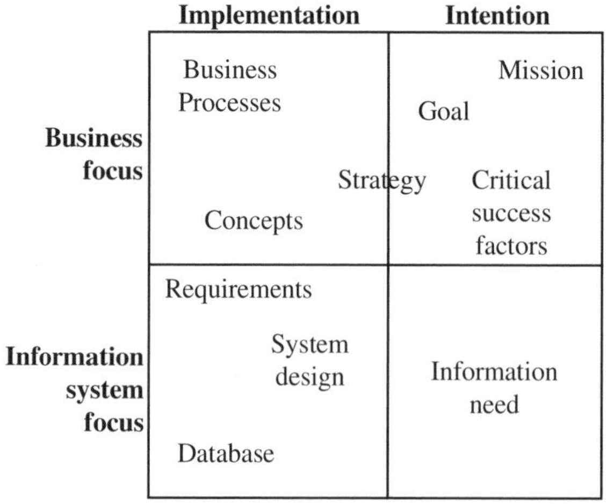

|  | Implementation | Intention |
|---|---|---|
| **Business focus** | Business Processes<br><br>Strategy<br>Concepts | Mission<br>Goal<br><br>Critical success factors |
| **Information system focus** | Requirements<br>System design<br><br>Database | Information need |

*Figure 4. IBM AD/Cycle Information Model, enterprise sub-model. Some concepts and where they belong in the framework.*

To illustrate what the four areas in the framework contain we can use the IBM AD/Cycle Information Model (IBM, 1992) which is a conceptually fairly rich model which attempts to cover many of the issues from business analysis to requirement analysis. In that model, an enterprise sub-model is defined. In that sub-model a number of concepts are used. Introducing the concepts in that sub-model to the framework would look something like Figure 4, above.

## *Inter-quadrant dependencies*

Figure 5 illustrates another important thing, the inter-quadrant dependencies. The organisation of an enterprise, i.e. the business processes, the administrative organisation etc., should be structured in order to support the achievement of the goals and nature of the business in the best possible way. Different enterprises have different goals. For example, a library may have different goals than a car manufacturer and need a different type of organisation than the car manufacturer.

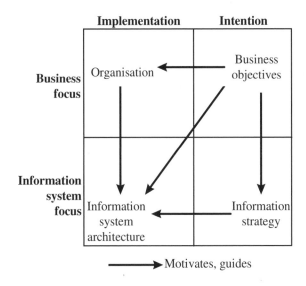

*Figure 5. The inter-quadrant dependencies.*

The information strategy is also dependent on, and should reflect the business objectives. If the business objectives state that, for instance, all new information systems must integrate with all old information systems within the enterprise, the information strategy must reflect this.

The computerised information system supports the organisation in the achievement of its goals. The information system architecture is therefore dependent on the goals of the enterprise, its organisation and information strategies.

Changes to the business goals, the administrative organisation, the business processes or the information strategies etc. all have effect on the information system and on the development of information systems. In a rapidly changing environment it is therefore important to have methods, tools and techniques that can make the implications of changes clear and support the implementation of changes in the information system in a fast and controlled way.

## Requirements engineering

In traditional requirements engineering, the starting point for the analysis-development cycle has been a description of the way the organisation works along with ideas of what the information support to be developed should do. The task for the requirements engineer has been to formalise the ideas into requirements and later to verify that the system design meet the requirements, see Figure 6.

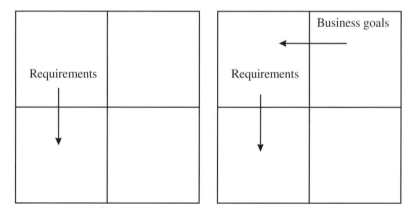

*Figure 6 (left). The scope of traditional requirements engineering methodologies.*

*Figure 7 (right). The scope of modern requirements engineering methodologies.*

Modern requirements engineering methodologies also include analysis of business goals, what effect they have on the business organisation and information systems requirements. See Figure 7, above.

So far there are very few commercially used development methodologies that cover the development of information-, information system- and information technology strategies, (the lower right field in the framework).

In the future it is likely that strategic business planning and information systems development will be part of the same development process. One way of working in such a process would be to start with the strategic planning of the business and then analyse the dependency chains from the business objectives, via organisation and via information strategy to information system design (links A, B, C, D and E in Figure 8) in an iterative manner.

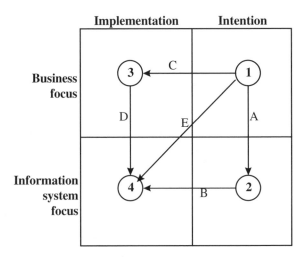

*Figure 8. The general movement over time in a design and development process for information system is from area 1 to area 4 iteratively via area 2 and 3.*

The analysis must not take too much time since the business will change continuously and if too much time is spent on the business analysis, the early requirements for the information system may become out of date and therefore of no use, no matter how detailed they are.

In these four quadrants different requirements on the information system can be discovered and because of the dependency between the quadrants, requirements originating from all quadrants are needed to ensure that the right system is developed. For this reason, we need good tools, techniques and methodologies to discover, identify, analyse and develop these requirements.

# Applying the framework

The framework was developed as a tool for classifying methodologies and models according to focus and scope. For example, one methodology might focus mainly on IS/IT strategy issues but with some aspects on how IS/IT strategies link to business objectives and how IS/IT strategies should be used when designing a systems architecture. Such a methodology would have a coverage in the framework that looks something like Figure 9.

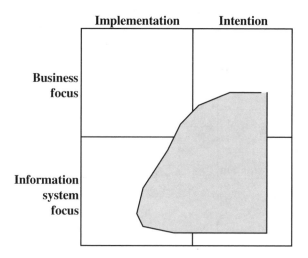

*Figure 9. Illustrating possible coverage of a development methodology having a focus on IS/IT strategy questions.*

A different methodology would get a different coverage in the framework. Figure 10 shows an example of a methodology with a focus on the organisation, its processes and the design of information systems.

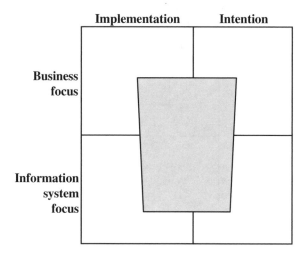

*Figure 10. Methodology with emphasis on the processes and organisation of an enterprise and on the design of information systems.*

The methodologies in the above two examples have some overlap in focus but are basically complementary. They might therefore be suitable to integrate. Further, more detailed, analysis of the two is necessary to find they are suitable to integrate on a more detailed, conceptual level.

## *The framework applied to Porter, Process Management and OOA*

The Value Chain by Michael Porter (Porter, 1985) is one of the more well known and referred ideas for strategic business planning. The idea can roughly be described as a way to describe the business functions, their contributions to customer value and how our business fit in with suppliers and customers in a value system. The main objective with using the Value Chain is to have a profit that is above average in the long run. This is achieved through creating and maintaining competitive advantage. The competitive advantage is based on product differentiation and low product cost.

Some of the basic concepts are strategic business unit, primary activity, support activity, and customer value. In the framework, the Value Chain would get an approximate coverage as in Figure 11.

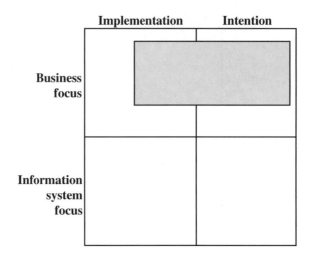

*Figure 11. The framework applied to Porter Value Chain.*

Process Management (Steneskog, 1991) builds on the idea that an organisation can improve its performance regarding cost and customer value by organising the company in processes, well structured and with a clearly defined customer focus. Main objective is to achieve better performing processes. Basic concepts are process, sub process, process owner, process interface, customer, process object and measurement. In the framework, Process Management would approximately have a coverage as in Figure 12.

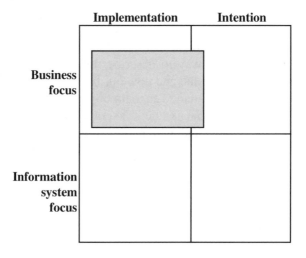

*Figure 12. The framework applied to Process Management.*

Object Oriented Analysis (Coad & Yourdon, 1991) is an example of a methodology for analysis and design of object-oriented programs and systems. The main objective is (roughly) to analyse and structure the information system needs and describe them in terms of (object-oriented) classes and information systems services. Basic concepts are class, object, subject, attribute and service. In the framework, OOA would cover something like in Figure 13.

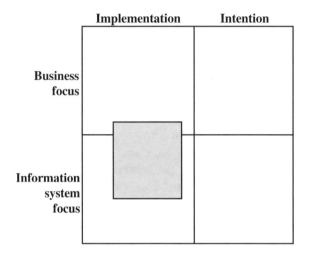

*Figure 13. The framework applied to OOA.*

From this very simple analysis we can conclude that there is some overlap between the Values Chain and Process Management but not very much overlap between OOA and the others. This is not surprising. What may be surprising, or at least interesting, is to note that not one of the three addresses the intentionality aspect of the information systems.

The semantic analysis used in the example is of course very surface. To really understand what methodologies can or can not be used together fruitfully one must investigate how they are used in practice and also do a more thorough semantic and pragmatic analysis of the concepts in each of the methodologies. However, on an overview level, the framework does provide a simple tool for showing the focus and ambition for methodologies.

# Further work

Further work will focus on empirical studies regarding the use of methodologies and on theoretical studies and classification of the metaphorical underpinnings to methodologies.

# Conclusions

A framework for classifying development methodologies based on simple semantic analysis has been presented. Through examples we have shown that through a graphical illustration technique, overlaps and gaps in methodology chains can be detected. We have also discussed the role of information strategies in relation to business development and information systems development. Also, we have discussed the role of the requirements engineer in relation to the framework, indicating that the role will change from focus on information system requirements to focus on the analysis and description of problems related to the integrated business- and information system. Maybe the name of the role will change as well. From information system requirements engineer to, perhaps, business system requirements engineer?

# Acknowledgements

The research was funded by NUTEK, the Swedish National Board for Industrial and Technical Development.

# References

Coad, P., & Yourdon, E. (1991) *Object Oriented Analysis*, Prentice Hall, Englewood Cliffs, New Jersey.

Curtis, B., & Krasner, H. (1988) "A Field Study of the Software Design Process for Large Systems", *Communications of the ACM*, Vol. 31, No. 11, pp. 1268-1287.

IBM (1992) *AD/Cycle Information Model Overview*, IBM.

Nellborn, C. (1996) "Dependencies between Business Development and Information System Development", in Dahlbom, B., Ljungberg, F., Nuldén, U., Simon, K., Stage, J. & Sørensen, C. *Proceedings of IRIS 19*, Gothenburg Studies in Informatics, Report 8, Department of Informatics, Göteborg University, Göteborg, Sweden, pp.198-212.

Porter, M. (1985) *Competitive Advantage: Creating and Sustaining Superior Performance*, Free Press, New York.

Steneskog, G. (1991) *Process Management: Konsten att styra och utveckla ett företags administrativa processer*, Liber, Malmö, Sweden [*Process Management: The Art of Managing and Developing a Company's Administrative Processes*].

# Part III:

# Description of Different Aspects

.

# 12

# The Business Developer's Toolbox: Chains and Alliances between Established Methods

*Anders G. Nilsson*

*Many companies are trying to create useful toolboxes for their method application in business development work. The main problem here is to build fruitful links between different methods in use. This chapter will show a framework for method integration using chains and alliances of established methods in the market. The framework is based on some techniques for meta-modelling and method-evaluation. The perspective taken is how a business manager can communicate with a systems expert by applying common methods.*

## Method use – some needs in practice

Business managers and systems experts often experience frustration when information support for business operations is being discussed. A major part of the problem is due to lack of essential communication and accusation from both sides is often the result. "The business people do not know what they want!" or "The systems people do not understand what we need!" However, communication is more than talking. It requires a firm base for common understanding, a common language.

It is in this sense a specific method can be a useful tool to create a common language between business and systems people. By a method we mean concrete guidelines or prescriptions for a systematic way of working with development tasks in organisations. It is possible to distinguish three main constituents of a method (see Nilsson, 1995):

- *Perspectives*; basic principles, views and assumptions which influence the proposed work between affected interest groups in business development

- *Work tasks*; guidelines to manage different issues and decisions during the development process. The development work is divided into a number of perceivable and delimited tasks, e.g. creation of different types of business models

- *Interest groups*; list of actors who could participate during the development process together with possible forms of collaboration. Specify "who is responsible for what" during the development work.

Successful management and planning of business enterprises require rich and precise models (descriptions) of both the real business operations and its links to the supporting information systems. Business modelling is a way of working to achieve such descriptions. Today, we have many established methods and models for development work in the market. See e.g. Avison & Fitzgerald (1995).

There has been much debate over the years of the actual effects of method use in practice. Below we summarise some needs for using methods to support development work:

- *Requirement specifications*; the need to produce exact, consistent and complete requirement specifications for designing the future business and information operations

- *Explain IT possibilities*; the need for explaining how new IT possibilities can improve business processes and sharpen corporate strategies in organisations

- *Describing business flows*; the need for describing and co-ordinating the complex nature of material flows, information flows and cash flows in enterprises

In today's business world, information support has become a more integrated part of business operations and, in many cases, a vital part of the business mission itself. In fact, the information systems can also create new business opportunities for the companies to reinforce their competitive edge in the market place.

In most cases development of corporate strategies, business operations and its information support are often carried out as separate change processes and as independent projects in companies. There is very limited or no organisational co-ordination and timing between business and systems development. The challenge here is to use efficient methods to make a progress in reaching a more holistic view of development work in organisations.

# Business developer's toolbox – a framework

A general view in business administration research is that products are going through a life cycle. In the same way we can regard business and information operations from a life cycle perspective. See Nilsson (1995). A proposal to such a life cycle could be as follows:

1. Business development

2. Operation and maintenance management

3. Business termination

We will here focus on the first stage of the life cycle, namely business development. Business development generally consists of different tasks. See Österle (1995), Earl et al (1996) and Tolis & Nilsson (1996). We can recognise three levels of development work in practice with a distinct scope and focus (see Figure 1):

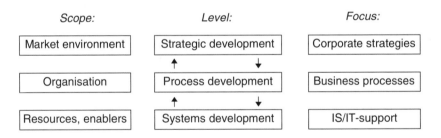

*Figure 1. Three levels of development work.*

- *Strategic development*; focusing on corporate strategies for improving the relations between our company and the actors in the market environment (e.g. customers, clients, suppliers and business partners).

- *Process development*; focusing on how to make the business processes more efficient within our company. The workflow between different functions in the organisation is designed in a new and better way.

- *Systems development*; focusing on how support from information systems (IS) and information technology (IT) can be useful resources and efficient enablers for running the business operations more professionally and strengthen the competitive edge of our business achievements.

Today no "super" method giving support to the whole development work in a company is to be found in the market. On the contrary, the current methods are delimited to a concrete level of development work according to Figure 1. Furthermore, methods for the same level somewhat "attack" different problems or perspectives in business and systems work.

There is not a need to work at a "top-down" fashion from strategic development through process development down to systems development. In a real case one can start at certain development level and let the outcome of this work trigger some other levels upwards and downwards often in several rounds (indicated by the arrows in Figure 1). We can therefore regard the development levels as essential inquiry areas during a whole change process.

In a concrete situation, a combination of methods that suits a specific company and its organisational culture has to be chosen. The policy for our research work is to take existing and well-known methods used in practice as a starting-point. One good argument for this is that established methods continuously would be refined and improved by their vendors (e.g. consultant agencies). The main idea is to work out how these methods for business development can or should be integrated in different situations.

The company's purpose of its own work with business development guides how the method integration should look like. There are two possible ways to link methods to each other (see Nilsson, 1992):

- *Method chains*; integration of methods between different levels of development work. This approach to combine methods is a kind of vertical integration. We create transitions or "roads" between methods through all three levels of development work.

- *Method alliances*; integration of methods within the same level of development work. This approach to combine methods is a kind of horizontal integration. We create alliances of methods from the same area (or level) in order to tackle several problems or perspectives in concrete situations.

We have so far presented a framework for method use in business development. Many companies today face several problems in linking different methods to each other. Sometimes a vision of a so called business developer's toolbox is presented. Such a toolbox should be a practical guide for companies to connect selected methods with respect to their specific situation for development work. We will here sketch a business developer's toolbox using the concept of method chains and alliances.

# Method engineering – research directions

Companies often stress the need for overall encompassing methods in order to be able to manage the broad spectrum of situations that may appear during development work in practice. Many attempts have been made to expand and enlarge existing methods in the market to comprise different levels of development work. As an example we can create a simple and straightforward method as a starting point and from this recommend several expansions or additions for different types of special cases. If we look at the front-line in research about method engineering today it is possible to identify some promising directions:

- *Method fragments*; to identify building blocks for development work through coherent pieces of existing methods. It is possible to distinguish product fragments (deliverables and results) and process fragments (outlines and procedures) for a specific method. Method fragments can have different granularity or range for development work. See Brinkkemper (1996).

- *Method components*; to identify generic and flexible components behind existing methods in an object oriented way of thinking. Method components should be exchangeable and adaptable in order to form integral parts in different application contexts. There is a possibility for re-using components between different methods. See Röstlinger & Goldkuhl (1996).

- *Method integration*; to combine sufficiently similar methods within or along the whole life cycle. Method combination could be performed by inter-process or intra-process integration. Inter-process integration of methods occurs across two or more phases (sub-processes) in the life-cycle. Intra-process integration of methods occurs within a specific phase of the life-cycle. See Ryan, Kronlof & Sheehan (1996).

The idea to partition specific methods in a set of delimited parts facilitates an analysis if methods from the same or different levels of development work can be combined or integrated in an efficient manner. In other words the possibility to create chains or alliances of several methods to support the entire development work. A method chain is a kind of inter-process method integration, while a method alliance is a kind of intra-process method integration. For investigating suitable method integrations we will now propose some techniques for meta-modelling and method-evaluation.

# Meta-modelling – a base for method integration

Meta-modelling or method-modelling is a sharp instrument to investigate possible connections between methods for business and systems development. By such a meta-modelling we describe the functioning of the development methods in a company environment (see Tolvanen & Lyytinen, 1993). In order to catch the main ideas behind the methods for business development, we may use three types of meta-models regarding (see Figure 2):

- *Intentions*; meta-modelling of goals, visions, problems, strengths, interest groups and critical success factors for using a specific method

- *Concepts*; meta-modelling of essential constructs, conceptions and definitions building up a specific method ("building blocks")

- *Ways of working*; meta-modelling of activities (phases, steps) and main deliverables (models, documents) from development work applying a specific method

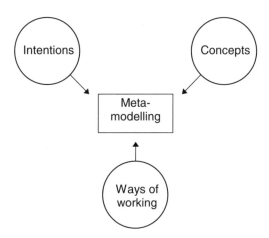

*Figure 2. Meta-modelling from three perspectives.*

Meta-modelling shows us, in this sense, three perspectives for studying specific methods (Figure 2). Meta-modelling gives a deeper understanding of the logic behind different methods and it facilitates creation of appropriate method chains and alliances. This could be done from work that tries to overlap meta-models for different methods. We can hence analyse if two methods e.g.:

- are contradictory or supplementary in character *(intentions)*
- have joint or dissimilar elements *(concepts)*
- can be connected in a sequential or parallel way *(ways of working)*

Such research efforts about meta-modelling will result in a general map or reference model for possible combinations of methods according to different business situations.

# Method-evaluation – for creating chains / alliances

Method-evaluation means that we do a critical review of specific methods and their parts in order to fulfil some declared purpose – in this case as a foundation for work with method integration. This evaluation should follow a systematic approach that comprises a set of well-defined steps of analysis. See e.g. Jayaratna (1994) and Olle et al (1991). Usually a method-evaluation is based on some selected criteria for judgement.

We will in this respect use the three types of meta models regarding intentions, concepts and ways of working as a base for evaluation of possible alternatives for method integration (see Figure 2). The work with method integration is here focused on how to find suitable chains and alliances between established methods in the market. Figure 3 shows a general map or reference model of some well-known methods for the three levels of development work in a company:

- *Strategic development*; e.g. The Balanced Scorecard/BSC (Kaplan & Norton, 1996), Porter's Value Chain (Porter, 1980 & 1985) and Ansplan (Ansoff & McDonnell, 1990)

- *Process development*; e.g. Business Process Reengineering or Redesign/BPR (Davenport, 1993), Total Quality Management/TQM (Ishikawa, 1985) and Rummler & Brache Group/RBG approach for process management (Rummler & Brache, 1995)

- *Systems development*; e.g. Yourdon Systems Method/YSM (Yourdon, 1993), Information Systems Work and Analysis of Changes/ISAC approach (Lundeberg et al, 1981) and Objectory (Jacobson et al, 1993 & 1994)

The general map for method integration in Figure 3 gives several ways to work with the development levels presented in Figure 1. We will now use some of the above mentioned methods when performing a few experiments with possible chains and alliances (indicated with lines in Figure 3) as a base for working with method integration.

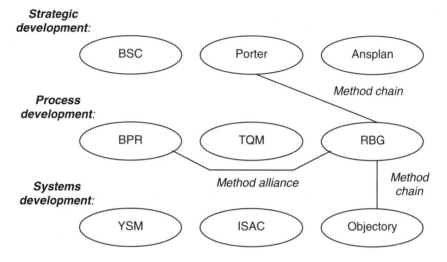

*Figure 3. General map of methods for integration into chains and alliances.*

# Method chain – experiment with three methods

We will now illustrate some concrete examples of how it is possible to combine several methods in a business developer's toolbox. The presented examples are based on some larger experiments of method-evaluations, carried out in our Business Modelling consortium. As a technique for method integration we will use the three types of meta-models regarding intentions, concepts and ways of working (Figure 2). We will start to show a proposal for a method chain, linking specific methods from the three levels of development work (Figure 1): Porter's method for strategic development, RBG's method for process development and the Objectory method for systems development. See Figure 3.

We recommend to start with an analysis of the *intentions* behind the studied methods. This could be done in several ways, but in this case we will analyse some goals stated by the creators of the three specific methods. An interesting thing is to find out if the methods are supplementary or contradictory in relation to each other. The argument to start with the "intention" aspect is just to sketch out whether the methods are in harmony or are disparate in character. In the latter case we should not try to do a method integration! We here focus on finding some overlaps between the meta-models of the three studied methods.

Figure 4 below shows extracts of meta-models regarding intentions or goals for the specific methods. The interpretation rules are the same as for ordinary means/ends models. The filled arrows always denote "contribute to". In Figure 4 the most important goal for the three specific methods is highlighted in a shaded form. Then we have tried to sketch supporting goals in two steps for each method. The small meta-intention-models only describe overall goals behind the three studied methods because of our limited space. But for our purposes we can do some interesting observations.

The main mission behind the Porter method is creating buyer value for the company's products. The reason for taking a customer perspective is the drive for companies to make a good marginal or profitability in order to survive in the business industry. A special competitive advantage influence both the customer value and the profitability of the company (strategic business unit). A competitive advantage can be achieved from a cost leadership strategy, differentiation strategy or a focused strategy on costs/differentiation. The Porter method also stresses the importance of sustaining superior performance in order to achieve competitive advantage.

The most important goal for the RBG method seems to be sustained performance improvement for a certain company in the marketplace. In order to achieve that we have to focus on both productivity issues for the organisational level and quality of work life issues on a job/performer level. The company should seek for adaptability in the process design for promoting the productivity as well as the quality of work life. The RBG method is based on a systems approach for creating adaptable systems inside the organisation.

The main goal behind the Objectory method is that systems development should be performed as an industrial process. The logic behind this is to minimise the system's life cycle cost. A leading idea is to work out reality-based business models for influencing the life cycle cost and making the development process more efficient. An analogy to systems entropy will guide the management of system's costs. Applying reusable objects will make it easier to achieve reduced costs and reality-based models.

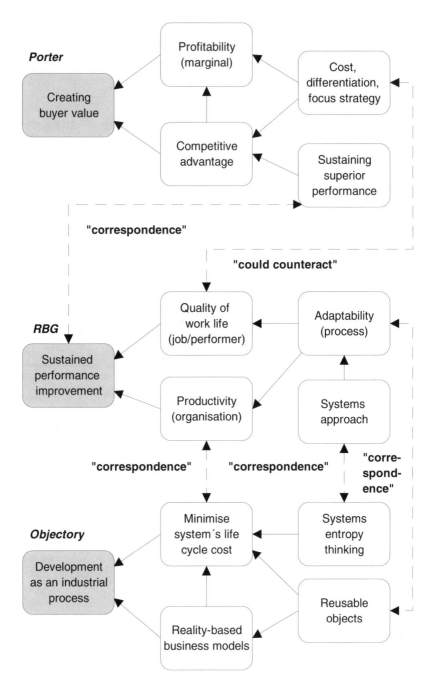

*Figure 4. Meta-models of intentions (goals) – method chain.*

After presenting the three small and limited meta-intention-models for the Porter, RBG and Objectory methods, we turn to analyse possible connections between the meta-models. Figure 4 shows some identified overlaps with help of dotted arrows. The three methods seem to be much in harmony with each other. There are some interesting relations between the overall goals for using the methods. Both the Porter method and the RBG method stress the importance of achieving sustained performance for a company to be competitive in the business industry. The RBG and Objectory methods have a correspondence: (i) when focusing on productivity and cost issues, (ii) in using principles from systems theory, and (iii) promoting flexible design through adaptability or reusable objects. A possible contradiction between two goals from the Porter and RBG methods has been noticed. The Porter method is not emphasising the importance of people or co-workers in the organisation. Therefore the goal quality of work life (RBG) could counteract with a too biased attention on cost and differentiation matters (Porter).

We have concluded from the meta-intention-models that the three specific methods have much in common when analysing the general view on business and systems development. It is now recommendable to do a more deep analysis of how the methods are structured or edified. A sharp instrument to support such an analysis is to make conceptual models of the three specific methods. Figure 5 below shows extracts of meta-models regarding the essential *concepts* or constructs in the specific methods. The interpretation rules are the same as for ordinary data models (conceptual models). We focus also here on finding some overlaps between the small meta-models of the three studied methods. More precisely we find out if the methods have some joint or dissimilar elements. If the studied methods have to many incompatible concepts it is worthless to try to do a fruitful method integration!

In Figure 5 the core concepts of three specific methods are highlighted in a shaded form. The main constructs of the Porter method is the value chain for a company (strategic business unit) and the value system for the whole industry. The value chain (and system) consists of value activities that are either primary for the value adding parts of the company or of a support character. The Porter method focuses on analysing the linkages between value activities within the company (internal linkages) or to other business actors in the industry (external or vertical linkages). The lessons learned is the fact that well-designed linkages often promote to strengthen the competitive advantage of our company. The pressure for a higher degree of competitive advantage requires that the value activities should be transformed to a certain degree.

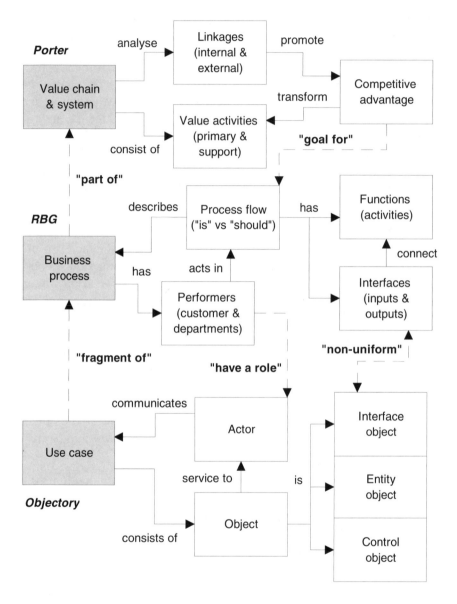

*Figure 5. Meta-models of concepts – method chain.*

The core concept of the RBG method is to study the business processes of our company. On a crude level the method distinguishes between primary, support and management processes that is similar to Porter's classification of value activities. A business process has several performers acting in different parts of the process flow. The performers could be customers to the company or various departments inside the company. The process flow describes the business process and has two building blocks: functions and interfaces. The interfaces connect functions (or activities) along the whole process flow by illustrating necessary inputs and outputs. The process flow could be sketched out both in the present state ("is"-flow) and in the desired future state ("should"-flow).

The core concept of the Objectory method could be the construct "object". This is natural because the method is classified as an approach to object-oriented systems development. But we have found out here that it is better to highlight the unique concept of "use case" in the Objectory method! This has to do with the context of trying to link Objectory to the other two methods and their core concepts (see below). In the Objectory method an actor communicates with a certain use case. A use case consists of objects which are of three kinds: interface object, entity object and control object. The objects in the use case give service to the actor.

After presenting the three small and limited meta-concept-models for the Porter, RBG and Objectory methods, we turn to analyse possible overlaps between the meta-models. Figure 5 shows some identified overlaps with help of dotted arrows. The three methods seem to be much in harmony with each other. There are some interesting connections between the core objects in the methods. A use case in the Objectory method can be regarded as a fragment of a business process in the RBG method. In a normal case a business process is a collection of use cases along the whole process flow. In special cases a use case could be the entire business process. A business process in the RBG method is a part of the value chain & system in the Porter method. The business process crosses some of the value activities within or between companies.

We have also found some other interesting results when comparing the three methods. A desired level of competitive advantage (Porter) could be a goal for managing the process flow (RBG) to a more efficient performance. Performers or users in the process flow (RBG) could have a role as an actor for triggering a certain use case for delivering desired services (Objectory). Despite these facts it will perhaps not be a straightforward task to do a method integration of the Porter, RBG and Objectory approaches. As an example we will pinpoint the fact that interfaces in the RBG method does not correspond to as a uniform construct to the interface object in the Objectory method. Possible solutions to this problem could be to introduce an intermediary (bridging) concept or maybe connect interfaces (RGB) with the more corresponding idea of entity objects (Objectory).

We have concluded from the meta-intention-models and the meta-concept-models that the three specific methods are possible to integrate in a method chain. This could be done in several ways. A more precise analysis of the *ways of working* with the methods would give more information of how to design a method chain between the Porter, RBG and Objectory approaches. Several methods in a chain can be connected in a sequential and/or parallel way. In the worst case we can have a situation where the ways of working in the studied methods are inconsistent with each other. Therefore we have to investigate the working procedures behind the methods. Figure 6 below shows extracts of meta-models for the ways of working in the three specific methods. The interpretation rules are the same as for ordinary data-flow models (diagrams). Also some possible links (overlaps) between the methods are marked with dotted lines.

The Porter method has not so explicit procedure for the exact way of working with strategic development in a company. But we have tried to grasp the main activities and deliverables in the Porter approach. Signals from the market or external environment could trigger the company to start an analysis of the competitive forces in the business industry. The purpose is to determine the industry profitability and the company's relative position within the business industry. The identified competitive profile is a good basis for analysing the potentials for one or more strategic business units (SBU) in the company.

The Porter method recommends in this sense to sketch a so called value chain model for the company and its business partners (customers, vendors). This model includes essential value activities and important internal and external linkages. The value chain analysis is a foundation to formulate concrete business strategies for the company. The strategy should position the competitive advantage (lower cost or product differentiation) and the competitive scope (broad or narrow target). The business strategies will be implemented in some way and assessed according to the business results. The Porter method is more focused on guidelines for strategy formulation than for strategy implementation.

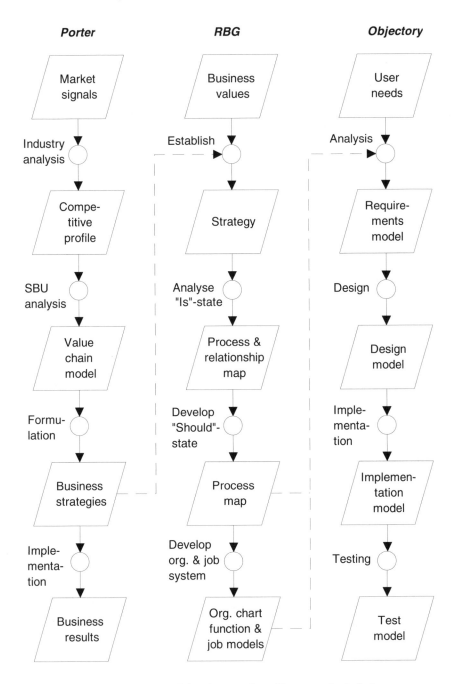

*Figure 6. Meta-models of ways of working – method chain.*

The RBG method has a concrete procedure for designing an organisation structure in several steps. We will here focus on the main activities and deliverables in the RGB approach concerning this respect. The starting point for the development work is to establish a clear strategy for guiding the business direction of the company. Then we analyse the business operations in the current situation. The "Is"-state is documented for both the organisation system in a relationship map and the existing process flow in a so called process map. In the next step we analyse the desired future situation ("Should"-state) for strategically significant processes that will be documented in a revised process map. Considering this process design we develop a new organisation structure and job/performer system. This work is documented in an organisation chart, function models for each department and necessary job models.

The Objectory method has a clear procedure for managing the systems development work. Systems development is defined as model building and is based on an object-oriented approach. The development work starts with a precise analysis of user needs and is documented in a requirements model with necessary use cases and including objects. This requirements specification is a basis for the construction phase. The construction phase consists of two steps: design and implementation. If possible we can here utilise ready-made components. The systems development ends up with a testing phase in order to verify if the complete system could be delivered. The test model consists of results from unit testing, integration testing and a holistic system testing.

After presenting the three small and limited meta-ways of working-models for the Porter, RBG and Objectory methods, we turn to analyse possible overlaps between the meta-models. Figure 6 shows some identified links with help of dotted arrows.

The three methods seem to be able to integrate with each other in a rather sequential way. The business strategies that have been worked out in the Porter method can be used as a valuable input to the starting phase in the RBG-method. Here we can establish the business strategies and try to relate them to the following process development work. The process map for the future situation ("Should"-state) together with the function/job models from the RBG method would be a good basis for working out the use cases in the requirements model according to the Objectory method.

# Method alliance – experiment with two methods

We will continue to illustrate a concrete example of how it is possible to combine several methods from the same development level (or inquiry area) in a business developer's toolbox. As a technique for method integration we will use the same types of meta-models regarding intentions (goals), concepts and ways of working. We will show a proposal for a method alliance within the process development level, linking RBG's method for process management and Davenports BPR method on process innovation. See the earlier presented general map in Figure 3.

We start with an analysis of the *intentions* or goals behind the methods. Figure 7 below shows extracts of meta-intention-models for the BPR and RBG methods. The small meta-model of goals for the RBG method is the same as shown before in Figure 4 about the earlier analysed method chain. What is new is the small meta-intention-model for the BPR-method.

The most important goal for the BPR method is to strive for dramatically improved business performance in customer value, delivery time and productivity. This should be achieved from a radical change in the key processes of the company – labelled process innovation by Davenport. A prerequisite for dramatic results and radical process change is a clear strategic vision from top management. A special focus in the BPR method is on identifying change levers or enablers for process innovation. These are of two categories: IT enablers versus organisational and human resource enablers. An enabler could represent both opportunities and constraints for practical work with process redesign.

There are some similarities and differences between the BPR and RBG methods when comparing the two small meta-intention-models. Figure 7 shows some identified overlaps with help of dotted arrows. The two methods share a common base of values. Both methods emphasise improved performance in business operations by process development work. In that matter the two methods do not differ in kind but slightly in difference – dramatic results (BPR) versus sustained results (RBG). There is also a correspondence in taken active part for a people or co-worker perspective. A difference of opinion is noticed regarding the view on pace of change. The BPR method proposes a radical change in contrary to the RBG method who proposes an adaptable approach depending on the particular situation how much change work is needed. A special feature in the BPR method – not found in the RBG method – is the conscious use of IT enablers for process development work.

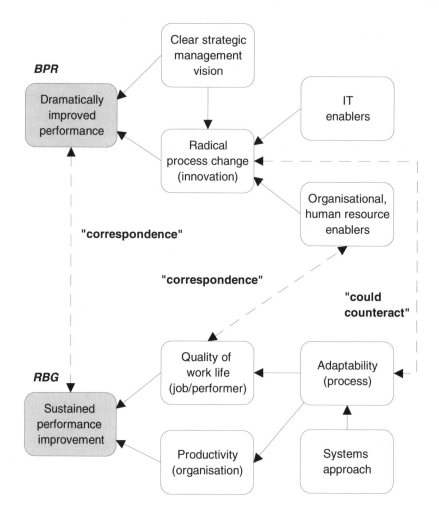

*Figure 7. Meta-models of intentions (goals) – method alliance.*

We can conclude from the meta-intention-models that the two methods could supplement and strengthen each other. It is now possible to take a closer look at the conceptual framework behind the BPR and RGB methods. Figure 8 below shows extracts of meta-models regarding some essential *concepts* or constructs in the specific methods. The small meta-model of concepts for the RBG method is the same as shown before in Figure 5 about the earlier analysed method chain. What is new is the small meta-concept-model for the BPR-method.

The core concept of the Davenports BPR method for process innovation is obviously the construct business process. According to Davenports definition represents a business process a specific ordering of work activities, connected by clearly identified inputs and outputs, and at the end designed to produce output to customers. Enablers in the shape of IT-factors and human/organisational factors are important to take care of in order to improve or innovate the business process under study.

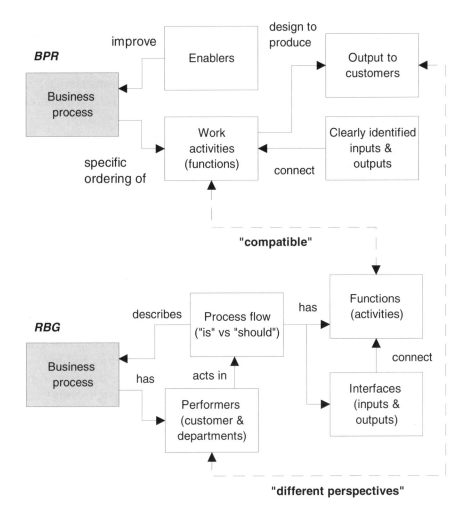

*Figure 8. Meta-models of concepts – method alliance.*

The BPR method (according to Davenport) and the RBG method (according to Rummler & Brache) have a rather similar perception of the business process concept. This is evident from studying the small meta-concept-models. Figure 8 shows some identified overlaps with help of dotted arrows. The definitions of the concept business process in the two studied methods are compatible with each other. It is only minor differences, e.g. work activities in the business process belonging to certain functions (BPR) or functions executing different activities along the process flow (RGB). A much bigger issue is the different perspectives taken about business actors. Davenport is through his BPR method more focused on creating a tangible process value to the customers while Rummler & Brache are more oriented towards keeping a good order on the processes and their performers for managing the "white space" in the organisation chart. This is in line with the distinction between external and internal process perspectives on development work (see Tolis & Nilsson, 1996).

We can conclude from the meta-intention-models and meta-concept-models that the two methods have many joint characteristics and a few crucial differences. It is a good forecast for making a method integration in the form of a method alliance for the process development level. But we now have to check the degree of correspondence concerning the *ways of working* in the two specific methods. Figure 9 below shows extracts of meta-models illustrating activities and deliverables in the BPR and RGB methods. The small meta-model of ways of working for the RBG method is the same as shown before in Figure 6 about the earlier analysed method chain. What is new is the small meta-ways of working-model for the BPR-method.

The BPR method according to Davenport is a rigorous approach concerning detailed activities for work with process innovation. Process innovation is a kind feasibility study or change analysis leaving out the rest of the development work such as detailed process design, systems construction and deployment. Figure 9 shows on a crude level the way of working with process innovation. A possible trigger is perceived needs for change in the organisation or by the customers. The development work starts up with identifying key (critical) processes for redesign and investigating change enablers suitable for the specific situation in the company. After that we develop visions and objectives for the key processes in order to facilitate measurement and assessment of business performance. Then comes a phase with understanding and improving existing processes according to the business objectives. A process map of the current flow is prepared.

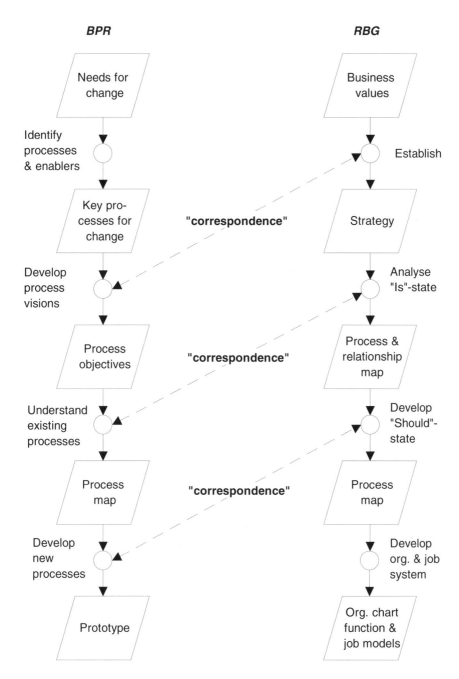

*Figure 9. Meta-models of ways of working – method alliance.*

The process innovation work ends up with a rough development of new processes. This will be done as prototypes because of the high risk of radical process change.

The BPR method and the RBG method have much in common when comparing the two meta-way of working-models. Figure 9 shows some identified overlaps with help of dotted arrows. Three activities from the two specific methods have a high degree of correspondence. This is a good basis for method integration. We could join the best of these activities to a more holistic approach for process development. What is more interesting is that the two remaining activities (from different methods) could supplement and enrich such a holistic approach in the beginning and end of the process development work. If a thorough document analysis of the main deliverable "process map" is made we will find that the RBG method has more precise drawing guidelines and a richer set of symbol legends. In other words using the process maps from the RGB method would sharpen the way of working with Davenports BPR-method.

## Methods in concert – What to keep in mind?

It is important to select methods that are in a harmony with the company's way of working with business and systems development. There is also a need to adapt the selected methods to the specific, unique situation of the company. Lessons learned from practice are that methods for business modelling could not be used in a straight-forward manner according to the schoolbook!

Perceived goals and intended purposes for different kinds of development work should guide the selection and adaptation of suitable methods that will be integral parts of a business developer's toolbox. Applied methods should be in a good concert! We have presented a framework for linking established and well-known methods from the same or different levels of development work. The constructs "method chain" and "method alliance" are introduced as roadmaps in a business developer's toolbox.

An advice to companies, which are about to implement business modelling in their organisations, is to work out an own "requirements profile" of method application. As a guideline we can use the above mentioned general map or reference model for sketching out possible integration of methods for strategy, process and systems development (see Figure 3). This could bridge the perceived communication gap between business and systems people in change projects. In such a situation there are good possibilities to create business driven systems that really would strengthen the company's competitive edge in the marketplace.

Finally some reflections on how to penetrate methods for business modelling in an efficient manner by using techniques for meta-modelling. We have proposed three types of meta-models regarding intentions (goals), concepts and ways of working. Some limited experiments have been performed using meta-models as a base for linking well-known methods to each other. This type of meta-modelling is a sharp instrument to catch the main ideas behind the selected methods for business modelling and for investigating possible connections between them.

The impression is that the established methods are very well packaged and documented in handbooks and publications. But during the work with meta-modelling we have found some interesting results in general terms:

- The *intentions* or goals for using the methods are often implicit and seem much to be inside the "head of the method creator"

- The *concepts* or "building blocks" are relatively easy to identify in the methods but rather difficult then to relate or connect to each other in a purposeful way

- The *ways of working* or proposed activities/deliverables in different methods varies very much in clarity, distinction and precision

There is a need for more research on principles for and effects of meta-modelling (together with method-evaluation) as an instrument for creating "method chains" and "method alliances". We need e.g. deeper knowledge about how to add or modify methods before combining them to more comprehensive approaches for business development. This study shows that the research about method integration or method engineering represents a vital part of the Information Systems area, but should be met with a great respect because of its complexities in many respects!

# Acknowledgements

The research was funded by NUTEK, the Swedish National Board for Industrial and Technical Development.

# References

Ansoff, I. & McDonnell, E. (1990) *Implanting Strategic Management*, 2nd ed., Prentice-Hall, New York.

Avison, D.E. & Fitzgerald, G. (1995) *Information Systems Development: Methodologies, Techniques and Tools*, 2nd ed., McGraw-Hill, London.

Brinkkemper, S. (1996) "Method Engineering: Engineering of Information Systems Development Methods and Tools", in Wrycza & Zupancic (eds.) *Proceedings of The Fifth International Conference on Information Systems Development – ISD'96*, Gdansk, Poland, pp. 69-78.

Davenport, T.H. (1993) *Process Innovation – Reengineering Work through Information Technology*, Harvard Business School Press, Boston, Massachusetts.

Earl, M.J., Sampler, J.L. & Short, J.E. (1996) "Relationships Between Strategy and Business Process Reengineering: Evidence From Case Studies", in Earl, M.J. (ed.) *Information Management – The Organizational Dimension*, Oxford University Press, Oxford, pp. 171-195.

Ishikawa, K. (1985) *What is Total Quality Control? – The Japanese Way*, Prentice-Hall, Englewood Cliffs, New Jersey.

Jacobson, I., Christerson, M., Jonsson, P. & Övergaard, G. (1993) *Object-Oriented Software Engineering – A Use Case Driven Approach*, revised fourth printing, Addison-Wesley, Wokingham, England.

Jacobson, I., Ericsson, M. & Jacobson, A. (1994) *The Object Advantage – Business Process Reengineering with Object Technology*, Addison-Wesley, Wokingham, England.

Jayaratna, N. (1994) *Understanding and Evaluating Methodologies – A Systemic Framework*, McGraw-Hill, London.

Kaplan, R.S. & Norton, D.P. (1996) *The Balanced Scorecard – Translating Strategy into Action*, Harvard Business School Press, Boston, Massachusetts.

Lundeberg, M., Goldkuhl, G. & Nilsson, A.G. (1981) *Information Systems Development – A Systematic Approach*, Prentice-Hall, Englewood Cliffs, New Jersey.

Nilsson, A.G. (1992) *Business Modelling as a Base for Information Systems Development*, EFI Research Paper 6479, The Economic Research Institute (EFI), Stockholm School of Economics, Stockholm.

Nilsson, A.G. (1995) "Evolution of Methodologies for Information Systems Work – A Historical Perspective", in Dahlbom, B. (ed.) *The Infological Equation – Essays in Honor of Börje Langefors*, Gothenburg Studies in Information Systems, Göteborg University, Göteborg, Sweden, pp. 251-285.

Olle, T.W., Hagelstein, J., Macdonald, I.G., Rolland, C., Sol, H.G., Van Assche, F.J.M. & Verrijn-Stuart, A.A. (1991) *Information Systems Methodologies – A Framework for Understanding*, 2nd ed., Addison-Wesley, Wokingham, England.

Porter, M.E. (1980) *Competitive Strategy – Techniques for Analyzing Industries and Competitors*, The Free Press, New York.

Porter, M.E. (1985) *Competitive Advantage – Creating and Sustaining Superior Performance*, The Free Press, New York.

Rummler, G.A. & Brache, A.P. (1995) *Improving Performance: How to Manage the White Space on the Organization Chart*, 2nd ed., Jossey-Bass Publishers, San Francisco.

Ryan, K., Kronlof, K. & Sheehan, A. (1996) "Method Integration", in Jayaratna, N. & Fitzgerald, B. (ed.) *Lessons Learned from the Use of Methodologies*, Proceedings of the Fourth Conference of the British Computer Society (BCS), Information Systems Methodologies Specialist Group, University of College Cork, Cork, Ireland, pp. 235-246.

Röstlinger, A. & Goldkuhl, G. (1996) *Generisk Flexibilitet – På väg mot en komponentbaserad metodsyn*, VITS, Research Report LiTH-IDA-R-96-15, Linköping University, Linköping, Sweden [*Generic Flexibility – Towards a Component-based View of Methods*].

Tolis, C. & Nilsson, A.G. (1996) "Using Business Models in Process Orientation", in Lundeberg, M. & Sundgren, B. (eds.) *Advancing Your Business – People and Information Systems in Concert*, The Economic Research Institute (EFI), Stockholm School of Economics, Stockholm.

Tolvanen, J.-P. & Lyytinen, K. (1993) "Flexible Method Adaptation in CASE Environments – The Metamodelling Approach", *Scandinavian Journal of Information Systems*, Vol. 1, No. 5, pp. 51-77.

Yourdon, E. (1993) *Yourdon Systems Method – Model-Driven Systems Development*, Yourdon Press, Prentice-Hall, Englewood Cliffs, New Jersey.

Österle, H. (1995) *Business in the Information Age – Heading for New Processes*, Springer Verlag, Berlin.

# 13

# Improving the Quality of Requirements Specifications by Enterprise Modelling

*Janis A. Bubenko jr.*
*Marite Kirikova*

*An Enterprise Model (EM) is a system of knowledge about the Enterprise, that can be maintained by a software tool. The EM is regarded as an essential part of a requirements specification (RS). The framework of the EM can reflect different views of the enterprise, such as the intentional view, the process view, the information view, and the actors view. It is argued that Enterprise Modelling supports and amplifies human thinking, reasoning, and co-operation. The quality of an EM is maintained by systematic and continuous participation of relevant stakeholders of the RS. The quality of an EM and a RS is also supported by different computer-aided quality control procedures. The methodology is suitable also for analysing enterprise change and evolution, and applicable in the area of business process re-engineering.*

## Introduction

The term "Requirements Engineering" (RE) is relatively new compared with more traditional terms such as "Information Engineering" (IE). Requirements Engineering denotes the area between business modelling and development and information system modelling and development. A number of journals and annual international conferences related to RE exist. A reason for the interest in this area is the observed problem that many expensive information system development efforts do not arrive at systems that are aligned with and support the business at hand. Understanding of a particular application domain and its activities, when stating information system requirements, has been found an essential problem.

The Requirements Specification (RS), ideally, serves as a bridge and as a basis for a contract between stakeholders and developers of a software application. The quality of the specification is, in cases where a procurement relationship holds, a necessary condition for achieving good quality of the software application, as well as for supporting effective communication and contractual negotiations between different groups of people involved in the procurement process.

According to Kant (1993), each thing can be considered as a "thing for others" and as a "thing itself". Applying this to the quality of RS, user satisfaction (specification for others) and, in particular, "internal" quality of a RS as an artefact (specification itself) accordingly have to be assessed and achieved (Dahlbom & Mathiassen, 1993).

Concerning the requirements specification as a "thing for others", the question "who is the stakeholder?" usually becomes difficult to answer (Vidgen, 1994). We consider as a stakeholder everybody whose work is directly or indirectly affected by the ideas reflected in the RS. Not only representatives of the application domain should be considered as stakeholders. Also representatives of the business environment as well as the work of system designers and programmers is RS dependent. "Working languages" of different stakeholders may be rather different. Therefore, in order to achieve good quality of a RS, flexible enough forms of representation of the contents of the specification are necessary.

"Internal" quality of the RS as an artefact requires evaluation of the RS according to standards that reflect the level of the quality believed to be achieved by the existing methodologies, technologies, methods, and tools. Davis (1990) points out the following quality characteristics concerning a RS: correctness, nonambiguity, completeness, verifiability, consistency, understandability, modifiability, traceablility and annotateability. At the same time he draws our attention to the fact that "there is no such a thing as perfect requirements specification". The problem is rather a negative correlation between some of the characteristics, when using conventional requirements acquisition and documentation techniques, e.g., Davis (1990) and Lubars et al (1993):

- the attempt to eliminate inconsistency and ambiguity (for instance, by reducing the share of natural language in a specification) makes the RS less understandable to non-computer specialists;

- striving for understandability raises the necessity to document requirements in a different way than they are analysed, so inconsistencies can easily creep in;

- attempting a detailed and complete RS requires more time than normally available, leads to extremely large documents, difficult to analyse;

- eliminating of redundancy rises ambiguity.

We suggest to develop a RS using Enterprise Modelling approach (Bubenko, 1993). This approach permits us at least to reduce some of the contradictions between the quality characteristics of RS. It is also helpful in dealing with different groups of stakeholders and in trying to satisfy their needs by stating more understandable and, hopefully, more relevant requirements. Enterprise can be here interpreted in a very wide sense. It could actually mean the whole enterprise or a small part of it. We consider as "enterprise" the object of particular efforts of management, analysis, investigation, development or design, performed by a particular group of persons.

The core of the Enterprise Modelling approach is an Enterprise Model (EM). The EM serves as an additional source of knowledge, when an enterprise is analysed with the purpose to clarify its basic objectives and requirements for a new or improved information system. The approach can also be used when the purpose is to solve some "one-shot" business problems, such as developing a new personnel policy, or solving a business process effectiveness problem.

In the next section we present the EM framework and a way how to use EM during requirements acquisition. Thereafter we discuss different quality issues and perspectives of enterprise modelling as well as ways of meeting quality characteristics of RSs. In order to discuss the relevance and quality of the EM methodology as an approach for requirements engineering, related work is considered in the following section. Our conclusions are presented in the last section.

# EM and the Enterprise Modelling process

Basic ideas related to Enterprise Modelling were introduced in the beginning of the eighties by Plandata, Sweden (Willars, 1988) and refined by SISU in the late eighties (Willars, 1991). SISU – The Swedish Institute for System Development, was founded in 1984. It has carried out more than

50 business and system analysis projects, where the Business Modelling methodology has been used. The Enterprise Modelling methodology presented here has evolved from this work.

The significant contribution of the above work was the notion to consider also *intentional* components of a specification, e.g. the goals (intentions) of a business, in addition to traditional model component types such as entities, relationships, and processes. The use of this approach in many different applications during the last ten years showed that the reason of success was not only the Business Model itself (the product), but the also appropriate management of the process of business and requirements engineering. SISU's concept of the Business Model was later extended to the Enterprise Model and further developed in the ESPRIT project F3 (From Fuzzy to Formal) (F3 Consortium, 1991 & 1994). The F3 Enterprise Modelling was then further elaborated in the Esprit project ELKD and is now being applied in the Esprit project ELEKTRA (ELEKTRA, 1997). The modelling framework of ELEKTRA is denoted EKD – Enterprise Knowledge Development which includes EM as a part. In this section we will discuss first the contents of the EM itself, and then briefly characterise the process of Enterprise Modelling.

## *EM – a system of knowledge of an enterprise*

The EKD structural framework includes a number of interrelated model types (Figure 1). In the information system modelling and design phase, semantic links are established from the information systems (IS) model to the EKD models, reflecting the rationale, or the motivation, for designing specific IS components. For instance, when selecting a component of the Information Systems Model (e.g. a data model component), it should be possible to trace its rationale and origins (e.g. why has it been introduced? which components in the information model does it represent? which business process uses it? etc.) back to a set of EKD model components.

The EKD model types contain each a number of components, i.e. objects and relationships of different types, which are typical for that model type. Relationships can be internal to a sub-model ("intra" relationships) or "external". External relationships relate components of two or more sub-models ("inter" relationships). Objects as well as relationships may have attributes. Populating model types and their relationships is, furthermore, controlled by a number of static as well as dynamic consistency rules, which control their state consistency as well as their permissible state transitions.

The Enterprise Model

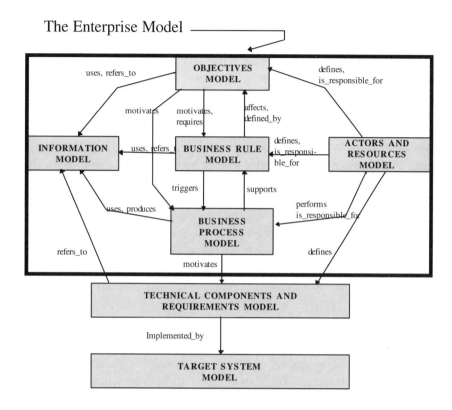

*Figure 1. The sub-model structure of the EKD framework.*

Each model type focuses on a specific aspect of the enterprise as will be describe in the sequel. Note that every model type may be used to describe an existing situation or a hypothetical (future) situation of the enterprise.

## Objectives modelling

The *Objectives Model* (OM) focuses on describing intentional aspects of the enterprise. Here we wish to describe what the enterprise and its employees want to achieve, or to avoid, and when. Important components of a objectives model are descriptions of goals the enterprise wants to pursue. Goals are described on different levels of increasing precision (operationalisation), and by using different classification of goals. It requires the modelling participants to reflect over and state their short as well as long range intentions about the enterprise. It also requires the

modelling participants to discuss and agree upon the individual importance, criticality, and priority of goals as well as discussing and evaluating
alternative ways of achieving goals.

While goals and goal structures are the target components of the objectives model, a number of other components are used in acquiring goals.
Additional OM component types used in EKD are *problem, constraint,
weakness, threat,* and *opportunity.* By documenting perceived problems
"hidden" goals can be detected, otherwise the problem would not have
been perceived. Weaknesses and threats are seen as two types of problems. Problems typically hinder the achievement of some goal. If a
stated problem cannot be seen as hindering some goal, then either the set
of goals is incomplete, or the problem really is not a problem of the
enterprise. Opportunities are, on the other hand, seen as "resources" or
"capabilities" that can make certain goals easier to achieve. Opportunities may also suggest new goals of the enterprise. For instance, more
powerful communication technology may facilitate possibilities of an
enterprise to achieve a goal to "enlarge the international market of its
products".

Developing an objectives model is initially a "brain-storming" activity.
Views and contributions from all participants must be considered. This
normally makes the initial set of objectives model statements unstructured
and difficult to perceive. Tools exist that can help structuring as well as
organising of this set of statements. Objectives model development phases
include structuring, classification, and operationalisation of objectives
model components. This is normally done by model "designers" in an
iterative fashion, where stakeholders are continuously involved and con-
sulted in order to validate progress.

## Business rule modelling

The *Business Rule Model* (BRM) is used to define and maintain explicitly
formulated business rules. The view put forward is that a major aspect of
information systems development is about formalising and documenting
knowledge about the application domain and this knowledge should be
represented explicitly (Bubenko & Wangler, 1993). In the EKD approach
we consider three types of rules:

- *Constraint rules,* which are concerned with the enterprise activities and
  their permitted behaviour. A dynamic constraint is, for instance, "the
  salary of a library employee must not decrease".

- *Derivation rules,* which define how different attributes or entity types are derived. For instance, "A bad library client is a client that does not return a loan on time after two consecutive reminders".

- *Event-action rules,* which control the initiation of activities and processes. For instance, "If the return of a loan is more than 4 days overdue, send a reminder".

Business rules must be consistent with the Objectives Model. Typically a rule can be seen as an operationalisation of a business goal or a constraint.

## Information modelling

The *Information Model* (IM) is used to strictly define the "things" and "phenomena" one is talking about in the other models. We use here a simple, extended entity-relationship like way to represent enterprise entity types, attributes, and relationships. Entity types are used to more strictly define expressions in the OM and the BRM, as well as to define the content of information sets in the business process model. For instance, the goal expression "To maintain and improve the library's services", requires a definition in the information model of the concept "library service". In the BRM above we need to formally define the concept of a "bad customer" as a specialisation of customer. Roughly speaking, the IM defines the "business language" used in the enterprise domain. Some temporally oriented applications may require more powerful information models. In that case a more powerful model may be used, e.g. the TEMPORA ERT (The Tempora Consortium, 1990).

## Business process modelling

The *Business Process Model* (BPM) is used to define and discuss different enterprise activities and processes, the way they interact, and the way they handle information as well as material. A business process is assumed to consume input in terms of information and/or material and produce outputs of the kind information and/or material. The BPM also includes a description of external processes which supply information and/or material (source) and external processes which consume information and/or material (sink). Processes as well as their input and output flows, can be decomposed into processes at a finer level. In general, the BPM is similar to what is used in traditional data-flow diagram models. An example of a library business process can be "Management of loan returns" which can be decomposed into "de-register a loan" and "manage the waiting list". The BPM also includes notation to express control flows in a process network.


## Actors and resources modelling

The *Actors and Resources Model* (ARM) is a vehicle to force developers and users to consider the actor and performer situation and roles in systems development as well as in the use of systems. Actors and resources can be organisational units, roles, individuals or groups of individuals, non-human actors, such as machines, etc. The purpose of AM is to describe how different actor and resources are related, and how they are related to components of the objectives model, e.g. goals, and to components of the BPM, i.e. processes. For instance, an actor can be the responsible of a particular process in the BPM, or the actor to pursue a particular goal in the OM. By studying the actors model and its relationships to other models, we can see how different actors exhibit dependencies between themselves, e.g. an actor may be dependent on a number of other actors with respect to performing a certain task or process (Yu & Mylopoulos, 1994).


## Technical components and requirements modelling

The *Technical Components and Requirements Model* (TCRM), finally, turns the development teams' attention to the technical IT system to be designed, needed to support the processes, and actors of the enterprise, and, indirectly to work for the goals of the enterprise. First we need to develop a set of high level requirements, goals, for the information system as a whole. On the basis of them, we make an attempt to structure the information system in a number of subsystems, or technical components. For each subsystem we have to define a set of more specific goals and requirements. These goals and requirements have to be derived from and consistent with the earlier sub-models discussed above. The TCRM is an initial attempt to define the overall structure and properties of the information system to support the business activities, as defined in the BPM. The TCRM is the basis for designing the Target Systems Model.

## Target system modelling

The *Target System Model* focuses on modelling the functionality of the intended information system, i.e. its data structures, its processes and its processing rules. Of particular importance is to show how the relationships to information system requirements in the TCRM are realised, e.g. how a particular requirement has been considered.

## Inter-model relationships

In developing a "complete" enterprise model, links between components of the different sub-models play an essential role. For instance, statements in the OM motivate different concepts to be defined more clearly. This is done in the IM, and a link is specified between the corresponding OM-component and the concept(s) in the IM. In the same way, goals in the OM motivate particular processes in the BPM. The processes are assumed needed in order to achieve the goals stated. A link is therefore inserted between the objective and its "motivated" processes. Links between models make the model "traceable", i.e. it is possible to see why certain processes and information system requirements have been introduced or, alternatively, how certain high level goals have been taken into consideration in the system design.

## An illustration

To illustrate the kinds of models we have described, we use a simple library case since most readers should be roughly familiar with this type of application domain. The scenario is as follows.

The management of a university library has issued a directive that the library's financial support from the university will be decreased by 10%. The management has initiated the task to reconsider the library's goals, operations, and processes in order to cope with the financial situation. An enterprise modelling process, involving a modelling group of representatives of the library's staff, has started. The process started with a brainstorming session where the library's major goals, problems, and opportunities were suggested by the modellers. A (small) fraction of an EM, reached after the initial session, is shown in Figure 2 (to show a model of a realistic size is not possible in a book chapter).

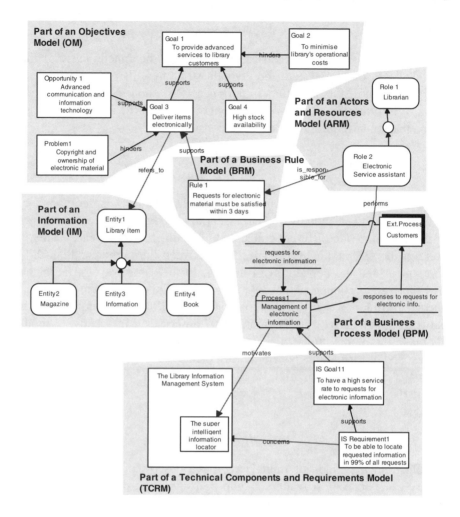

*Figure 2. A partial illustration of an Enterprise Model.*

The OM shows two conflicting (as it first appears) high level goals: to provide advanced library services and to minimise the library's operational costs. A new goal has been suggested: to be able to deliver library items to customers electronically. This supports the goal of advanced services, but seems to be hindered by copyright and ownership problems regarding electronic material. The goal of electronic delivery is further operationalised by introducing a business rule (in the BRM) saying that requests for electronic material must be satisfied within three days. Talking about delivering "library items" electronically somebody poses a question what a "library item" really means. This moves the modelling group's attention to the Information Model (IM) where a first attempt to describe library items as magazines, books, or "information" is documented. It is obvious that this will need further discussion and refinement. At this stage is it not clear what the term "information" means and how it relates to magazines and books. Developing the electronic delivery goal further brings the group to the Business Process Model, where a new business function, "Management of Electronic Information", is introduced. Introducing this new function seems to create the need for a new kind of staff, the actor role "Electronic Service Assistant".

The business function "Management of Electronic Information" introduces the need for an advanced information support sub-system, "The Super-intelligent Information Locator", as part of the library's Information Management System. Some goals an requirements of this technical support system are shown in the Technical Components and Requirements Model.

In this scenario we have described a typical situation in the very beginning of a modelling process. At this stage the models and their components are typically ill-defined, ill-described, and fuzzy. The models are incomplete and contain many "holes". To some this situation may even appear "chaotic". Much work remains to make all descriptions as clear as possible and to make the models reasonably complete. Making better and stricter formulations is typically the responsibility of the modelling technicians, but the correctness and validity of the models is the responsibility of the stakeholders. Next section has a few more words about the modelling process.

# The process of Enterprise Modelling

The process of Enterprise Modelling is mainly based on participatory group work. It preferably takes place in a specially equipped room with a "live-board", supported by a software tool, and guided by an experienced modelling facilitator. All the elements, introduced in the EM, are visible for participants on the large screen, they can be discussed, changed or deleted, if necessary. The software tool is intended for graphical representation of model information and maintaining it in a knowledge base. The tool supports different forms of knowledge representation: natural language texts, conceptual schemes, diagrams, as well as formal descriptions. The purpose here is to maintain knowledge acquired in different phases of the modelling process. The tool may also contain software for model analysis, "filtered" presentation as well as for quality checking.

Developing an adequate software support for Enterprise Modelling is an intricate matter. It is still under continuous improvement and development.

The modelling process is issue driven and situation sensitive. We can say that an "issue" here is a particular need of knowledge, or problem, of some knowledge system and the possibility to meet that need or problem by another knowledge system. By "knowledge systems" we mean here knowledge, situated in the head of a human being, participating in the session, or "artificial" knowledge represented by the EM. We further distinguish issues as "managerial" or "technical". A managerial issue typically concerns problematic, social relationships between participants in the modelling exercise. A technical issue concerns problems related to modelling enterprise phenomena, i.e. the way to abstract things, etc. A number of heuristics and modelling hints are suggested in (F3 Consortium, 1994).

The EM also has its own "needs": goals in the OM have to be supported by processes in the BPM; information sets of the BPM should be explained in the IM, and that like. In other words, good quality of the EM is based on discussions about explicit relationships between elements belonging to different EM sub-models. To achieve this, the enterprise is considered from different points of view (the objectives view, the process view, the information view, etc.) by involving a variety of groups of people with different knowledge and background. The EM gives in a natural way a possibility for participants to get insight into the things and phenomena that are related with their own part of the business and see the impact of their decisions or requirements to the overall intentions and processes of the enterprise. Working with EM, therefore, gives benefits to the organisation's culture and learning. It also provides a platform for achieving agreements concerning information system requirements.

The modelling process usually (but not necessarily) starts with objectives analysis, where the main problems and goals are suggested, discussed, and reflected in the OM. The process can also start with analysis of the existing activities or of the organisational structure, and representation of so acquired knowledge in the BPM or the ARM respectively. Requirement engineers are typically seeking for an explicit structure of the environment in which the information system will be embedded. They also look for actors with whom the system will communicate, and try to determine the explicit contents of required information. The modelling process is discussed in more detail in (F3 Consortium, 1994) and (Bubenko & Kirikova, 1994).

# Towards quality of requirements specification

Using the EM approach, a requirements specification is considered as a result of development of the EM (actually, the EM itself is part of a requirements specification). Seeking for quality of the specification, general principles for achieving quality of a product have to be respected (Sage, 1992; Dahlbom & Mathiassen, 1993). These state that quality of the product is reachable through the quality of the development process and its management. We will distinguish here between quality of the tool, the methodology, and the application of methodology in the process of requirements engineering (Figure 3).

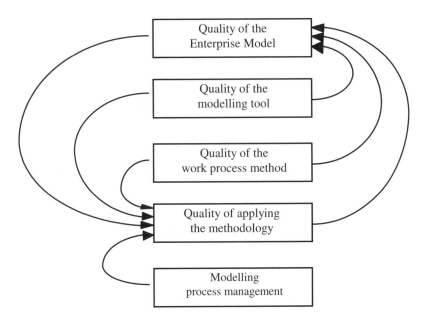

*Figure 3. Dependencies between issues of quality in Enterprise Modelling*

By quality of the EM we mean user satisfaction with the stated requirements as well as the "internal" quality of the EM as an artefact. To some extent this internal quality could be considered as user satisfaction as well. In this interpretation, system analysts are playing the role of users, and their need to be sure that the "stated requirements" of the information system are aligned with the "enterprise" has to satisfied.

Quality of a tool means quality of computer aided as well as of manual methods and techniques used during modelling activities. Visibility of graphical interpretations of the models, response time, and navigation possibilities, are some of the quality characteristics here.

Quality of the methodology reflects the adequacy of ideas, reflected and exploited by the methodology. The methodology is knowledge that should be applied in particular situations by specific human actors. Quality of applying the methodology depends on how well the fit between the methodology and the situation is understood, and how strictly and carefully the methodology is followed.

Quality of a requirements specification requires quality of the EM, that is dependent on the quality of the tool, the methodology, and applying the methodology. Quality of applying the methodology is project and enterprise management dependent, e.g., it is dependent on time and financial resources allocated, authority and guidance given, etc. Quality of the methodology and quality of the tool affect possibilities to apply the methodology successfully. Good quality of the Enterprise Model, i.e., appropriate knowledge provided, in its turn, improves quality of applying the methodology and can improve the quality of project and enterprise management as well.

We will discuss the quality of Enterprise Modelling and the process of applying it, concerning different perspectives of quality assurance, and possibilities to meet quality requirements of the RS. Project and enterprise management dependent quality issues will not be considered here. The discussion about quality of the methodology continues also in the next section, by comparing Enterprise Modelling with other related approaches.

## Ways of assessing and ensuring quality

A number of frameworks for quality assurance can be found in different scientific and practical quality assurance attempts (Sage, 1992; Dahlbom & Mathiassen, 1993). "User satisfaction" and "quality standards" are perhaps the most exploited notions. The first notion emphasises the subjective nature of quality, while the second observes some objective peculiarities. Both are necessary. Looking only to user satisfaction, the notion "quality of the user" becomes important. Estimating user quality seems currently to be out of scope of computer system developers. Therefore, correspondence to standards seems to serve as a balance to subjectivity, and should perhaps be considered in quality assurance, even if it may be felt as a barrier for creativity and advanced ideas. On the other hand, the "quality of standards" themselves have to be taken into the consideration. We can see that the concept "quality" indeed consists of a system of different notions of qualities, and requires further investigations in order to be properly understood.

Here we will, more pragmatically than scientifically, consider quality of the EM from different perspectives as suggested by Garvin (1984). This is one of the richest frameworks presented for assessing quality of a product. It does not explicitly separate "subjectivity" and "objectivity", but, instead, prescribes different, simultaneously subjective and objective, "viewpoints" to be maintained. Our intention is to expose the Enterprise Modelling methodology from the following perspectives:

- *User-Customer Perspective.* This perspective reflects subjective views of quality. In enterprise modelling, this perspective is supported by early and intensive involvement of users in the modelling process and the use of user-friendly forms of knowledge representation. When users are participating in EM development from the very beginning, understanding and even using the EM before final documents are elaborated, they have a exceptional possibility to influence the process, to reflect their requirements adequately, and to improve quality of the EM during "walk-throughs", critical reviews, and other procedures.

- *Transcendental Perspective.* From this perspective the things are evaluated as a whole or unified patterns of experience without necessity to view the whole through examination of each of the parts that comprise the whole. We interpret the transcendental perspective as investigation of inter-model links in the EM. For acceptance of the EM, the goals stated have to be supported by processes in the BPM, processes should be related with performers, information system requirements – with information sets and concepts, etc.

- *Product Based Perspective.* The whole now is seen through the examination of the parts of it. Each of the sub-models in the EM (the ARM, the OM, etc.) as well as their elements, are parts of the Enterprise Model. The quality of the EM is then seen as the "sum of qualities" of the contents of sub-models, their elements and relationships. It means that it is necessary to be sure that all relevant goals are considered in the OM, all processes described appropriately in the BPM, and that like.

- *Manufacturing Perspective.* From this point of view, quality is interpreted as a conformity to the requirements and standards, including cost and schedule restrictions. It is not necessarily true, that Enterprise

Modelling methodology makes the process of requirements engineering shorter than by using other approaches. The Objectives Model, that reflects the "why?" component of the EM, used in the early stages of modelling, requires more time from the requirements holders than by using "traditional" methodologies. We believe, however, that understanding of real problems and issues makes agreements between stakeholders more natural and saves time in coming, more detailed, activities of Enterprise Modelling.

- *Value Perspective*. This perspective blends quality as a measure of the goodness with quality as a measure of utility: a qualitative product is one that provides sufficient performance at an acceptable price and time. The value of an information system can be determined by its capacity to change the users' pattern of actions (Stolterman, 1994). From this point of view, quality assurance in Enterprise Modelling is supported by the possibility to model the impact of stated requirements to the overall enterprise and thereby see how the fulfilment of requirements will affect processes in the enterprise and the work of involved actors.

We have argued that, considering all perspectives of quality assessment, as suggested by Garvin (1984), different ways to improve quality of the requirements specification are supported by the EM methodology. The next section focuses particularly on the manufacturing perspective, and shows how quality can be maintained concerning different issues of quality (Figure 3).

## *Meeting quality characteristics of requirements specifications*

Desirable quality characteristics of a RS are listed in several publications (IEEE, 1984; Martin, 1987; Davis, 1990). The terminology and definitions of them are similar, but not equivalent. We follow notions suggested by Davis. All issues of striking for quality (Figure 3) are concerned with each quality characteristic. Tables 1 and 2 reflect how the suggested issues, the structure of the EM, the EM tool, the EM Methodology itself, and the application of it, benefit in improving the quality of a RS. Quality criteria are reflected by rows of the tables. Columns depict particular quality issues. Each cell observes some Enterprise Modelling attributes that support the corresponding quality characteristic.

| Characteristic | The EM itself | The EM tool |
|---|---|---|
| **Validity** (a RS is valid if and only if every requirement stated therein represents a relevant problem and if all relevant problems are addressed by the RS) | The EM forces stakeholders to explain how business as well as IS requirements are related to business goals and problems. | The tool facilitates upwards (the "why") as well as downwards (the "how") of tracing between intentions and solutions. |
| **Non-ambiguity** (a RS is non-ambiguous if every requirement stated therein has only one interpretation) | Relating IS requirements to components of other models improve their correct interpretation. | No direct support. |
| **Completeness** (a RS is syntactically complete if the RS contains all prescribed details) | The EM prescribes a structured model for expressing requirements. Completeness with respect to the model is easy to check. | Certain completeness characteristics can be automatically checked. |
| **Verifiability** (a RS is verifiable if and only if there exists cost effective processes to verify that the software built meets the requirements) | The EM promotes a more detailed, complete, and operational RS. This RS should be more easy to verify with respect to the IT solution. | No direct support. |
| **Consistency** (a RS is consistent if no subset of the therein stated requirements are in conflict) | The structured EM with intermodel links promotes the build-up of a consistent RS. | A tool can provide a limited set of automatic consistency checks of the IM, BPM, and the ARM. |
| **Understandability** (a RS is understandable if all stakeholders can constructively reason about it) | Experience has shown that the EM facilitates understanding of the total business problem and its IT-support. | A tool can provide "complexity reducing" projections (filtering) and displays of the EM. |
| **Modifiability** (a RS is modifiable if changes to it can with reasonable effort be made easily maintaining the above characteristics) | The structured EM facilitates analysing effects of changes to other EM components. | A tool can provide considerable support in managing the change of an EM. |

*Table 1. Quality aspects of the EM and the EM tool*

| Characteristic | The EM method | Application of the EM method |
|---|---|---|
| **Validity** (a RS is valid if and only if every requirement stated therein represents a relevant problem and if all relevant problems are addressed by the RS) | The method focuses on active stakeholder participation and analysis of intra-model as well as inter-model relationships. | Application of the method presumes facilitator guidance as well as critical walk-throughs and working sessions. |
| **Non-ambiguity** (a RS is non-ambiguous if every requirement stated therein has only one interpretation) | No direct support. | No direct support. |
| **Completeness** (a RS is syntactically complete if the RS contains all prescribed details) | The structured EM defines what a syntactically "complete" specification is. | The method's guide-lines for working strive for achieving improved completeness. |
| **Verifiability** (a RS is verifiable if and only if there exists cost effective processes to verify that the software built meets the requirements) | No direct support, but the method strives for definition of "measurable" information system requirements. | A facilitator can "drive" the process towards measurable information system requirements. |
| **Consistency** (a RS is consistent if no subset of the therein stated requirements are in conflict) | A number of consistency preserving rules regarding the EM are specified in the method. | Consistency issues are detected and resolved in "integration" sessions and walk-throughs. |
| **Understandability** (a RS is understandable if all stakeholders can constructively reason about it) | Step-wise development, from natural language to structured specifications, improves stakeholder understanding. | The use of adequate audio-visual aids and support for group work may improve stakeholder understanding. |
| **Modifiability** (a RS is modifiable if changes to it can with reasonable effort be made easily maintaining the above characteristics) | Separation of concerns in different sub-models of the EM makes the RS more easy to change. | The relationship between a design decision and its actors is maintained. |

*Table 2. Quality aspects of the EM methodology*

Using the EM as part of a RS, or as a background of documents for a RS, it is possible to cover (more or less) all the quality characteristics listed above. In Enterprise Modelling the problem of contradictions between the quality characteristics (see the first section of this chapter) seems to be less pronounced, for instance:

- Different forms of representation, including natural language, as well as mappings between the forms, are maintained in the EM. Therefore it is not necessary to sacrifice nonambiguity for having a satisfactory consistency of an RS.

- User-friendly frameworks of sub-modules and continuous user involvement in the modelling process support coexistence of understandability and consistency.

- Graphical representation and computer-based maintenance of the EM permit easy modification of requirements without loosing the concreteness of an RS.

- Possibility to distinguish between the internal and the external representation of the EM gives an opportunity to present for different groups of users concise documents, that are consistent with the internally completely documented EM.

- Mappings between different forms of representation of requirements permit to eliminate redundancy without rising of ambiguity.

The Enterprise Modelling methodology shows that it is possible to do something to follow each of the "standard" quality characteristics stated for a RS. It seems also that the negative correlation between the particular characteristics is not a law in requirements engineering, but depends on the strength of our methodologies and its tools.

The possibility to follow standards, stated for the product, is not the only quality issue to be expected from the requirements engineering methodology. Usually, in practice, the quality of some object is evaluated by comparing it with the other available ones. In the next section we will use this approach of comparison in order to further assess the Enterprise Modelling methodology.

# Related work

This section reviews some related works in the areas of Requirements Engineering and Knowledge Acquisition. We are considering both areas, because knowledge acquisition is a problem that has to be solved during Requirements Engineering, and, on the other hand, Requirements Engineering is one of the application domains of Knowledge Acquisition. Our purpose is to reflect some relevant issues found in other published works, and discuss Enterprise Modelling in the light of them.

## *"Voice of the customer" and "the filter of analysts"*

The term "Voice of the Customer" comes from work (Kihara & Hutchinson, 1992), where the Quality Function Deployment (QFD) model is introduced. Three decomposition phases are indicated in the model's application procedure: (1) decompose Voice of the Customer, (2) prioritise Voice of the Customer, (3) obtain program module, respectively. The conclusion made by the authors of QFD concerning the first phase is that "it is important to collect the accurate *original language* of the customers, since any misinterpretation at this stage will also carry forward to each following stage".

Some research works in knowledge acquisition (Sandahl, 1987; Eriksson, 1991) show that better results concerning knowledge bases have been achieved, when the expert is directly communicating with a knowledge acquisition tool, and not through the "filter of knowledge engineers". This seems true in requirements engineering as well. Many problems in the area are concerned with communication difficulties between analysts and stakeholders of the requirements (Bubenko et al, 1992).

In Enterprise Modelling there is a possibility to document accurately "original language" of the requirements holders, and to return to those descriptions from the latest versions of the EM. In group sessions users are the ones who are introducing and formulating elements of the EM. There are no "filter of analysts" here that might change the acquired knowledge inappropriately.

## *Variety of sources of knowledge*

Previous work in the field of knowledge acquisition has shown that excellent interviewing methods and powerful tools usually are not the main key for achieving high quality of the knowledge bases. Acquiring knowledge from several different sources is now seen as a main advantage in building satisfactory knowledge acquisition systems (Gaines, 1988).

In Enterprise Modelling a number of necessary sources of information are involved by facilitating group sessions and selecting group members appropriately. Some sources of knowledge can be considered using interviewing as well as some other knowledge acquisition techniques, e.g., obtaining information from documents.

## Family of models

Different "families" of models have become popular in requirements engineering as well as in knowledge acquisition. Two examples are shown in what follows.

The first example is an integrated model architecture, consisting of the following models (Ramackers, 1994): the Strategic Business Model, the Operational Business Model, the External Information System Model, the Conceptual Information Systems Model, the Implementation Model (user interfacing), and the Implementation Model (system processing). Data, behaviour, processes, objects, analysis, and design perspectives or views are supported inside and between the models.

Another example is the Common KADS model set for knowledge acquisition (KADS II Consortium, 1992). The set consists of the Organisation Model, the Task Model, the Agent Model, the Expertise Model, the Communication Model, and the Design Model.

We can find similarities between meta-structures of the EM submodels and meta-structures of the members of the two "families" considered above. The difference is that the EM is the only one containing a pure "intentional component" – the Objectives Model. Existence of the OM stresses the attention of system developers to the "why?" perspective of requirements acquisition. We see this perspective as the, perhaps, most significant one for stimulating human reasoning and learning, for achieving a good result in the overall modelling procedure, and for correctly embedding requirements in their environment.

## Sequence of modelling activities

Perhaps the most common trait of the works considered above, is the top-down approach, (Kihara & Hutchinson, 1992; Ramackers, 1994). In the Common KADS case, the modelling process starts with a configuration of template models, i.e. decisions are made which parts of the templates will or will not be filled during the project. The project manager has to define activities that will fill the configured models. These contents must be assessed against the target(s), e.g., quality criteria defined for a particular state. If the model contents achieve the criteria, a specific landmark state is achieved, and development can continue with the next set of activities of the workplan.

The process of Enterprise Modelling does not follow some prescribed sequence of activities. However, guide-lines exist for different modelling situations (F3 Consortium, 1994). It is a matter of further investigations, to see how the EM methodology could benefit from using template models. Quality assessment in Enterprise Modelling is mainly human-agreement dependent. Therefore, it is not possible to precisely define the sequence of actions to be performed. In EM development is focusing at different times on different sub-models depending on the need to further elaborate or to seek explanation for some statements.

# Conclusions

Important objectives of Requirements Engineering are:

- to improve and to document the participants' knowledge about the current enterprise situation as well as about desirable or possible future situations;

- to improve their possibilities to reach a clear, structured, and documented agreement on important concepts, properties, processes, and goals for the future enterprise situation;

- to develop a basis, as complete as possible, for designing an adequate information system, conforming to the enterprise objectives;

- to develop a set of interrelated documents, that in the future can be re-used, when re-designing enterprise objectives, processes, and information system requirements.

The chapter suggests the Enterprise Modelling methodology as an appropriate approach for development of a requirements specification (RS). The requirements specification is constructed on the basis of the Enterprise Model which guarantees that the information system is better aligned with the business. The Enterprise Modelling methodology exhibits the following characteristics:

- structure of components of knowledge, suggested by the EM, has been found effective for knowledge elicitation. It also supports human thinking, reasoning and learning;

- transparent, structured representation of pragmatic (the OM, the BPM, the ARM, the TCRM), as well as semantic (the IM) issues of enterprise modelling, have been found to provide a good basis for collective decision making and achieving agreements concerning requirements;

- quality assurance, based on human reasoning, can be complemented by computer aided quality assessment procedures.

The Enterprise Modelling Methodology gives a possibility to assess quality from user, transcendental, product based, manufacturing, as well as value perspectives. It prescribes particular activities for improving quality of a RS concerning its correctness, nonambiguity, completeness, verifiability, consistency, understandability, and modifiability. It is, however, a movement towards those characteristics, and not a deterministic method how the characteristics could be achieved to 100%. Even if the components of an EM are rather structured and "hard", the way of working and quality assessment is "soft". The key issue of using EM is avoiding contradictions, usually experienced between different quality characteristics of a model. In this chapter, the quality of a RS was discussed without considering such notions of quality as "quality of users", "quality of management" and "quality of standards". They are, however, important preconditions for performing modelling and requirements acquisition exercises using EM. Failure to observe them lead most likely to failures in the modelling process itself (F3 Consortium, 1994).

Analysis of related work shows that ideas incorporated in the Enterprise Modelling methodology are in harmony with several other ideas found in related research works. The methodology is, however, still under the development, and is being tested in practical cases (see, for instance, Persson, 1997). Its current version is supported by a number of prototype software tools. Some tools are oriented towards group work support. Better flexibility and navigation possibilities, as well as more advanced analysis procedures are future plans for development of the tools.

This chapter is related to and complements several other chapters of this book, in particular 8, 11, 14, and 15. In chapter 11, Nellborn presents a framework for classifying modelling methodologies and their ability to cover the span from strategic planning to information system development. In chapter 14, Nilsson asks the question "On why to model what and how" and suggests an architecture similar to that of this chapter. The chapters 8 and 15 by Lindström and Willars, respectively, present important lessons learned from practical modelling and suggest a number of "Dos" and "Don'ts" in modelling practice.

# Acknowledgement

The authors' work on this problem was in part funded by NUTEK, Swedish National Board for Industrial and Technical Development, in its support for ESPRIT project F3 (6612).

# References

Bubenko, J.A. & Kirikova, M. (1994) "'Worlds' in Requirements Acquisition and Modelling", in Kangassalo, H. & Wangler, B. (eds.) *The 4th European – Japanese Seminar on Information Modelling and Knowledge Bases*, Kista, Sweden [later published by IOS, The Netherlands].

Bubenko, J.A (1993) "Extending the Scope of Information Modelling", in Olivé, A. (ed.) *Proceedings of the Fourth International Workshop on the Deductive Approach to Information Systems and Databases*, Report LSI/93-25, Department de Llenguatges i Sistemes Informatics, Universitat Politecnica de Catalunya, Barcelona, Spain

Bubenko jr., J.A., Gustafsson, M.R., Nellborn, C. & Song, W. (1992) *Computer Support for Enterprise Modelling and Requirements acquisition. From Fuzzy to Formal*, Esprit III Project 6612: Deliverable 3-1-3-R1 Part B, SISU, Electrum 212, SE-164 40 Kista, Sweden.

Bubenko, J. & Wangler, B. (1993) "Objectives Driven Capture of Business Rules and of Information System Requirements", in *Proceedings of the 1993 IEEE Systems, Man, and Cybernetics Conference*, Le Touquet, France,

Dahlbom, B. & Mathiassen, L. (1993) *Computers in Context: The Philosophy and Practice of Systems Design*, NCC Blackwell, Cambridge, England.

Davis, A.M. (1990) *Software Requirements: Analysis and Specification*, Prentice-Hall Inc., Englewood Cliffs, New Jersey.

ELEKTRA, (1997) *ELEKTRA – ELectrical Enterprise Knowledge for TRansforming Applications*, ESPRIT Project 22927 [Summary available on http://www.dsv.su.se/~js/elektra.html (February, 1997)].

Eriksson, H. (1991) *Meta-Tool Support for Knowledge Acquisition*. Linköping Studies in Science and Technology, Dissertations No. 224, Linköping University, Linköping, Sweden.

F3 Consortium, (1991) *From Fuzzy to Formal*, Technical Annex Part II, ESPRIT Project 6612, The F3 Consortium.

F3 Consortium. (1994) *The F3 Requirements Engineering Handbook*, SISU, Box 1250, SE-164 40, Kista, Sweden.

Gaines, B.R. (1988) "Second Generation Knowledge Acquisition Systems", in Boose, J.; Gaines, B.; Linster, M. (eds.) *Proceedings of the European Knowledge Acquisition Workshop (EKAW'88)*, Studien No. 143, GMD, Sankt Augustin, Germany.

Garvin, D.A. (1984) "What Does 'Product Quality' Really Mean?", *Sloan Management Review*, Vol. 26, No. 1.

IEEE (1984) *An American National Standard. IEEE Guide to Software Requirements Specifications*, ANSI/IEEE Std 830-1984, The Institute of Electrical and Electronics Engineers, Inc. 345 47th Street, New York, NY 10017, USA.

KADS II Consortium (1992) *The Common KADS Model Set.* KADS-II/WP I – II/RR/UvA/018/4.0, University of Amsterdam, Amsterdam.

Kant, I. (1993) *Critique of pure reason.* A revised and expanded translation based on Meiklejohn, Polotis, V. (Ed.), Dent, London.

Kihara, T. & Hutchinson, C. E. (1992) "QFD as a Structured Design Tool for Software Development," in *Transactions from The Fourth Symposium on Quality Function Deployment*, Novi MI, pp. 369-383.

Lubars, M., Potts, C. & Richter, C. (1993) *A Review of State of the Practice in Requirements Modeling*, in *Proceedings of the IEEE International Symposium on Requirements Engineering*, IEEE Computer Society Press, Los Alamitos, California, pp. 2-14.

Martin, C.F. (1987) *User-centred Requirements Analysis*, Prentice-Hall Inc., Englewood Cliffs, New Jersey.

Persson, A. (1997) "Using the F3 Enterprise Model for Specification of Requirements – an Initial Experience Report", *The 3rd International Workshop on Requirements Engineering: Foundation for Software Quality*, CAiSE'97, Barcelona, Spain.

Ramackers, G.J. (1994) *Integrated Object Modelling: An Executable Specification Framework for Business Analysis and Information System Design*, Dissertation, Thesis Publishers, Amsterdam.

Sage, A.P. (1992) *Systems Engineering.* John Wiley & Sons Inc., New York.

Sandahl, K. (1987) *Case Studies in Knowledge Acquisition, Migration and User Acceptance of Expert Systems.* Linköping Studies in Science and Technology, Licentiate thesis 127, LiU-Tek-Lic 1987:28, Linköping University: Linköping, Sweden.

Stolterman, E. (1994) "On Critical Studies of Information Systems", in Kerola, P., Justila, A. & Jarvinen, J. (eds.) *Proceedings of the 17th IRIS*, Department of Information Processing Science, University of Oulu, Finland, pp. 979-988.

The TEMPORA Consortium (1990) *Concepts Manual*, ESPRIT Project No. 2469, UMIST, Manchester, England.

Vidgen, R. (1994) "Information Systems: Identifying Customers and Understanding Quality Requirements", in Kerola, P., Justila, A. & Jarvinen, J. (eds.) *Proceedings of the 17th IRIS*, Department of Information Processing Science, University of Oulu, Finland, pp. 989-1000.

Willars, H. (1988) *Handbok i ABC-metoden*, Plandata Strategi, Stockholm [*Handbook of the ABC method*].

Willars, H. (1991) "Amplification of Business Cognition through Modelling Techniques", *Proceedings of the 11th IEA Congress*, Paris.

Yu, E. & Mylopoulos, J. (1994) "From E-R to 'A-R' – Modelling Strategic Actor Relationships for Business Process Reengineering", in Loucopoulos, P. (ed.) *Entity-Relationship Approach - ER'94, Business Modelling and Re-Engineering, 13th International Conference on the Entity-Relationship Approach*, Lecture Notes in Computer Science, Vol. 881, Springer, Berlin, pp. 548-565.

# 14

# On Why to Model What and How: Concepts and Architecture for Change

*Björn E. Nilsson*

*Having spent more than a quarter of a century in practical model-ling work, I fear that, in many cases, we tend to model the wrong things during the wrong work phases for the wrong reasons using the wrong instruments. Searching remedies for these problems, we will look into the basic reasons for introducing concepts to be used in modelling as well as an architecture within which to apply selected concepts in a profitable manner.*

## Some problems

Over the years, model based development of the business and its informa-tion support has emerged as a predominant way of working. What then is the contemporary thinking behind the usage of models in the realm of business modelling?

One driving force is to improve the business of organisations using models to bridge the gap between business managers and system developers thus creating a stable basis for understanding and communication. Bridging this gap, has an enormous economic impact. However, maybe even more important reasons are totally unrelated to information technology. In most cases, the paramount effect from modelling the business is the establish-ment of a working social contract on how to view the business and how to relate to and communicate about phenomena related to the business. Ade-quate models act as enablers for development of both the business itself as for development of its information support systems.

In most human enterprises, value addition results from co-ordinated action. In any organisation of even moderate complexity, co-ordinated action is by necessity based upon effective human communication. Today, information-technology-based systems are instrumental in the control and management of most organisations. Often, business operation and information technology are hard to separate. IT is also a vital technology for the value addition itself. The prime business or process object is often information. This holds not only for financial institutions but also for many other types of enterprises today.

Although current development models and methods may employ powerful and sophisticated techniques for a great variety of analysis, some fundamental aspects of analysis and design of information systems seem to be lacking:

- *Information system principles – not established.* The basic goals behind, and the working principles of, information systems have not been analysed in sufficient depth.

- *Information usage – unknown.* Even as basic a question as how information actually is used in the decision process is not properly researched, as pointed out in Langefors (1966 b) and Earl (1989). This means, in essence, that we do not know what effects we are creating. The contribution of information in value addition activities seems to be virtually unknown.

- *Philosophical foundation – unstable.* A bit unsettling is also that the very concept of information as such has no generally accepted philosophical basis. The research has no working paradigm – which is the rationale behind the work of Falkenberg et al (1996).

- *Value of information – unknown.* A bizarre situation is the inadequacy of accepted principles regarding the setting of value of information and information systems. The resulting lack of proper economic incentives has led to an improper basis in both the use of and further development of methods.

Now, if the above refers to the academic scene, what is then going on in practice?

To start with, the customer has not got the time to wait. The reaction from a business executive "We don't have IT-projects any more, we just have business projects" reflects an adequate management reaction which, in the long run, is beneficial for the community at large. The practitioner has not got the time to wait either. As research is not focused on relevant needs, the leading edge in methods development is today not to be found in the academic world but in the consultant companies. At the same time, the practitioners seem over and over to favour fashion rather than efficiency. In modelling, we may easily see the following examples:

- *The business reengineering fallacy:* Today, the core of business reengineering revolves around processes. For an example, see Davenport & Short (1990). However, the most fundamental business development is neither done during process analysis and design nor in goal or market analysis. Rather, concept or object analysis is the fulcrum of business change. Why? In conceptual analysis we are forming the bearing business abstractions, the core of the culture, the very fundament for change. Changing the business abstractions and the business language means changing the mental models in peoples heads – sometimes changing the notion of what the business is all about.

- *The process reengineering fallacy:* The most important part of early process analysis is not creating an efficient flow. Rather, goal formulation is the critical success factor in process design. Why? The goal formulations determine the architecture of control mechanisms to be established in the organisation. This is a higher order structure which to a large extent determine the process flow. The goal formulations determine in what ways processes should work together. Changing the goals in business operation often implies changing the mental models on the ways specific control mechanisms have to be established. The understanding of the basic value adding process is necessary but the gains are usually achieved by improving the control systems or, rather, processes.

- *The natural object fallacy:* With the advent of object orientation, the error of believing objects to be in some way natural or easy to perceive resurfaced after some ten years of better practice. Even if the problem is diminishing, it is still, today, a serious one. It is a costly mistake to think that the objects of the business are natural, just there to be found or that they could be easily identified. Why? What we perceive to be there is to a large degree a social agreement. Business modelling cannot be done as a pure analysis or objective mapping, it contains always a large element of design and, thus, social agreement. *High quality* object or concept modelling aims at making profitable abstractions, thus forming the business language in a effective manner.

- *The 1:1:1 fallacy:* An implementation driven view is the thought that you have a natural, direct correspondence between reality, the object model of the business and the implemented objects. Why? The goals for implementation in terms of reuse and effectiveness do not match the goals of business change in such a straightforward manner. Different structuring mechanisms are at work in these two areas. What makes this fallacy extra tricky is that it is not in all respects a fallacy but also a goal to strive for. However, it is a very dangerous goal to push too far.

- *The measurable goal fallacy:* A couple of analysis methods require goals to be quantitatively measurable. This is a rather fundamental mistake. Why? The most important goals work as motivational forces on a rather high level of abstraction. Their nature is basically intentional and permits management by making sense. Thus, execution is taking human judgement and value into consideration.

- *The invoice syndrome:* Avoid modelling administrative objects, like order, invoice etc., into the core of the business model. Why? The administrative documents reflect a specific way of working, not the task to be solved. Modelling them into the core of the business models might petrify the business processes and destroy the possibility for finding new business solutions. These kinds of objects should be regarded as very volatile while their underlying, far more stable abstractions should be made visible. The underlying abstraction for, say, invoice might be debt. Debts may be regulated in many ways, not only by conventional invoices.

Even if these simple examples are just small indicators that something is lacking in our methodologies, they also contain fragments of a basis for resolving problems. Which method constructs are we to introduce to reduce the problems of our discipline?

# On criteria for introducing method components

The basic criterion is actually very simple.

The introduction of any component, be it a working process, a concept, an architecture or any other tool to be used in a method, should ultimately contribute to the creation of value in the processes of organisations where the method is applied. In our case, the contribution of value by an established component originates from its final effects on the organisation – as a consequence of its proper application during the analysis and design of processes and their possible IT-support. Naturally, the application, and thereby the value addition, of a certain component might be both direct and indirect. However, anything introduced into a method which is not ultimately contributing to these ends ought to be severely questioned within a system of concepts for analysis.

In the text, based upon this criterion, we will follow two different but connected lines of reasoning.

The first line concerns the need for concepts in modelling, notably handled in Ackoff (1971), Sundgren (1974), Bunge (1977, 1979) and Griethuysen (1982). The argumentation follows different semiotically determined levels of analysis, outlined in Stamper (1973). Those semiotic levels will, eventually, turn out to be important economic levels of analysis with corresponding demands for adequate concepts in a modelling framework. We will also introduce new names for these levels such as culture economy, communication economy and information economy.

The second line of reasoning concerns the need for an architecture or structure within which to apply these modelling concepts. We will introduce a fractal, multi-perspective architecture applicable on the indicated levels of analysis and give the motivation behind the structure in psychological and managerial terms.

# On the need for concepts in modelling: A line of reasoning based on semiotics

A framework for reasoning about and, ultimately, for developing methods and techniques for analysis and design, may have a variety of starting points. Concerning the mentioned gap in communication between the business and the analysis and development people, we have found the following to be the most obvious and fundamental question to ask:

*In an organisation, why do we develop information systems at all?*

The answer is, actually, very simple:

*Information systems ought to be developed only to support or perform value addition.*

Supporting or performing value addition will be our basic criterion of relevance. when reasoning about method components. See Falkenberg et al (1996).

To short-circuit the long line of reasoning, a compact matrix will sum it up (see Table 1).

| Realm of design | Question | Answer |
|---|---|---|
| **Business economy** Aspects of organisational value addition | Within an organisation, why do we actually design and implement information systems in the first place? | Information systems ought to be designed and implemented with the sole aim to perform or support adequate action such that value addition may be achieved. |
| **Culture economy** Social aspects: | What is the context within which actions actually are performed? | An organisation constitutes a social system where, based on decision, action is performed within the frame of more or less well established norms or rules of behaviour and other mental pictures of the world. |
| **Communication economy**: Pragmatical aspects | How do we acquire the necessary basis for decision and co-ordinated action? | The primary basis for co-ordinated action is established through communication, often aiming at establishing reasonably well shared mental models |
| **Information economy** Semantical aspects | What is actually communicated? | Models are communicated. |
| **Representation economy** Syntactical aspects | How are models represented? | Models are expressed as sentences in defined languages |
| **Storage and transmission economy** Empirical aspects | How are sentences made time persistent, i.e. manifest? | Sentences are made manifest in patterns. |
| **Encoding and detection economy:** Physical aspects | How are patterns implemented? | Patterns are made detectable on physical substrates. |

*Table 1. A semiotics based line of reasoning (adapted from Falkenberg et al, 1996).*

We will now study how this line of reasoning relates to the need of concepts in modelling. Later on, we will place some of these concepts in a model architecture.

Let us start all over again with the basic question: Within an organisation, why do we design and implement information systems?

## Business economy

The only reason for information systems to be designed and implemented within an enterprise is to support or, indeed, perform its value addition.

Value addition is achieved in action. Within a business, value is normally produced consciously and in an organised way. The patterns, the organised forms for repetitive behaviour, are often called processes – whether these forms are known or not. Note that value may be produced by both deliberate action and non-action. Value may also be produced at random, but the very core of business systems is deliberate and controlled value creating action.

Value is produced by consuming resources to create new resources. A consumption of resources may lead to state changes of objects including, as a special case, their transition from existence to non-existence. All objects relevant to the business may be seen as resources at one time or another – if not, why bother about them? Sometimes the resources are created for usage in external processes, the business has then by definition a customer. Now, based on this reasoning, a reasonable set of concepts to include in a method might be (*please read the following text as one long sentence*):

- organisation – for which different directions and aims are set, as
- goals – towards which the organisation strive in order to create
- value – which, in a controlled way, is accomplished by coherent
- actions – performed according to patterns called
- processes – within which
- actors – act and cause change on
- resources – which can be seen as changing the
- states – of objects related to the business

Note that we may not restrict ourselves to human, responsible actors, but also take into account non-responsible ones like machines or programs. Moreover, a resource might well be abstract, as information. With respect to the concepts mentioned, how do current methods measure up?

Current methods of analysis and design are quite adequate in dealing with things such as value chain analysis and work-flow or process management, including the formal aspects of sequencing and synchronising actions as well as logistics as illustrated in Sibley et al (1991). On the other hand, progress is hampered by lack of methods encompassing efficient analysis and design of goal structures with contribution calculus – as well as lack of good mechanisms for formal coupling between goals and processes.

We are suggesting that goal-oriented, value-adding, action is paramount to survival and success of organisations. This leads to yet another question: What is the context within which actions actually are performed?

## *Culture economy*

Goal-oriented action is performed within, and cannot be separated from, its social context.

An organisation constitutes a social system, where action is performed within the frame of social contracts or in violation of these. As a consequence of the view expressed, an organisation may be seen as a system of social contracts during analysis. When contracts are reasonably well established and generally accepted, they are sometimes said to constitute norms. When mental models of different types are sufficiently well established, we will talk about shared mental models which are constituting part of the social contracts. These contracts control the behaviour within a social grouping. Within the frame of such contracts, possible actions and their consequences are evaluated, decisions are taken, and actions are performed.

The norms of our society also shape our world view or philosophical position. They actually form our very ability to conceive and reason about the world. They also underlie the surface level of our notional actions and value systems. See Nilsson (1979), Gibson et al (1984) and Weber (1947).

Based on this reasoning, we may conclude that a method ought to take into account concepts like:

- social system – within which the
- behaviour – to a large extent is controlled by agreed-upon
- mental models – containing normative aspects in
- norms – which normally are in correspondence with established
- value systems – underlying the formation of explicit organisational
- rules – often called business rules which, in turn, often determine
- responsibility – and authority concerning making
- decisions – affecting action in the organisation.

Now, on this social level of abstraction which is mainly concerned with questions concerning culture economy, how do our methods measure up?

With a few exceptions, contemporary methods in large scale practical usage, tend to disregard culture economy. Most often, adequate facilities for analysing and further dealing with the cultural or social aspects of information systems is lacking. The economic effects of applying proper methods for analysis and design of information systems on this level of abstraction seems to be severely underestimated. As a consequence, aspects of organisational culture – the fundament for the driving forces at play within an organisation – normally are not analysed as part of the information systems development process. To the shame of our profession, this is still today a significant factor contributing to the low acceptance and, hence, the low effectiveness of many information systems.

Most contemporary methods also provide very weak facilities for business rule analysis. Object-oriented approaches suffer the same weakness, in spite of a pretence to the opposite.

Business development methodology, on the other hand, in some areas, shows passably strong techniques for the analysis of social aspects. Some of these and other similar techniques are slowly migrating into contemporary information system development methods. See Leonard-Barton (1988), Checkland (1981) and Mumford (1983).

To sum up the view adopted so far, coherent and goal-oriented action is considered paramount to survival and success of organisations. Action is taken to be performed within a social system with more or less well established mental models, contracts or protocols, that are expressed in terms of norms or rules. Action is, furthermore, based on evaluation and decision. This begs a further question: How do we acquire the necessary basis for decision and co-ordinated action?

## Communication economy

The primary basis for co-ordinated action is established through communication.

Within the context of an organisation, seen as a social system, co-ordinated action is brought about either by communication between actors or through direct observation of the state of affairs – where adequate action is determined by common experience and norms, which, in turns, are the effects of earlier communication (see Berger & Luckmann, 1966). Sometimes it is said that as much as 90% of our experience actually is indirect, through linguistic communication.

Communication has the ultimate purpose of sharing intentions or keeping the world view up to date. Naturally, communication may substitute direct observation, by merely providing a description of the state of affairs. On the other hand, in special cases, when norms are sufficiently action-oriented, direct observation of the state of affairs might substitute explicit communication acts, things will be done anyway. Communication also serves the purpose of enabling the evaluation of alternative actions and negotiating alternatives between various interested parties.

Reasoning about the organisation on the pragmatic level of abstraction, concerning communication economy, a method may benefit from employment of concepts such as

- observation – and other perceptions may lead to formation of
- intentions – which may be communicated or conveyed in
- speech acts – which are performed in accordance with established
- protocols – which are sometimes explicit to ensure
- effects – in terms of actions to be performed.

At this level, intentions behind as well as effects of various messages are in the focus of analysis. Yet, contemporary methods are very weak in analysing these aspects.

Future methodology development, in general, might benefit from a paradigm shift. Tradition of the past two decades has been that the fulcrum of the information system is its database. It contains data that has to be acquired, processed and delivered to various parties at the right points in time. In business, this paradigm is increasingly invalidated because of the extent to which the modern organisation is making itself dependent on fresh information for decision making. While most traditional approaches in information analysis have worked well for situations that are controlled by a sender or distributor, those approaches do neither work well for a consumer-controlled information acquisition situation nor for a negotiation-oriented work situation with more autonomous actors.

Positive trends may be observed in the emerging application of speech act theory and, to a limited extent, object-oriented methods for organisation analysis and design. Speech act theory is slowly gaining recognition, bringing the pragmatic level of business abstraction into focus. The theory has to be further developed to encompass other types of acts as well as being broadened in context. See Austin (1962), Auramäki et al (1988), Auramäki et al (1992), Flores et al (1988), Habermas (1984), Medina-Mora et al (1993) and Searle (1979). Object-oriented organisation analysis methods, where messages are modelled so as to invoke protocol determined services from the objects they are sent to, may also lead to improvement in the basic conception of how an organisation works. So far, however, existent analysis methods are fairly technical and lack the necessary integration of knowledge from different disciplines such as philosophy, organisation science, sociology, psychology and linguistics. Inclusion of such views is indispensable if relevant effects on relevant semiotic levels of information systems are to be captured by one's method.

Naturally, communication in itself constitutes action. It follows more or less established protocols or norms. Taking part in such an action demands sufficient adherence to applicable norms (or protocols in terms of social contracts), so as to achieve controllable effects. This begs a further question: What is actually communicated?

## *Information economy*

Exclusively, models are communicated.

Basically, communication aims at establishing sufficient conceptual correspondence or dissonance between actors to enable adequate action. Sometimes, this is thought of as degrees of (mental) model correspondence. Note that a model is a conception and can be given a multitude of denotations or representations. Models may convey beliefs concerning ordinary state of affairs as well as intentions.

We often forget our complete dependence on models. When a person tells something about something to another person, matters are, of course, about the persons conceptions of that something, the mental model, not about the something as such. Even if mechanical instruments are used for direct measurements, underlying assumptions – often called the observation model, which is a model on a higher level of abstraction – will affect both the outcome and the interpretation of one's findings. See Michael et al (1991).

The formulation above is very strict. It means that when communication takes place on a non-linguistic level, as passing the salt without any comment, this sign has to be interpreted in the correct context in the same manner as a linguistic message. The world is the text to formulate it a bit provocatively.

Another, semantically equivalent, answer to the question above, is that information is what is communicated. Generally, information is that what is made known without regard to how that is done. Semantically, we are completely indifferent to what medium, e.g. speech or handwriting, or what language – is employed – as long as the effects are the intended ones.

Meaning (semantics), as a concept, is recognised within a variety of more or less unstable theories. Often, the notion of semantics is equated with the intended or actual interpretation of an observed sentence. It may also relate to a correct and/or useful interpretation of observation of state of affairs. This means that concepts such as usefulness, truth and correspondence are treated at this level of reasoning. See Langefors (1966a).

Meaning and semantics is often treated as an absolute concept, dubiously coupled to the notion of total understanding. At the same time, conveying to a receiver all the connotations a sender has to a certain concept is impossible. However, in daily life and in running an enterprise, there is no need for total understanding. To achieve sufficient model correspondence between actors to facilitate adequate action is close to the goal of most information systems. Often, not even understanding, but rather adequate response in terms of action, is what is demanded. An alternative definition of information is to regard it as the effect over time that a message creates (Nilsson, 1979).

If we treat the concept of information as the meaning of a sentence, in reasoning, we have to handle the semantic and syntactical levels simultaneously. Also, the concept of communication has both a semantic and syntactic aspect which have to be considered together. For reasons of simplicity, this complication has not been taken into account.

When reasoning about the organisation on the meaning level of abstraction, thus handling aspects of information i.e. interpretation and expression economy, a method ought to be concerned with concepts such as;

- model – which can be seen as
- information – inherent in a structure of
- concepts – having certain
- meaning – and where those models may be evaluated in terms of
- truth – which is a tricky concept sometimes handled as
- correspondence – concerning descriptive or intentional matters

Now, to what extent do contemporary methods cover this level of abstraction? To some extent very well, to some extent only poorly.

The cost of misinterpretation of available data is very high, although it may be difficult to assign a motivated value in every instance. At any rate, this is a totally neglected area with vast economic consequences. See Carnap (1947), Chomsky (1968), O'Connor (1975), Langefors (1966 b) and Leech (1974).

Understanding data about the organisation requires a context for correct interpretation. In an IT-environment, this context is normally provided for by a mapping between a business concept model and a data model. Within such models, rules for interpretation are given by structural implications (part of the semantics is the placement in a conceptual structure) and by general textual descriptions of different conceptual components.

Concept modelling as well as process modelling and the interplay between these techniques have been given very much attention during the two last decades. There is, still, a most unfortunate focus on theory concerned with the syntactical aspects of concept modelling, while the problems related to model semantics and pragmatics of the utilisation of models are often neglected. This leads to unnecessary costs for change of applications and databases. Although the practitioner is well aware of the fact that a multi-perspective view is needed in modelling, the academic concentration on a few perspectives has lead to an unfortunate lack of well founded theory and instruments.

Earlier, we stated that coherent and goal-oriented action is based on evaluation and decision which, in turn, is based on the availability of information in terms of results from direct observation or communicated models. Now, this leads to a further question: How are models expressed?

## *Representation economy*

Models are expressed as sentences in defined languages.

When reasoning about the organisation on the syntactical level of abstraction, we are concerned with (agreed rules for) languages. This means that on this level of abstraction, we deal with the economics of formulation, presentation and manipulation and are concerned about concepts such as:

- model denotation – which is equivalent to a defined set of
- sentences – which are expressed in a
- language – which has a defined
- grammar – stating the structure within which
- references – or terms are to be interpreted, i.e. related to concepts.

Again, please note that we are not bound to traditional linguistic phenomena. A thing is in itself information bearing. Actually, like the rest of the levels of abstraction treated so far, proper reasoning about central concepts is not possible within one level only. This is done only as a didactic instrument. A central concept like reference, for instance, has to be treated on both the semantic and syntactical level in parallel.

Nevertheless, we are now on a level of abstraction where good theory is available as well as good working models and procedures. Actually, most of the methods available concentrate on this level.

As we have covered the most important aspects of business related analysis, we will stop the walk-through of the matrix here and revert the order of reasoning to check its validity.

## Climbing up the semiotic ladder

Let us assume that an actor, who has seen some business opportunity, wants a value creating activity to be performed. The action fits well within the business culture so the actor packages a message for good effect and, in the end gives it a certain encoding on, for example, a piece of paper. This time, we will start at the very bottom line of the matrix. Every layer in the matrix will now act as a filter or link in a chain. What is filtered out will not be there or, to take the analogy of a chain, one faulty link will break the chain. Whenever something goes wrong, value as intended will not be produced in proper action. What happens from the receivers standpoint?

On the level of encoding and detection economy, the requirement is that something has to be detectable. As humans we may well detect that somebody is trying to say something, without being able to hear what is said. We often know that a message is there before we know its contents. Some things are detectable with simple means, some things require special instruments. A colour-blind person might for instance totally miss a colour signal on a VDU. If parts of a message is not detectable, things might go wrong.

On the level of transmission economy, defined simple patterns or tokens has to be discernible with a reasonable accuracy. For instance it must be determinable if patterns are belonging to a defined vocabulary or not. Patterns which fulfil demands concerning requisite variety may still be subject to distortion (Shannon & Weaver, 1949). In this case, countermeasures such as redundancy and algorithmic error correction may come in handy. On this level, we often optimise with respect to storage and transmission economy on a basic level. On this level, from a human standpoint, things like overambitious use of short codes instead of ordinary text may cause problems, as may the opposite.

On the level of representation economy, vocabulary or references must hang together in larger patterns determined by the grammar of a language. Certain rules has to be followed and those must be known to all parties involved. It must be formally possible to judge if a sentence is syntactically correct. In storing or presenting data, we often introduce very artificial grammars adopted to records or tables on this level. On this level form of representation may determine if things succeed or not.

On the level of information economy, we are concerned whether a sentence or set of sentences is carrying meaning. Certain rules has to be followed both in interpreting and producing sentences. In this case, a set of sentences should be interpreted thus influencing model components in the interpreters mind. Note that the old definition of information as new knowledge fits in very well here. Naturally, a proper context has to be established for interpretation to be possible – either by earlier direct knowledge or by second order or meta knowledge. Bad definitions of terms may cause misinterpretation and spoil things.

On the level of communication economy, we have to take the total communication situation and interplay into consideration. Having understood a message, its contents has to be judged and intentions evaluated as well as the rights for participants to demand what might be asked for. In ordinary communication, this is done in a dialogue but, when submitted via IT-based systems, the reaction to, for instance, an order or invoice is often presupposed. Within such communication acts, roles of the participants normally are required to be well defined – for example in terms lines of command within an organisational structure or process. Sometimes we design processes where patterns of action are much more open and dependent on situation. Even such a simple thing as who has issued a message may cause trouble on this level.

On the level of culture economy, having established contents including intentions and rights, we value required action from a social or cultural standpoint. Here, motivating forces within the organisation complement the structures of allowance and command. A culture with rigid processes will have predetermined responses to a high degree while a permissible culture allows for a more flexible response and behaviour. As an example, efficiency on this level makes management by making sense possible. Unclear process interfaces, rule systems and personal mandates create problems on this level. Unclear vision and strategy creates severe problems, especially on higher levels in the organisation.

On the level of business economy, the aimed at action is taken by the receiver and value addition is performed. We have two classes of value addition. One is value addition within the organisation from a cultural perspective which is actually on the cultural or social level. Generally speaking, however, value must be seen from a standpoint outside the delivery process. In business, value is often seen in the perspective of the next process within the organisation or the external customer process. Unclear strategies concerning self sufficiency of business areas or products create problems as does a variety of principles for internal billing and auditing

As we have walked through this it has probably become clear that the situation is far more complex than described.

- One point which has to be observed, and which complicates things in analysis, is that in reality, we act in parallel on all levels of the table. Analysis, on the other hand, is often performed on the different semiotic levels as if they were unconnected.

- Analysis perspectives as well as analysis levels have to coexist within the analysis process but still form a coherent whole.

In practice, this means that a certain concept has to be looked upon from different angles or perspectives during an analysis. This begs for a further question: In which framework should the set of concepts be applied?

# On the need for architecture in modelling: A fractal, multi-perspective view

Like value, fundamental principles of or goals for any system, have to be found outside the system in question itself. What would be a natural context in this case?

In our view, a sound architecture of models and basic concepts for modelling have to be based on reasons adherent to:

- *Human action.* On what premises do we act – what are the basic motivations?

- *Management principles.* How do we direct and control business affairs – how is action obtained?

- *Philosophical and formal basis.* Can we use it in a controlled and reasonably secure way?

On a more trivial level, a sound architecture also has to support an efficient work process, efficient communication etc. It must also, be sufficiently adaptable or configurable to meet the demands of different analysis and design situations.

Let us, again, short-circuit the deeper discussion and directly look at a
generic version of the structure (see Figure 1). Initially, we will keep to a
minimal set of concepts and perspectives to communicate structural
aspects without complications.

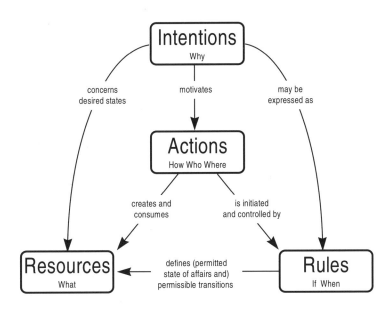

*Figure 1. Generic perspectives in a model architecture.*

The basic architecture of the generic perspectives fractal is very simple.
Intentions motivate actions. Actions create and consume resources and are
controlled by rules. Rules determine permissible transitions of state of
affairs. In popular terms, we may talk about a why, a what, a how and a
when or under-which-conditions perspective.

To relate back to the earlier reasoning, value is mainly created by action.
On an abstract level, to create value is equivalent to create resources or
change their state. In the process of creating resources, other resources are

consumed or their state changed. Note that resource is a very abstract concept.

In modelling, the perspectives just described are applied on one and the same object of study, the business. The business or part thereof is studied from an intentional, a behavioural, a resource and a rule perspective – the same object of study but, different glasses or filters.

How would these perspectives correspond to a simple model of human behaviour?

## *Human action in focus*

The basis for survival is clearly adequate action, but what makes us, human beings, act?

Motivation, both in terms of desires and fear, seems to be linked to, on one hand, beliefs concerning state of affairs and their evolution over time and, on the other, to conceptions of desirable state of affairs over time (see Figure 2). Action is normally performed on the basis of such beliefs and aims at changing of, or conservation of, states. Naturally, a state should not be regarded as something static in a narrow sense. The actual place for a car may be viewed as a state, as well as its speed or its acceleration. An action, where these states may be changed, is pressing the accelerator.

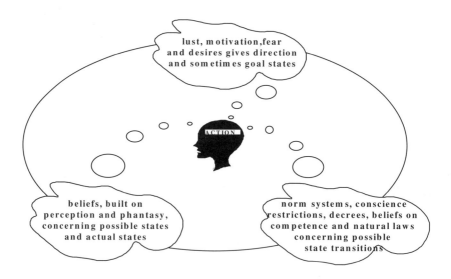

*Figure 2. Human action in context.*

Action is also normally restrained by what we perceive as norms, natural laws etc. On all levels of reasoning, however, there seems to be a choice involved, maybe, to some extent excluding the actual state of affairs.

In general terms, human action seems to fit into a realm of models concerning possibilities and actualities which seems to correspond well to the generic structure (see Figure 3).

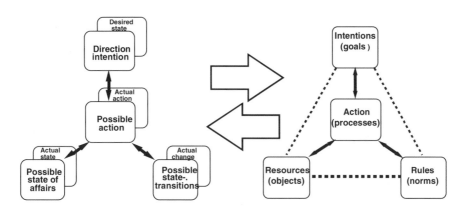

*Figure 3. The architecture applied to modelling human action.*

Let us take a simple example to get a better flavour of the architecture at work. Assume it is raining and that we decide to use an umbrella. Since long, we know how an umbrella works and which effects it may have in different situations, we have an established basis of action patterns and also an action readiness. We know the rules and procedures, we are aware of the process. When we expand the umbrella, which, of course, is to be regarded as a resource, we do that with the intention of remaining dry, i.e. to create another resource, a dry space. In this case we want to uphold a certain state of affairs threatened by natural causes. At the same time, the umbrella gets wet which may be perceived as a decrement in status when we return indoors. It may even require an drying action, which may need a spatial resource at home. Now what does the example tell us?

Intentions concern state of affairs. Our actions may create resources – even of an abstract nature. At the same time, however, resources are used to create other resources. Intentions, which motivates our actions, are a specific kind of rules, where the rule is not absolute. We may not succeed, for example. Some rules seem to be fairly absolute, like natural laws while other rules seem to be more loose like the rule of not placing a wet umbrella on the sofa. But, are not rules and behavioural patterns in themselves resources?

Actually, when standing outside the model looking at the business, the perspectives might seem rather unrelated. When standing inside the model, regardless of the perspective within which we stand, we will detect aspects of this perspective in all the other perspectives. It is also the case that given good instruments, all perspectives can, more or less, be described by any other perspective.

- When modelling, we find that everything mentioned in any class of model may be treated as a resource – and also modelled as an object.

- Given a sufficiently powerful way of modelling rules, everything could be modelled as rules, including object existence and behavioural patterns.

- Any rule could be also be implemented in behavioural patterns, i.e. procedural terms. In this case, flexibility might suffer heavily.

We also, in practice, find that things like permitted state of affairs almost always is modelled directly it the object models, as indicated above. The rule perspective has here migrated into the resource perspective.

Earlier, we said that co-ordinated action was based on shared or available models. Starting from a humanistic standpoint we state that providing for goal models, action or process models, resource or object models and rule models seems to be fundamental. Will this hold if we apply a management perspective?

## *Management principles in focus*

Control information in a business situation seems mainly to revolve around the same categories as in the person centred situation. Controlling information like orders contain aspects of goals to be achieved, resources allowed to consume and rules within which to act as well as already established procedures. For instance, in many military organisations, an order has mandatory points concerning objectives, resources available for the task and restrictions on action – rules and standard procedures to be followed. In this case, by keeping the restrictions or demands on action to a minimum, the aim to allow for maximum freedom to solve the task within given boundaries is secured.

Over the years management principles or, rather, clichés have developed which concentrate on one of the aspects mentioned at a time (see Figure 4). Over time, a balanced view or, rather, a situation dependent mixture of these aspects has emerged. Today, fast action in an increasingly complex situation where rules and procedures take too long to develop has called for principles like management by making sense. This requires the basic intentions of the organisation to be made known together with the rule system within which to act but also demands competence with a wider span than earlier.

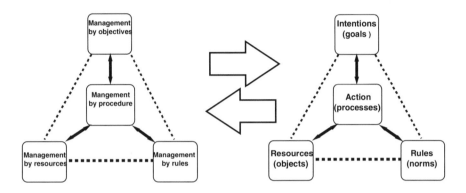

*Figure 4. Management styles and the model architecture.*

It looks as if the perspectives as proposed are quite natural also in a business environment. What does this means in terms of classes of models?

## Modelling the business and its information support

To facilitate the reasoning, we will discuss things in classes of models or model types. Observe that this is a rather brutal simplification for a practitioner even if contemporary modelling tools as well as contemporary research often make this assumption. In practice, model aspects are often mixed for a variety of very good reasons. We will further simplify the reasoning by adopting a very conventional attitude to developing information systems.

As stated earlier, in business, co-ordinated action is enabled by communication. We will call the basic or composite elements of communication business messages (see Figure 5). These messages might contain models of the business with intentional as well as descriptive aspects.

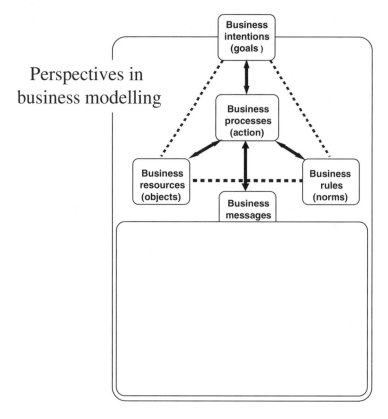

*Figure 5. Generic perspectives applied to conventional business modelling.*

Business action is explicitly controlled by messages. When modelling the business, messages are normally also components of the commonly used process models. If we talk about business in general, classes of messages may well be regarded as special kinds of objects. But what is actually isomorphic between the business and its IT-support systems – can we use the same structure?

It seems as if we can. If we analyse an information system in terms of processes, resources intentions and rules, we may link this structure to the structure of perspectives in modelling the business. Let us start with the process or action perspective.

The process perspective on an information system is close to an application perspective – a process model of the business is similar to an application model of the information support system. Now, on which resources does an application operate?

Normally, the major resource would be data. Not any data though, but data describing the business objects. The business resource model or the business object model is similar to an application resource model, i.e. an information or data model. What would be the system intention?

In most cases, the system intention would be seen as the competence for message production as a result of messages received. This is to say the system services provided. From an external perspective, this is also very close to the services provided by a business – or any kind of system. However, this also means that we have a link between the model of the business and the model of the information support system in the message model, which is defining which services the system should give the business processes (see Figure 6).

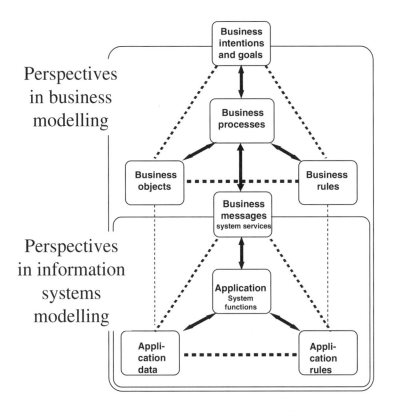

*Figure 6. Generic modelling perspectives applied in modelling the business system and its information support system, conventional version.*

As said, an application or, rather, a system function, has as its basic resource, not the objects of the business, but, the data about these objects.

The processes of the business want services from the system, normally information services. In this case, the application creates new data from data in the same way as resources in general are created from resources. This means that most external goals of an IT-based information support system can be stated in terms of messages as well as their properties of a non-functional character like timeliness etc. In practice, caution has to be observed, as both information- and data-oriented aspects may find their way into the business demands on a system.

Just to complete the picture, in the same way as state transitions in the business is regulated, state transitions in data is also regulated by certain rules. Please note once more that the information handling might well be the value creating core process of the business.

Let us for a while return to the intentional part of the information systems architecture. The message model defines an interface between the business processes and the information support system

The interface model is the only model that simultaneously belongs to the set of business and IT-oriented models.

The interface-model is the fulcrum of concerns between IT-oriented models and the business oriented models. What is then an interface?

Think of an interface as – nothing – just a surface as between water and air. Where one stops, the other starts. To use another metaphor, think of an interface as a infinitesimally thin piece of paper which could be written upon and read from one side by the user side and from the other side by the information system. On one side, things just appear when so decided by the other. Forget concepts like "intelligent interface". We have seen the architecture at work on two levels, would this be sufficient for ordinary usage?

## *Expanding the utilisation of the architecture*

Within a model based method, we clearly have to partition the analysis in smaller chunks. A standard application of the structure would be in a four or five layered analysis. Within this structure, we have applied the fractal on two levels of reasoning roughly corresponding to the operational business level and the conceptual information system level (see Figure 7).

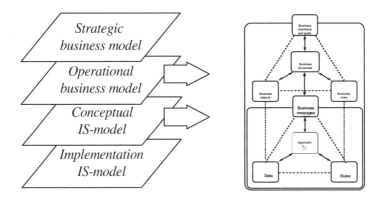

*Figure 7. Standard four levels of application.*

Let us start the expansion with a brief look at the operational and strategic levels of analysis in combination. On the strategic level, the action perspective might lead into analysis of a variety of market and customer processes, trends behaviour etc. The resource perspective might lead into analysis of products on the market – as well as their producers and production facilities searching possible partnerships, evaluating competition etc. The rule perspective might lead to international analysis of market and product legislation, ethics etc. Now, with the focus outgoing from the operational business model, would the same model interaction perspective hold?

Let us study a limited case (see Figure 8 below).

In the illustrative example above, an analysis might encompass the consumers, their needs over time and in prognoses as well as the development of the own production and sales processes to supply adequate products and services to meet foreseen demands.

Observe that we have the same interface thinking replicated. The potential or actual customer sees only the products and services provided, including advertising and such, but not the internals of the business.

Observe also that the models in this case are encapsulated. The market environment contains the business contains the information system.

Sometimes it is preferable to analyse the information system in a larger number of separate levels than indicated in the standard model. The information system in a broad sense, encompassing the human information processing, is then analysed separated from the information system in its narrow sense, the IT-based one. In this case, the information system in its broad sense would encapsulate the narrow sense system. This would just add yet another level in the architecture. Now, how about implementation strategies with respect to the structure?

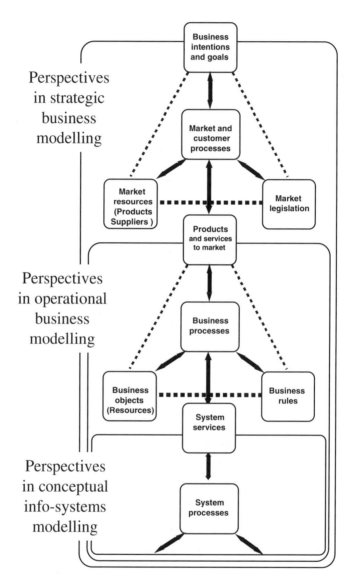

*Figure 8. Example of strategic and operational models in interplay.*

In a classical implementation, we would have set up a data manipulation interface, a control interface (possibly with a rule base as its kernel) and a presentation and manipulation interface round the application. This would give a good structure. However, the fractal is not used in the same encapsulated fashion in this case. Rather, the same fractal is used but this time expanding and deepening the analysis on the previous level.

Using an object orientated approach, everything works well on the surface except for the rules. There is no direct correspondence as rules will have to be spread and converted into methods. This happens to be one of the weakest points in object orientation, where rule allocation leads to severe problems. In complex environments, a rule base may complement the class definitions.

In practice, though, object oriented thinking has lead to a very profitable definition in the architecture for implementation. For object oriented implementation, process objects were introduced to exclusively handle the process logic of the organisation. This means, if a business process has work flow support, that there is a corresponding process class and that the process instances will be treated as objects.

We also work with basic business logic in the "business objects" and, naturally, with view-objects. The introduction of process objects has lead to good results while the dilemma around ordinary control objects stays.

# Why and when to model what: Motives related to some classical model types

Very briefly, we may say that different perspectives and classes of models on different levels of analysis contributes to our main goal, supporting value creation in an effective manner, in rather dissimilar ways, and on different levels in the semiotic structure.

## *Business intention and goal models*

- *Rationale:* To secure long term efficient evolution of the business, to give direction, stimulate business development and ensure relevant business operation and strategy. To support organisational culture, allowing effective management. *All decisions. in the analysis and design process should be traceable to these analyses.*

- *Major concepts:* Culture, value, goal, intention, belief

- *Forms:* Vision statements, scenarios, goal models, problem statements, action plans etc. with representations from text to formal diagrams.

## Business process models

- *Rationale:* To secure an efficient operation of the business.

- *Major concepts:* Social system, behaviour, process, information, actor, responsibility, action, observation, decision

- *Forms:* Process models, organisation models, logistics models, function models, actor models, action workflow models etc. with a variety of representations such as CATN-networks, petri nets, life cycle diagrams etc.

## Business rule models

- *Rationale:* To guarantee a stable basis for controlling the business.

- *Major concepts:* Norm, rule, logic, condition, state, transition, event

- *Forms:* Rule models, legal documents in the form of text, formal notation, transition diagrams etc.

## Business resource or object models

- *Rationale:* To secure a reasonable view of what the business concerns. To develop a business language with abstractions independent of operational issues as a basis for change.

- *Major concepts:* Concept, resource, object, property, relation, state

- *Forms:* Object models, terminologies, definitions in the form of diagrams, formal languages and text.

## Business messages or business communication models

- *Rationale:* Normally, to ensure correct and effective supply and usage of information.

- *Major concepts:* Communication act, speech act, protocol, message, language, grammar, sentence.

- *Forms:* Dialogue structure diagrams, message types (including screen layouts etc.) EDI-definitions

### Application or system function models

- *Rationale:* To ensure an adequate and flexible development, with a high degree of reuse

### Information system resources, information or data models

- *Rationale:* To secure the information demand and supply in adequate base data.

### Information system rule models

- *Rationale:* To secure data quality and give a stable basis for applications development

Above, we have exemplified different perspectives using different classes of models. When configuring the architecture for a certain work, we certainly have a lot to choose from. But have we really exploited the perspective approach enough?

# Mixing model perspectives: A note on process analysis

We will use the fractal again, but in a slightly different way. Earlier, we used the pattern to look at an object of analysis from different perspectives. The fractal could be used in another way, by standing in a model and looking in on the other models or, rather, perspectives of analysis. Let us take the process and have a look at it from the other perspectives.

If we start with studying the process from the resource perspective. First we may distinguish physical from information resources as being used and produced by the process. Information resources may be divided into general information, event information, which just is a special case, and signal information which has the role of direct synchronisation.

If we move to a rule perspective, we might like to define start and stop criteria for processes, conditions for signalling etc.

Earlier, we also asserted that the most important part of a process model is the goal formulations. If we study the process from this perspective, goals, efficiency measurements and the like will show, but many of these will be formulated as rules in practice. A goal is a not necessarily fulfilled rule or condition.

In a process model, as the link to resources is obvious, we tend to include elements from many different model types into one model and we often work along the following mixed scheme (see Figure 9).

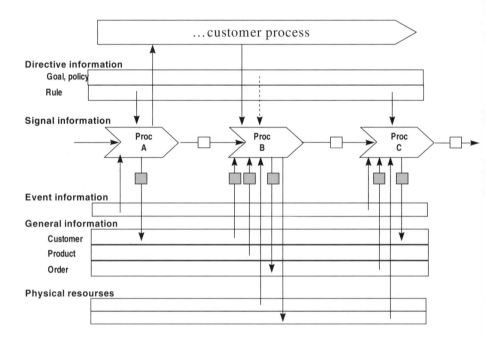

*Figure 9. Mixing classes of models in one analysis and presentation.*

The following things may be observed:

- Analysing the interplay between the customer oriented business processes at hand and the customer process is often a key factor for creating a really purposeful operational pattern. This is often called mirroring the delivery process and the customer process.

- The introduction of the resource level (the score or partitur) makes desynchronisation of process components more easy to illustrate. By not keeping to a conventional process model, we may handle complex event driven situations.

Still, process or workflow definitions express rather static patterns on how things are to be done. These very powerful instrument are used to great advantage, but can we find more flexible ways to go?

# On linguistic and cultural grammars

To stimulate further research on business analysis and design methods, we will take a short look at the concept of grammar. We will not actually expose experience – as very little is at hand but, rather, try to provide for inspiration.

- When we utter a sentence which has never been uttered by a human being before, it may still be understood. We can also detect if it is correctly or incorrectly expressed as well as if it is meaningful or not. This phenomenon is based on the existence of a linguistic grammar. Such a grammar provides for generative and interpretative capabilities.

- When we perform an action within a certain business context, this action may be understood and appreciated. People will also detect if the action is proper or dubious in character or if it indeed fall outside what is considered tolerable. This phenomenon can be said to be based on a cultural grammar. Such a grammar generates behaviour and allows also interpretation and judgement thereof.

Patterns for action may be fixed as in workflow definitions or more open as defined by cultural grammars. Instruments to properly analyse and express business grammar might be a key element in coming generations of business analysis methods. However, such instruments do not exist for practical usage.

Before ending this chapter it might be prudent to ask: Are there critical elements in our own cultural grammar, being modelling facilitators, that is of outstanding importance?

# On basic philosophy and modelling

In modelling, we work according to very different grammars on different levels. Differences concerning linguistic grammars and the syntax of graphical or lexical model expressions are nowadays of minor importance.

As the profession advances and the problems are getting more sophisticated, elements of the cultural grammar – the driving forces behind how we approach things – seem to be of increasing importance.

- Basic philosophical issues are, in fact, the ones that have the most dramatic impact during practical modelling during the analysis and design of organisational systems and their information systems.

- In a reasonably complex situation, the choice of a hard-nosed Naive Realist's position will be a fairly good guarantee for creating a modelling disaster.

- In practice, a moderate constructivist approach seems to be the most viable one. The conception of reality is then seen as a product of a social process. As a corollary, the product of the modelling effort is to be seen as a social contract on how to effectively perceive and communicate about things in the business – not a description of how things really are, the truth.

With this final comment, we have linked back to the basic criterion of relevance, the creation of value and the interdependencies between language, model and effectiveness.

# Acknowledgements

This chapter is, in its first part, related to working paper contributions to the IFIP task group FRISCO creating a framework of fundamental information system concepts. Especially, I would like to thank Prof. Ron Stamper at the University of Twente for radically increasing my insight concerning the power of applying semiotics in practical analysis.

The second part is, to some extent, based on an invited contribution for the 1991 CAiSE conference. On this occasion, my presentation was based on results from a work for Ericsson, Sweden Post and Telia (Swedish Telecom). The layered model architecture, or, rather its enclosed, fractal properties, drew inspiration from a set of beautiful wooden Russian dolls.

For essentially all processes related thinking, I am greatly in dept to Gösta Steneskog, without whom this chapter, as well as much of my work as a consultant, would deliver lower quality.

# References

Ackoff, R.L. (1971) "Towards a System of System Concepts", *Management Science*, Vol. 17, July.

Auramäki, E., Hirschheim, R., & Lyytinen, K. (1992) "Modelling Offices Through Discourse Analysis: A Comparison and Evaluation of SAMPO and OSSAD and ICN", *The Computer Journal*, Vol. 35, No. 5.

Auramäki, E., Lehtinen, E., & Lyytinen, K. (1988) "A Speech-Act-Based Office Modeling Approach", *ACM Transactions on Office Information Systems*, Vol. 6, No. 2.

Austin, J. L., (1962) *How to Do Things with Words*, Harvard University Press, Boston, Massachusetts.

Berger, P. & Luckmann, T. (1966) *The Social Construction of Reality*, Doubleday, New York.

Bunge, M.A. (1977) *Ontology I: The Furniture of the World. Vol. 3 of Treatise on Basic Philosophy*, D. Reidel Publishing Company, Dordrecht, The Netherlands.

Bunge, M.A. (1979) *Ontology II: A World of Systems. Vol. 4 of Treatise on Basic Philosophy*, D. Reidel Publishing Company, Dordrecht, The Netherlands.

Carnap, R. (1947) *Meaning and Necessity*, University of Chicago Press, Chicago.

Checkland, P.B. (1981) *Systems Thinking, Systems Practice*, John Wiley and Sons, Chichester, England.

Chomsky, N. (1968) *Language and Mind*, Harcourt, Brace & World, New York.

Davenport, T.H. & Short, J.E. (1990) "The New Industrial Engineering: Information Technology and Business Process Redesign", *Sloan Management Review*, Summer, pp. 11-27.

Earl, M.J. (1989) *Management Strategies for Information Technology*, Prentice Hall International, New York.

Falkenberg, E.D., Hesse, W., Lindgreen, P., Nilsson, B.E., Oei, J.L.H., Rolland, C., Stamper, R.K., Van Assche, F.J.M., Verrijn-Stuart, A.A., Voss, K. (1996) *FRISCO: A Framework of Information System Concepts*, The IFIP WG 8.1 Task Group FRISCO, International Federation for Information Processing, Geneva.

Flores, F., Graves, M., Hartfield, B. & Winograd, T. (1988) "Computer Systems and the Design of Organizational Interaction", *ACM Transactions on Office Information Systems*, Vol. 6, No. 2.

Gibson, C.F., Singer, C.J., Schnidman, A.A. & Davenport, T.H. (1984) "Strategies for Making an Information System Fit Your Organization", *Management Review*, January, pp. 8-14.

van Griethuysen, J.J. (ed.) (1982) *Concepts and Terminology for the Conceptual Schema and the Information Base*, ISO/TC 97/SC5 Report – N 695, International Organization for Standardization, Geneva [Also available as ISO/TC 97/SC5 Technical Report 9007, 1987]

Habermas, J. (1984) *The theory of communicative action*, Beacon Press, Boston, Massachusetts.

Langefors, B. (1966 a) *Samband mellan object och verklighet*, Report IB-ADB 66 No. 1, Royal Institute of Technology and Stockholm University, Stockholm [*Model field and object field correspondence*].

Langefors, B. (1966 b) *Theoretical Analysis of Information Systems*, Studentlitteratur, Lund, Sweden [Also published 1973 by Auerbach, Philadelphia].

Leech, G. (1974) *Semantics*, Penguin Books, Harmondsworth, Great Britain.

Leonard-Barton, D. (1988) "Implementation Characteristics of Organizational Innovations," *Communication Research*, Vol. 15, No. 5, pp. 603-631.

Medina-Mora, R., Winograd, T., Flores, R., & Flores, F. (1993) "The Action Workflow Approach to Workflow Management Technology", in Turner, J. & Kraut, R. (eds.) *Proceedings of the 4th Conference on Computer Supported Cooperative Work*, ACM, New York.

Michael, J.B., Sibley, E.H. & Wexelblat R.L. (1991) "A modeling paradigm for representing intention in information systems policy," *Proceedings of the First Workshop on Information Technologies and Systems*, Massachusetts Institute of Technology, Sloan School of Management, Cambridge, Massachusetts.

Mumford, E. (1983) *Designing Human Systems*, Manchester Business School, Manchester, England.

Nilsson, B.E. (1979) *On Models and Mappings in a Data Base Environment. – A Holistic Approach to Data Modeling*, Statistics Sweden, Stockholm.

O'Connor, D.J. (1975) *The Correspondence Theory of Truth*, Hutchinson, London.

Searle, J.R. (1979) "A Taxonomy of Illocutionary Acts", in *Expression and Meaning: Studies in the Theory of Speech Acts*, Cambridge University Press, Cambridge, Massachusetts.

Shannon, C.E. & Weaver, W. (1949) *The Mathematical Theory of Communication*, University of Illinois Press, Urbana, Illinois.

Sibley, E.H., Michael, J.B. & Wexelblat, R.L. (1991) "An Approach to Formalizing Policy Management." *Proceedings of the Second International Conference on Economics and Artificial Intelligence*, Pergamon Press, Oxford, England.

Stamper, R. K (1973) *Information in Business and Administrative Systems*, Wiley, New York.

Sundgren, B. (1974) *Conceptual Foundation to the Infological Approach to Data Bases*, in Klimbie, J. W. and Koffeman, K. L., (eds.) Data Base Mangement, North Holland, Amsterdam.

Weber, M. (1947) *Theory of Social and Economic Organization*, Free Press, New York.

# 15

# Business Modeller's Checklist: "Dos" and "Don'ts" in Hands-on Practice

## *Hans Willars*

*As may be apparent by this book, there is a multitude of approaches, models and methods in the marketplace, giving opportunities to combine them in business modelling. However, good performance in business modelling practice demands more. Therefore, this chapter aims to sum up some hints and requirements for success, collected from experienced business modellers throughout the years. First, an adequate point of view is settled through a couple of "basic assumptions". Eternal questions, appearing in every business modelling situation, are discussed in "main issues of analysis". The human aspects are specifically important in "teamwork modelling", demanding good advice for team situation handling. Practicalities concerning material etc. is covered in "tools for business modelling". Finally, some advice is given for "yourself as a business modeller", covering how to perform and develop as a business modelling professional.*

## Background and justification

As may be apparent by this book, there is a multitude of approaches, models and methods in the marketplace, giving opportunities to combine them in business modelling. However, good performance in business modelling practice demands more than models and methods.

Therefore, this chapter aims to sum up some hints and requirements for success, collected from experienced business modellers throughout the years. The hints are given rather briefly, sometimes illustrated with examples.

In order to get some structure, the hints are organised under the following five headings:

- *Basic assumptions* in order to promote an adequate point of view.

- *Main issues of analysis* or "eternal questions", always burning regardless of method used.

- *Teamwork in Business Modelling,* to avoid obstacles and produce value.

- *Tools for Business Modelling,* manual as well as computerised.

- *Yourself* as a business modelling facilitator.

The chapter ends with some final conclusions for further research.

# Basic assumptions for Business Modelling success

## *About business models*

Every business model is an expression of thoughts and conceptions regarding the business and its environment. Actually, the *real* models are in the minds of people, and what we usually call "business models" are some simplified symbolic abstraction expressed in some medium. Bearing this in mind, much confusion and time-wasting disputes may be avoided.

Furthermore, the general purpose with business models is to promote understanding and new knowledge within the business in focus. Hence, the way to produce and express business models should take into account, and amplify, the human capability to create knowledge. Procedures and symbols must be chosen accordingly. (The role of business models is further discussed by Tolis in chapter 7).

## *About the modelled domain*

In this book, an approach to combine various methods and models is proposed. To avoid confusion, it is very important to make clear what each model (or part thereof) is attempting to be a *model of.* For example, business models and information system models are easily mixed-up, specifically if they are expressed in similar notations. They should be separated since they are of different kinds, addressing different issues and involving different professionals. Such reduction of confusion is a necessary pre-condition for bridging the gap between business people and systems people, as advocated by Nilsson, Tolis & Nellborn in chapter 1.

The synergistic approach to combine methods is specifically addressed by Nellborn in chapter 11 and Nilsson in chapter 12, explaining how method chains and alliances can promote a more integrated way of working. See also how Steneskog in chapter 9 recommends a distinction between modelling the physical and the virtual worlds, respectively.

Concerning the notation, there is usually one supplied with the method being used. It is frequently of practical importance not to get stuck in that notation but to combine it with other kinds of expression: Pictures, tables, plain text, etc.

## About the outcome from Business Modelling

Business modelling may yield a variety of benefits: More profitable concepts for products or customers (implying new business), efficient processes, valid and consistent requirements for IT, communicated business directions, etc. Hence, every presumed outcome should be kept in mind from the start, in order to implement it as soon as possibilities emerge.

It must not stay in the mind, though. In negotiating a business modelling assignment there are sometimes difficulties to explain and visualise all benefits. By some initial education, the demands of the customer may be raised. Then, a more clever contract can be designed, as discussed by Rapp in chapter 10.

## About the overall direction of Business Modelling

The usual direction of business modelling is *co-ordinated development*. Depending on the situation, other directions (or combinations) may apply:

* *Managing direction:* Management intentions/views are expressed to company staff.

* *Conflict direction:* Different points-of-view are confronted in order to force conflicting issues to the surface.

* *Knowledge direction:* Business knowledge is propagated in the organisation.

### *About the culture for Business Modelling*

Consciousness, openness and distinctiveness are the guiding stars for business modelling success. In a culture where issues are kept in the dark, where there is fear, or where distinctiveness is avoided, no analysis method can be successful. Other measures have to be taken.

Specifically, business modellers should be aware that in cultures characterised by a large amount of "politics", distinctiveness is usually not preferred but rather avoided!

And cultures regularly are difficult to change. In chapter 4, Andersson claims this as "a matter of destroying the dictatorship of current thinking".

# Main issues of analysis in Business Modelling

In business modelling practice it has been extremely beneficial to base the analysis on a model architecture, i.e. an overall structure for the modelled phenomena. Examples are given by Lindström in chapter 8 (MALDIV approach), by Bubenko and Kirikova in chapter 13 (Enterprise model), and by Nilsson in chapter 14 (Generic perspectives). Some main analysis issues, as they have turned out following chapter 14, boil down to:

- *Intentions,* the "Why-issue": Why does this business exist, and what do we want to achieve with it?

- *Actions,* the "How-issue": How do we act and perform, in business processes and procedures?

- *Resources,* the "What-issue": What business objects/resources are we attending to in our actions?

Since those issues are unavoidable in almost every business modelling activity, some hints and advice will be helpful.

As a consequence of the combinatorial approach, there is not one fixed sequence of steps specifying, once and for all, how to proceed in resolving the analysis issues. Treat the issues according to the primary problem of the situation. A few examples on how to get started:

- Unknown present state of business procedures and their actual usage of IT resources: Process analysis.

- Vaguely expressed directives/objectives: Goal analysis. (Generally, if nothing else is known, goal analysis is a sure starter: there must be at least one intention in a business! Get it clear and you are on the track.)

- Confused terminology in communicating business matters: Business objects analysis.

On the marketplace there are many models and methods suitable for addressing such problems. Learn how to use and combine them!

Based on the outcome you may decide how to continue. As shown in the chapters referred above, there is always a couple of possibilities for value-adding combinations step by step. You are never lost!

## About models in general

Let the aims and intended outcomes of the modelling assignment govern every step. There is a "why-issue" also for business modelling as such!

Avoid reinventing the wheel, learn how to reuse models and methods already in the marketplace. As Nilsson, Tolis & Nellborn explain in chapter 1, the main baseline for research on business modelling is to make use of *existing* knowledge. See also Nellborn (chapter 11) and Nilsson (chapter 12), proposing frameworks for assessing the adequacy of combining existing methods.

Avoid the mistake to believe that (or act as if) objects, processes or whatever you model, "are out there", and it is just to "go and get them". Modelling should not be seen as merely a reproductive activity, but a constructive one: a design activity. The designed pattern makes something well-known appear in a new, value-added way.

Make different points-of-view meet, and don't let one limited view dominate. Frequently this will be the financial view. The Balanced Scorecard approach is an example of how different kinds of goals may be viewed in balance, see Kaplan & Norton (1996).

Focus primarily on the core idea of the business at hand. Avoid modelling "the administrative system". This will come out by itself, related to the core business.

Establish the long-term stable base for change and development, common to all parties within the business. Example from banking: When the concept of *(savings) account* was generalised from "a way to *save* money" to "an aid in the *general handling* of money", new financial services may be developed, making use of this aid.

Make the language of the business at hand present in the models. Avoid "foreign" language with words not belonging to the domain. During the modelling, however, the language of the business may well be developed.

The interpretation of all models is clarified by the business objects model. In that model, all basic concepts and terms for the business at hand may be naturally defined in relation to each other.

Employ a relevant "base model" with assumptions and language accepted by the business. Examples: Avoid industrial assumptions and terminology when modelling health care, viewing patients as mere "objects" to be "repaired". As Andersson reports in chapter 4, the concept of "customer" may be controversial in social insurance. Also, as Steneskog explains in chapter 9, we should avoid using "physical" base models in analysis of the "virtual" world.

Make frequent use of general systems theory: Every model or part thereof may be further detailed/decomposed, and is itself part of a more embracing super-model. Consequently, avoid decomposition into a, once and for all, limited number of levels, thus deliberately putting strait-jacket on human abstraction capability. Example of strait-jacket thinking: A process may consist of sub-processes, each consisting of activities, and that's it. Example of liberated thinking: A process may consist of processes consisting of processes, etc., as many levels as needed in the current situation (cf. the discussion regarding Sweden Post by Nellborn & Tolis, chapter 3).

Look for logical and workable model decompositions, simplifying continued modelling. Decompose for separation into specific aspects.

Make sure that models connect consistently. No loose ends or isolated "islands". Model consistency is a necessary prerequisite for model quality. (The issue of model quality is more thoroughly discussed by Bubenko and Kirikova in chapter 13)

In general, try to work top-down, starting from an overall "helicopter view". But beware: In a top-down approach you may take the most important decisions when you know the least! Hence, be prepared to backtrack and "kill your babies" when you learn more. Some arguments about top-down are given in Jackson (1995).

Demonstrate and teach, by examples, what "structuring" may be in different models. Introduce structures gradually, referring to experiences: "At company X they did like this…". Example: basic ideas of how to structure insurance policies could in fact be "inherited" from the product structure in a manufacturing industry, just changing some words used.

## *Modelling business intentions/goals/objectives*

Relate the modelled business to its context. Focusing only on internal goals is misleading, there must be at least one external, superordinate goal. A goal is specifically relevant if it contributes, directly or indirectly, to business external effectiveness and efficiency. Example: A common external goal is "customer satisfaction".

Thus, every goal must be justified by its contribution, directly or indirectly, to superordinate goals. Relate goal statements to each other with the "contributes to" relation.

Look for goals giving multiple contributions "upwards", indicating possibilities to "kill many birds with one stone".

Investigate contribution power and basic assumptions underpinning a contribution idea. Are they valid?

Look for goal conflicts. Explore "prevents/hinders" relations between goals, and define actions for managing the conflict. It is important to sort out how goals are related and ranked, specifically if they are in conflict. In ranking goal importance, use the knowledge and experience present in the team.

Every goal should correspond to some action(s) to achieve it, otherwise you have just a pipedream. Goals may be challenging, but not impossible.

Use problem experiences to reveal the relevant goals, and use stated goals to track related problems. Example from health care: "The problem is that patients do not listen to what we say". Ask: "Why is this a problem?", and you force the goal to surface: "They should learn how to treat themselves". Continued analysis: "Is there any other means to achieve this?", and the problem may be avoided rather than solved!

State goals carefully with a full sentence. Practice sentence completion: "The goal is to… (achieve what?)". It is not adequate with just one or two words which usually give a rather vague understanding of what precisely is to be achieved.

Stress the question "Why?" to reveal the contribution of a goal and justify it in terms of a superordinate goal. Stress the question "How?" to reveal the requirements for a goal, making it more operative and measurable. (Those questions never fail, provided you have competent team!)

Avoid the common trap to measure what is easily measured, instead of what needs to be measured. Establish goals first, then measures for achievements.

Break down compound goals into several single-goal statements. Continue by compiling their structure. Example: "More, and wealthier, customers in order to yield more profit" contains two goals contributing to a third.

## Modelling business actions/procedures

Process models may serve as the hub in a holistic view of business and IT, with other models related to, and accessible through, the processes. Examples: The Lindström MALDIV approach in chapter 8, the Bubenko and Kirikova Enterprise model in chapter 13, the Nilsson Generic perspectives in chapter 14.

Regard a process as a pattern for value-adding actions in a workflow. Value added is the primary criterion of relevance in every process model. Define the values added! (Not necessarily *economic* value only)

Value is added through transformation of resources. Define the resources! This implies business object modelling, from a business usage point of view. Relate actions to objects: *What* is required *where*?

Transformations connect to each other by interfaces. Define the interfaces! This implies business object as well as object information analysis. What is communicated in order to make the business move? The interface objects between processes are easy to forget, as was shown in the experiences from Ericsson and Sweden Post (chapters 2 and 3).

Value added should relate to what is/was intended. Define the intentions! This implies business intention/goal analysis. Every business action should contribute to some business goal(s). Relate them.

Every piece of work may produce a value, also "support processes". Avoid the distressful insult that some parts of the business add no value! Value produced may be regarded by other transformations in various ways: directives, prerequisites or input to be further transformed. Define! Example: In negotiation processes with suppliers, the value produced is a couple of call-off agreements, which may be regarded/used as resources by call-off operations.

As a simple starter, approach a concrete physical workflow known by everybody. Introduce abstractions gradually. Example: Start with the process of producing a specific physical goods, before turning to the general production process covering goods and services in general. However, as Steneskog argues in chapter 9, business processes are becoming increasingly virtual, making the "simple physical starter" inadequate. Hence, we must learn to approach the virtual world with simplicity! According to Andersson in chapter 6 this is especially important for small & medium-sized companies, as they tend to use in-house non-experts for business development.

Business development requires attention to function and process, not organisation. Avoid getting stuck in disputes about "who", force attention to "why"! And then, by asking "May there be better ways to achieve this?", you are already into re-engineering.

## Modelling business objects/resources

The benefit of a business object depends on its benefit to business. Every object should be justified by fulfilment of business needs.

Practice, where appropriate, subdivision into "categories" (different kinds) and decomposition into "components" (parts), in order to get structure. Example: Customers may be categorised as private persons and enterprises, needing different kinds of attention. Enterprises may be decomposed in subsidiaries, whereas private persons are not decomposed.

A complete elementary statement "NP-VP-NP" (noun phrase – verb phrase – noun phrase) is the smallest meaningful part of the analysis. Example: Every customer (NP) should have access to exactly one (VP) person responsible for customer contacts (NP).

Test of object relevance: "*What* do we want to *know* about objects of this kind?" If relevant, properties and relationships to other objects will result. (This is the main question in infological analysis, pioneered by Statistics Sweden. See Sundgren, chapter 5, to benefit from their experiences.)

Look at an object as an individual. Check by putting "Each" in front of it and read the statements implied by the modelled relationships. Does it make sense?

Don't jump too fast into property details. Start with some rough categories and establish a pattern of relationships. Avoid the property trap: Irrelevant detailing of describing properties before a guiding context is established.

Every property "belongs" to a specific object of its own and must not be put elsewhere. No belonging for a property? Develop or invent the new object!

Every object must be of interest to some business action, and the information need for every business action should be specified through the object model.

Objects (and concepts in general) are defined primarily through their positions in the overall pattern of business models. Verbal definitions need only mention what is not evident through the model patterns. Example: *Products* are defined in relation to some *needs* they attempt to fulfil, and the needs in turn are defined in relation to presumed *customers* having the needs, etc. Everything is depending on everything else, through the principle of "distributed meaning".

Roadblock? Try verbal definitions to be able to move on or to promote concept inventions. "Hidden thoughts" often come out when forcing definitions and justifications. Define meaning ("What is this?") and justification ("Why is it needed?") for every object.

Often a word is missing for a developing, not yet well-formed concept. *Invent/construct a new word*, not yet loaded with an established meaning! Example: "Actually, we are producing *Components for Treatment of Air*" said the production engineer, trying to find an adequate new word, not too clumsy, for the new product. "So you are producing different kinds of CTA's?" was a good try. CTA became the accepted term.

Utilise the language consciously, as a tool to develop the relevant concepts. The ordinary conceptions surrounding a word are usually revealed through other words, such as applicable prepositions.

Beware of words with old, now invalid associations, they can never be wiped off. *Do not* try to reuse them with a new meaning! As an aid, bring a thesaurus in order to track alternatives to "poisoned" words. (As Sundgren recalls in chapter 5, strong emotions were provoked by words rather than by the underlying concepts.)

Word confusion? "Forbid the word", and everyone is forced to explain what they actually mean by using substitute words and phrases.

A graphical symbolism does not force established word labels for everything before it is put into structure. Take advantage of this freedom.

Beware of "document objects", such as invoice etc. They don't belong to the business core. For objects like "Information about x, y z": Continue the analysis with x, y, z themselves and put them right in their structure.

Practice "focusing the important": Let everyone select his/hers five most important objects. Mark with coloured dots. Practice "disregarding the unimportant": Let everyone dismiss his/hers two least important objects.

# Teamwork in Business Modelling

Teamwork dramatically increases the benefits of a modelling technique. A team is characterised by stimulating interactions, enhanced creativity, multiplied attention, expanded competence, self-amplification and chaos. All this can and should be utilised during the modelling process.

Assign team members carefully, taking into account their knowledge and personality. This is most important! In general, the modelling facilitator cannot make up for lack of professional knowledge in the team. In negotiating the assignment, make sure you get adequate supply of knowledge, capability, decision power and "go". But don't oversell modelling seminars: Everything difficult cannot be solved in a few days.

Always prepare a schedule for the analysis work, but be prepared to digress, doing what is important instead of what is in the schedule.

Take advantage of a chaotic situation. When issues are most unclear with much confusion around, business modelling can generate most benefits.

To get started, let everyone contribute with his/hers "five most important goals/objects/activities" (depending on analysis issue). Nobody is left out, and getting stuck on a narrow trail is prevented.

Another sure start is a short context analysis, for instance in terms of "factors influencing the business in focus". Group the results and evaluate their importance. In this way, the team gets a common view of the situation as a platform.

The "5-second-rule": Listen carefully to spoken language, and learn how to observe and catch new ideas in the fly before they fade away from short-term memory. Important statements frequently appear unconsciously. An utterer frequently forgets a clever utterance, or may not even be aware that it was, in fact, a clever utterance. Teach and train this in the team by intervening the spoken flow: "Did you hear what Jim just said about shipments-in-time? Jim, is your idea that…" etc.

Participants have different profiles and seek different roles. Take advantage of this situation, e.g. let them work together in team activities.

Don't show off! The modelling facilitators task is primarily to be a catalyst. Avoid the crocodile syndrome: Large mouth and small ears.

Force the Business Modelling activities to achieve results by posing "prompting questions", prepared from interviews and initial inquiries. If, for example, interviews reveal different opinions about customer satisfaction, ask "How, during the process, is satisfaction delivered to a customer?", or "What customer needs must be fulfilled to achieve satisfaction?".

Stop energy-consuming nonsense by focusing matters of common interest. Don't let anyone block the team with monologues. Conceptualise and condense verbal floods to a few building blocks and test them on the team. The team is your resource in such situations.

Move between creativity, conflict/criticism and consensus, but make the team keep the pace (c.f. Tolis in chapter 7 discussing model assumptions). Use the participants initial expectations to make everyone responsible for directing the modelling session.

Observe less talkative members of the team and make them some "space". "Go the round" will give everyone 45 seconds to *uninterrupted* time to express comments and ideas of individual importance.

Work in small teams (4-6 members), mixing competence, gender, organisation units and management levels. Use "points-of-view" to direct each team and create a propelling tension between teams: External vs. internal view, management vs. staff view, customer vs. supplier view, etc. Example: Put two structures in opposition (e.g. customer and product), assign differently to subgroups and take advantage of the inherent tension between customer needs and product ability to satisfy the needs.

Listen carefully to detect conflicts, or when members begin to block. Act immediately. Example: Bill suddenly becomes passive in spite of demonstrated competence. In a coffee-break chat with the facilitator, he reveals some disappointment: he just observed that the team is going to solve the problem he had adopted in order to get promoted. Realising that Bill may be resigning and become a competent enemy to any team solution, the facilitator immediately breaks the schedule and appoints Bill a teamleader in a small team of "juniors", specifically assigned to solve the issue *under professional direction of Bill*. Bill is back on the track, effectively becoming in charge of the solution, i.e. *his* solution!

Don't get stuck on exotic peculiarities, go for the common and general. Watch-out when members introduce pseudo-conflicts about unimportant concepts in order to take over and control the team. Counter prestige-games with "Business Modelling rules" and focus on subject matter.

Take advantage of the dynamics in subject matter conflicts. Visualise views in opposition, go for definitions and try to obtain a structure covering the views.

Beware of nonsense modelling, or modelling what is easy to model instead of what need be modelled! The latter is generally more difficult, being the focus of business attention. The most important business concepts are never atomic, they always have inherent structures! It is a severe mistake, and a too easy way out, to avoid them.

Preferably use two modelling facilitators. Being alone, it is difficult to pay enough attention to everything of interest.

Preparation of the team members in advance promotes a flying start, yielding modelling economy. Prior interviews may detect forthcoming difficulties in the team process. Avoid change of team members during the modelling session.

Plant ideas as seeds. "Water" now and then to make them grow. However, be humble and prepared to disconnect your ego: "You have to kill your babies!" Teach this difficult art to the team. Example: In a case of modelling technical concepts with a team of engineers, the facilitator presumptuously came up with a "perfect solution", not observing the team confusion. Two hours later the team was back to their point of departure, and valuable time for expensive professionals had been lost.

Consensus is not equivalent to compromise. Team modelling is no voting.

Make it clear that both actively participating team members as well as passive ones are responsible for the outcome. It is not permitted just to be an observer. Every team member is expected to act and contribute in his/her own way.

Establish the modelling work firmly at management level. Acquire management understanding for business modelling. They must accept some responsibility for the effort and its outcome.

Practice "vernissages" where subgroups exhibit their models to each other. Use the tension to promote comments; put them up in the model. Visibility check: Visiting team walks-through the model. What do they get out of it?

As a facilitator you are in position to give team members substantial "intellectual rewards". Hand out for free: Some words of recognition when someone deserves credit cost nothing and is very encouraging.

Avoid "parachuting" as a facilitator into an unknown situation, with a foreign team. If something is fishy, you will find out too late.

If passive managers are blocking the team: Establish a competition. Two subgroups, same task, one "blocker" in each group. Slow actions? Increase the pressure: "Report solution in 45 minutes!"

Be demanding as responsible modelling facilitator. *They* should sweat!

# Tools for Business Modelling

Tools in business modelling may be manual or computerised, and the ultimate aim is to promote human capability in the creation and use of business models. Means, media and functionality should be chosen accordingly.

## *About manual tools*

Make every modelling activity and model concrete and down to earth, by producing the models on wallpaper using tangible building-blocks created by the modelling participants themselves. Thus, the result will be theirs and promote their commitment.

Engage as many senses as possible, using forms, colours, dialogues, materials, etc. Be truly multimedial in order to amplify human cognition: Attention, perception, thinking, problem solving and communication.

Support participants linguistic capabilities by prepared forms for statements and utterances. Apply the "sentence-to-be-completed"-method, i.e. using forms with prepared statements like "The primary goal for the process X is to….". By completing the sentence grammatically correct, professionals may discuss it and make it as distinctive as required.

## *Computerised tools*

Tools should be easy to use by non-expert users whenever a business modelling situation occurs. Tools should visualise various business issues by producing proper "business drawings" adapted to the situation and styled for management attention. If widespread communication of business models is important, choose tools which are standard and in widespread use on the market. The tools must not be expensive, since this would prevent widespread installation and use.

Visibility is further enhanced by using very large paper formats (2*A0, etc.) for process overviews and related structural output. Such maps cannot, by their very nature, be hidden on the shelves. Instead, they are intended for the walls, where everybody concerned can study, rethink and comment on work procedures, etc.

In general, it is not adequate with typical CASE-tool capabilities (strict formalisation, code generation, etc.), since such (expensive!) capabilities are of little use in a business modelling situation. Unfortunately, the market is still lacking true CABE-tools: Computer-Aided *Business* Engineering, as opposed to Computer-Aided *Software* Engineering.

Finally, don't regard tools as strait-jackets. When tools, methods or even modelling patterns prevent progress, they must be abandoned! Be free.

# Yourself as a Business Modelling facilitator

Apart from general knowledge in business modelling technicalities, there are some extra requirements to be fulfilled by a full-fledged facilitator of Business Modelling workshops. Below is a number of recommended personal capabilities of the type that you either have, or with some effort, can acquire. Judge for yourself!

## *Generalist with the ability to abstract*

The modelling facilitator will often need to find the general and the common in a large number of special cases where many simultaneous considerations must be made. Generalisation from subcategories and aggregation from subparts must be frequently exercised in successive layers, in order to make a complex multitude perceivable. Not easy!

## *Pedagogue with the ability to make issues concrete*

Substantial pedagogical capability is required in all modelling situations: marketing of the approach, carrying out "in action", communicating the outcomes, etc. Take advantage of all teaching possibilities. The important but difficult trick is to make abstract phenomena concrete and down to earth, by adapting to the preferences of the audience addressed.

## *Creativity*

The modelling facilitator must be creative and be able to inspire others to be creative. This will further the facilitator's own development as much as the participants' development.

## *Capacity to analyse and synthesise*

The facilitator's job is not simply a matter of pulling situations apart and analysing the bits. It is also a matter of being able to put bits together to form wholes (synthesis) without leaving anything behind!

## *Holistic approach*

The facilitator must be able to see the whole, i.e., to look at the business and the issues surrounding it "from above" without favouring any particular angle – and getting the rest of the group to do the same.

## *Ability to co-operate and negotiate*

Some of the most difficult moments any modelling facilitator will experience are in negotiations between parties in questions about the proper description of the business. In such negotiations, the modelling facilitator can, if agreed between the parties, be the arbiter.

## *Ability to communicate*

The modelling facilitator's job will be much easier if he/she is able to communicate ideas effectively. May be both own ideas or others'. Remember also that communication is more than words.

## *A good listener*

A minimum requirement is that the modelling facilitator hears what people are actually saying and shows that he/she understands what is being said. By providing some feedback, the facilitator demonstrates real interest. Even more useful is the ability to also comprehend what is actually *meant* by what is being said. This might be checked by re-formulating or re-phrasing utterances. A modelling facilitator must be able to take in signals from the group and interpret these correctly. A pair of big ears are very useful!

## Authority

Note that there is a difference between authoritarian behaviour and possessing authority! The latter is something positive and should be a consequence of the modelling facilitator having the right qualifications and a certain role. It is also positive if the modelling facilitator is conscious of his or her authority and learns to use it when required. But *do* avoid authoritarian behaviour – it is a sign of lack of real authority!

## Courage

The modelling facilitator frequently ends up in the hot seat in business analysis, particularly with an aim of making changes! You might need to say the truth about a situation, balance separate interests and push issues that some in the group will regard as controversial. This requires a certain amount of courage – to go out into uncharted territory.

## Humility

A modelling facilitator usually learns fairly quickly to be humble in the face of a complex reality and other people's abilities. You should *never* imagine that you know more about the business than the group. Still, your input in terms of clarifying what is said might be invaluable.

## Openness

Openness means the acceptance of new standpoints and different views. Co-operation, negotiation and even teaching are all made easier by an open attitude. Listening without being open to the ideas communicated is a sham.

## Ability to conceptualise

This is an ability somewhat difficult to define. Its main feature is being able to distinguish and give form to central trains of thought, ideas and reasoning before they have become completely obvious. This is the ability to see a concept taking shape through a fog of words. Some just have it!

# Some final conclusions

As the "dos" and "don'ts" in business modelling have been gradually better understood, so has the understanding of what the important development issues may be for business modelling as such. Regarding this book, the subject is obviously very broad. Therefore, the conclusion will point out just a few research directions which appear challenging. The message is that someone ought to do further investigations.

Another conclusion regards the value of real-life cases, where research issues are brought to the surface and research solutions can be tested. Without a large amount of cases, such as those in chapters 2, 3, 4 and 5, this very checklist could never have been written!

## *Cognition*

Since every business modelling attempt is highly depending on human thinking capability, it must necessarily be founded on cognitive science. The general aim of business modelling is to amplify business cognition in the following ways:

- Direct *attention* to relevant business areas.

- Support *perception* of business situations.

- Enhance *understanding* of management and operational issues.

- Promote *communication* in business matters.

- Release *problem solving* creativity.

Each of the cognitive issues highlighted above may be studied in order to explain its contribution to "better business modelling". Start with Anderson (1995).

## *Concept formation*

Specifically in modelling business objects, there is frequently a need to form new or modified concepts, subsequently followed by finding or forming a word to use as concept label. Hence, concept formation in the

mind of humans is a valuable capability, yet to be understood. In Gärdenfors (1992), the prototype theory for concept formation is explained, and
criteria for concept usability in inductive reasoning are indicated. With the
assumption that most decisions in a business are based on inductive rather
than deductive reasoning, this research on concept formation ought to be
studied and, if possible, made operational. The research issue may be:
"What is a good business concept formation, and how can we go about to
achieve it?"

## Human competence

Human competence is a necessary resource for business modelling. In
Sandberg (1994) it is argued that the *conceptions* we have about our work
have implications for our operational performance as well as for our further professional development. This is interesting since the very
"material" we work with in business modelling is our conceptions. How
can they be influenced in order to improve our competence at work? Then,
it is put forth as a management issue to influence staff members conceptions of their work in a way that creates a *shared system of meaning*,
which in turn promotes competence at work. Thus, since a business model
is permeated with meaning, the question is: How can business modelling
be used as an instrument for *management-by-making-sense*?

# References

Anderson, J.R. (1995) *Cognitive psychology and its implications*, W.H. Freeman
and Company, New York.

Gärdenfors, P. (1992) *Blotta tanken*, Bokförlaget Nya Doxa AB, Nora, Sweden
[*The Mere Thought*].

Jackson, M. (1995) *Software Requirements and Specifications*, Addison-Wesley,
New York.

Kaplan, R.S. & Norton, D.P. (1996) *The Balanced Scorecard – Translating Strategy into Action*, Harvard Business School Press, Boston, Massachusetts.

Sandberg, J. (1994) *Human Competence at Work*, BAS, Göteborg University,
Göteborg, Sweden.

# Index

# Business Modelling

# Research Consortium

Research on business modelling requires existing knowledge from a number of disciplines such as Business Administration and Information Systems. Relevant knowledge areas include corporate strategies, business control, material/production control, marketing management, IS/IT support, and development methodologies. As a single research group cannot have a critical mass in all these areas, multidisciplinary research is needed.

In the Business Modelling research consortium, we have accomplished this through a highly co-operative network of participants from three Swedish universities: Stockholm School of Economics (HHS/SSE), The Royal Institute of Technology in Stockholm (KTH/RIT) and Linköping University (LiU). Established in 1994, the research consortium is managed by professor Anders G. Nilsson together with the researchers Jörgen Andersson, Christer Nellborn and Christofer Tolis.

In order to strengthen the practical experiences in business modelling, we have invited different companies to participate in the consortium. We have accomplished joint research projects with Ericsson, Sweden Post, Social Insurance Office and Statistics Sweden. In addition, we have carried out fruitful research hearings with ABB and Scania. These companies represent different environments for business modelling from private industry to public services.

In addition to the direct research work with the companies, we have established a reference group with recognised professors and professional consultants. The participants in the reference group have various interesting experiences in change work in organisations and therefore give a broader perspective on business modelling as a subject area.

Seven people are currently engaged in the reference group: three professors, Janis A. Bubenko jr., Birger Rapp and Bo Sundgren, together with four senior consultants, Claes-Göran Lindström, Dr. Björn E. Nilsson, Gösta Steneskog and Hans Willars. We have also co-operated with professor Marite Kirikova from Riga Technical University in Latvia. This book has contributions from all people connected to the research consortium.

The research consortium has been funded by NUTEK, the Swedish National Board for Industrial and Technical Development, during the period of 1995-1997

The consortium's Internet homepage is http://www.dsv.su.se/~chn/BM/

# About the Authors

## Jörgen Andersson, Econ. Lic.

Jörgen Andersson has a licentiate degree in Economic Information Systems and is a researcher at the Department of Computer and Information Science at Linköping University. His research interest concerns information technology, management control, and small and medium-sized enterprises (SMEs). He is co-operating with researchers from the Royal Institute of Technology and Stockholm School of Economics in the consortium "Business Modelling". Jörgen has participated in an EC-project about competitiveness of SME's through information technology. He has also co-operated with the Social Insurance Office of Östergötland in their work to introduce process management. He has also been a teacher and director of studies at Linköping University and responsible for an undergraduate course in accounting and budgeting.

Contact address: Economic Information Systems, Department of Computer and Information Science, Linköping University, SE-581 83 Linköping, Sweden. E-mail: joran@ida.liu.se

## Janis A. Bubenko jr., Professor, Ph.D.

Janis A. Bubenko jr. has a Ph.D. in Information Systems from the Royal Institute of Technology (KTH). He has been professor in Computer and Systems Sciences at University of Gothenburg and Chalmers University of Technology 1977-81, and at the Royal Institute of Technology and Stockholm University (SU) since 1982. In 1984 he initiated the establishment of the Swedish Institute for Systems Development, SISU, and was its managing director during 1985-92. Janis is the author/co-author of eight textbooks and more than 140 research reports and published articles. Current research includes methods for requirements engineering and enterprise modelling. He has participated in a number of ESPRIT projects since 1987 and is currently working with enterprise modelling in the project ELEKTRA.

Contact address: Department of Computer and Systems Sciences, KTH/ SU, Electrum 230, SE-164 40, Kista, Sweden. E-mail: janis@dsv.su.se

# Marite Kirikova, Associate Professor, Dr.sc.ing.

Marite Kirikova has a Dr.sc.ing. in Information and Information Systems at the Riga Technical University, Latvia. She has 26 scientific publications and works as a scientific researcher and lecturer at Riga Technical University since 1982. She has done fieldwork at Stockholm University, Royal Institute of Technology, and Copenhagen University. Marite currently lectures in system analysis, knowledge acquisition, requirements engineering and project engineering. She also participates in the research project "Intelligent Multi-Level Meta Model Processing System for Construction of Structural Modelling Methods and Tools."

Contact address: Department of Systems Theory and Design, Riga Technical University, 1 Kalku, Riga LV-1658, Latvia. E-mail: marite@itl.rtu.lv

# Claes-Göran Lindström, M.Sc.

Majoring in Statistics, Claes-Göran stayed with the Institute of Statistics, Uppsala University, for a couple of years after his exam, teaching and doing applied research and consultancy. Information Need Analysis and methodology for Requirements Analysis were – and still are – main topics of interest. In the 1970s, Claes-Göran was head of the department of Higher Education Statistics at Statistics Sweden. During the 1980s, he was employed as consultant in major Swedish consultancy firms (Statskonsult and PlanData), occupied mostly with requirements analyses, pre-studies and, to some extent, database design. Since 1990, Claes-Göran is running his own business together with five partners in IT plan, a consultancy firm specialising in strategic aspects of IT development and application. Typical clients are large Swedish organisations with global activities, e.g. Ericsson, IKEA and Wallenius Lines.

Contact address: IT plan, Nybrogatan 15, SE-114 39 Stockholm, Sweden. Email: claes-goran.lindstrom@itplan.se

# Christer Nellborn, B.Sc.

Christer Nellborn has studied Information Systems on a B.Sc. level at the Royal Institute of Technology (KTH) and Stockholm University (SU). He is since 1995 a management consultant at Astrakan Strategic Development and a part time researcher at the Department of Computer and Systems Sciences at the Stockholm University. Christer has previously been a researcher at the Swedish Institute for Systems Development (SISU) 1988-1995 where his research topics included business modelling, information systems design, knowledge modelling and expert systems design. He was there one of the designers of the Enterprise Modelling technique in the ESPRIT-project F3. His current research topics include the integrated use of models in strategic planning and information systems design. This research is performed mainly in the "Business Modelling" consortium and in the ELEKTRA project. Christer has also been a lecturer at the Stockholm University for more than 12 years.

Contact address: Department of Computer and Systems Sciences, KTH/ SU, Electrum 230, SE-164 40, Kista, Sweden. E-mail: chn@dsv.su.se

## Anders G. Nilsson, Professor, Ph.D.

Anders G. Nilsson has a Ph.D. in Business Administration with special focus on Information Management from the Stockholm School of Economics. He has been part-time professor in Economic Information Systems at Linköping University, and is now professor at Informatics, Karlstad University, Sweden. Anders is research leader for the consortium "Business Modelling," investigating Swedish companies' interest in business process orientation. As a research partner at the Institute for Business Process Development (Institute V), he has developed a practical method for helping companies to purchase standard application packages. Anders has been working for 25 years as a process consultant with different information systems projects in industry. He is author/co-author of 12 books in business development, such as the ISAC-method published in "Information Systems Development – A Systematic Approach" (Prentice-Hall, 1981).

Contact address: The Institute for Business Process Development (Institute V), Stockholm School of Economics, Box 6501, SE-113 83 Stockholm, Sweden. E-mail: Anders.Nilsson@hhs.se

## Björn E. Nilsson, Ph.D.

Björn E. Nilsson has a Ph.D. in Administrative Information Processing from Stockholm University. He has been vice president of the research institute SISU, Swedish Institute for Systems Development, 1987-95. Since then, he is a partner of the Astrakan consultant company. During 25 years as a methods developer and process consultant to different information systems projects in government, defence organisations and industry, his main objective has been bridging the gap between information science and actual ongoing development work. A passion has also been the development of strategies, bridging the gap between business- and IT-development. Working in a variety of standardisation groups, Björn is a co-author of the ISO-report "Concepts and Terminology for the Conceptual Schema". He is also a member of the IFIP 8.1 and a co-author of the FRISCO report "A Framework of Information System Concepts".

Contact address: Astrakan Strategic Development, Gävlegatan 22, SE-113 30, Stockholm, Sweden. E-mail: bjorn@astrakan.se

# Birger Rapp, Professor, Ph.D.

Birger Rapp has a chair in Economic Information Systems, Department of Computer and Information Science, Linköping Institute of Technology and Linköping University. He has been president of SORA (Swedish Operational Research Association) and EURO (The Association of European Operational Research Societies), and is now vice president at large of IFORS (International Federation of Operational Research Societies). He is program director in Management and Economic Information Systems at IMIT (Institute of Management of Innovation and Technology). He belongs to the editorial (advisory) boards of EJOR, IJMSD, JORBEL and Omega. Birger has published books in investment theory, in production planning and in control and principal agent theory. He is a senior consultant to many Swedish companies and was the first president of the Pronova Research and Development Board in Sweden.

Contact address: Economic Information Systems, Department of Computer and Information Science, Linköping University, SE-581 83 Linköping, Sweden. E-mail: birra@ida.liu.se

# Gösta Steneskog, M.Sc.

Gösta Steneskog is a management consultant and researcher at the Institute for Business Process Development (Institute V), Stockholm School of Economics. His competence areas are process management, systems development, maintenance and operation, project management and change management. As a consultant, he has been working for a number of large Swedish companies with a focus in the financial sector. He is participating in an EC-project – CEBUSNET – which is a co-operation between six business schools and universities in Europe. The project is about excellent business processes. Gösta is working as a researching practitioner as he is spending most of his time on management consulting. He has been a pioneer of Process Management in Sweden and he is author of "Process Management" (Liber, 1990; in Swedish) – the first book in Sweden on this subject.

Contact address: The Institute for Business Process Development (Institute V), Stockholm School of Economics, Box 6501, SE-113 83 Stockholm, Sweden. E-mail: Gosta.Steneskog@hhs.se

## Bo Sundgren, Professor, Ph.D.

Bo Sundgren has a Ph.D. in Administrative Information Processing from Stockholm University. He is a researcher and part-time professor at the department of Information Management at the Stockholm School of Economics and the Economic Research Institute. Bo also works as head of Statistical Informatics at Statistics Sweden. His research concerns areas such as business modelling, data modelling, database-oriented systems development, meta information systems, statistical information systems, and the corporation's information system as infrastructure. Bo is internationally active and heads a EC-project concerning meta information systems. His latest published books are "Databasorienterad systemutveckling" (Studentlitteratur, 1992; in Swedish), concerning database-oriented systems development, and "Advancing Your Business" (EFI, 1996; also available on http://www.hhs.se/im/efi/ayb.htm), edited together with Mats Lundeberg.

Contact address: Statistics Sweden (SCB), Box 24 300, SE-104 51 Stockholm, Sweden. E-mail: Bo.Sundgren@scb.se

## Christofer Tolis, M.Sc.

Christofer Tolis has a M.Sc. in Information Management from Stockholm School of Economics. He has prior experience of information systems in organisations, working with technical support and problem solving towards retailers and end-users. Christofer is currently working as a researcher and lecturer at Stockholm School of Economics. His research focuses on the role of business models in organisational development, viewed from a perspective of learning and knowledge. Christofer is co-operating with researchers from the Royal Institute of Technology and

Linköping University in the research consortium "Business Modelling". Within the consortium, he has been participating in development projects at Ericsson Radio and Sweden Post. As a lecturer, Christofer teaches in the areas of business and systems analysis, and has been responsible for an undergraduate course in information and business processes.

Contact address: Department of Information Management, Stockholm School of Economics, Box 6501, SE-113 83, Stockholm, Sweden. E-mail: Christofer.Tolis@hhs.se

# Hans Willars, M.Sc.

Hans Willars is a management consultant in business modelling and business modelling applications at Astrakan in Stockholm. Prior to joining Astrakan 1995, he was a consultant at PlanData 1978 – 1989, exploring conceptual modelling as a general tool for business, systems and staff development. 1989 – 1995 he was Technical manager of the Business Engineering research area at SISU (Swedish Institute for Systems Development). Within SISU, the general interest was technology transfer to membership companies and responsiveness to their research needs. Specific responsibilities included further development of business modelling techniques as well as the introduction of high-level modelling applications in membership companies. His primary aim is to make modelling theories operational for the benefit of business. He is a regular lecturer on the subject at the Royal Institute of Technology and Stockholm University.

Contact address: Astrakan Strategic Development, Gävlegatan 22, SE-113 30, Stockholm, Sweden. E-mail: hawil@astrakan.se

Printing: Druckhaus Beltz, Hemsbach
Binding: Buchbinderei Schäffer, Grünstadt